OCEANS AND OCEANOGRAPHY

THE LIVING EARTH

OCEANS AND OCEANOGRAPHY

EDITED BY JOHN P. RAFFERTY, ASSOCIATE EDITOR, EARTH AND LIFE SCIENCES

Britannica
Educational Publishing

IN ASSOCIATION WITH

ROSEN
EDUCATIONAL SERVICES

Published in 2011 by Britannica Educational Publishing
(a trademark of Encyclopædia Britannica, Inc.)
in association with Rosen Educational Services, LLC
29 East 21st Street, New York, NY 10010.

First Edition

Britannica Educational Publishing
Michael I. Levy: Executive Editor
J.E. Luebering: Senior Manager
Marilyn L. Barton: Senior Coordinator, Production Control
Steven Bosco: Director, Editorial Technologies
Lisa S. Braucher: Senior Producer and Data Editor
Yvette Charboneau: Senior Copy Editor
Kathy Nakamura: Manager, Media Acquisition
John P. Rafferty: Associate Editor, Earth and Life Sciences

Rosen Educational Services
Jeanne Nagle: Senior Editor
Nelson Sá: Art Director
Cindy Reiman: Photography Manager
Matthew Cauli: Designer, Cover Design
Introduction by Therese Shea Harasymiw

Library of Congress Cataloging-in-Publication Data

Oceans and oceanography / edited by John P. Rafferty.—1st ed.
     p. cm.—(The living earth)
"In association with Britannica Educational Publishing, Rosen Educational Services."
Includes bibliographical references and index.
ISBN 978-1-61530-334-2 (library binding)
1. Oceanography. I. Rafferty, John P.
GC11.2.O258 2011
551.46—dc22

2010032151

Manufactured in the United States of America

On the cover: A clown fish swims amid the anemones along the ocean floor. *Shutterstock.com*

On page x: A diver examines the many diverse marine life forms located within the Verde
sea passage, south of Manila, Philippines. *Jay Directo/AFP/Getty Images*

On pages v, 1, 49, 104, 139, 180, 226, 249, 250, 252, 260: A cresting wave. *Jean-Paul Nacivet/
Photographer's Choice/Getty Images*

CONTENTS

pull of the sun and
the Moon

Earth

sun

Moon   high tide

low ti

136

145

159

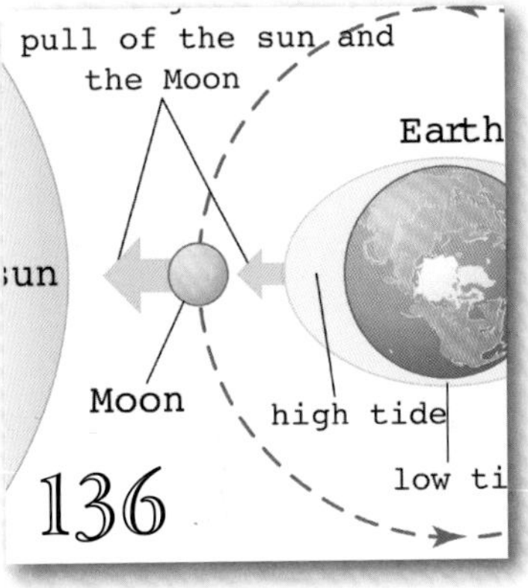

227

243

INTRODUCTION

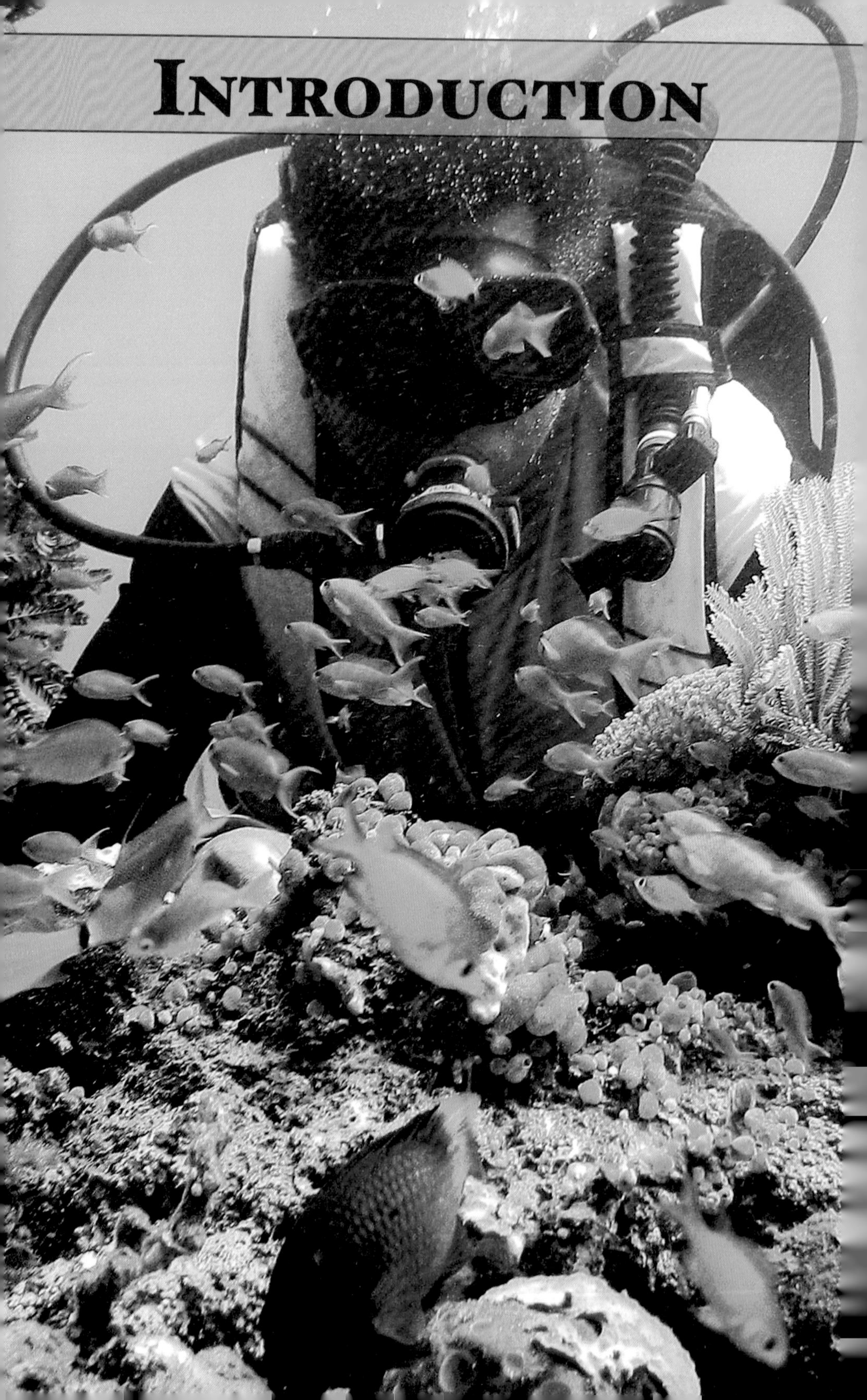

Of all the planets in the solar system, Earth is singled out as the "Blue Planet." This colorful label is indicative of the presence of water on the planet's surface. When viewed from space, Earth's oceans, which cover nearly three-fourths of the total sphere, appear blue. The sheer preponderance of water makes it easy to comprehend how the oceans influence nearly every life process on Earth. This volume takes a comprehensive look at the world's oceans, examining them from the tip of their wave crests to the depths of their basins. Topics covered include currents, sea life, the ocean's effect on climate, and the science of oceanography.

Although they are, in truth, one continuous body of water, the world's oceans are commonly referred to in the plural. Earth has three major oceans: the Pacific, the Atlantic, and the Indian Ocean. The Pacific is the largest in area and volume, and the Indian is the smallest. The Arctic Ocean is technically considered part of the northern Atlantic. While the waters surrounding Antarctica are sometimes called the Southern Ocean, they are considered by many to be part of the southern Pacific, Atlantic, and Indian oceans.

The origin of oceanic waters remains something of an unknown, though a few theories offer an explanation. One states that as the planet was forming, its developing crust reacted with water vapor and other gases in the atmosphere to produce liquid water. Of the two kinds of crust that solidified over Earth's mantle, the thicker oceanic crust formed a basin for the oceans and served as a cradle for Earth's early living organisms. The earliest fossils of algae and bacteria date from 3.3 billion years ago.

Topographical studies of the ocean floor have revealed that Earth's ocean basins possess several terrain features that would be familiar to land dwellers. Similar to its terrestrial counterpart, the ocean floor is covered with hills, mountains, featureless plains, and deep gorges. The majority of the ocean floor, however, lies at depths of between

4,000 metres (13,000 feet) and 5,000 metres (16,500 feet). The Mariana Trench, located in the western part of the North Pacific Ocean, plunges to over 11,000 metres (36,200 feet). Little was known about ocean basins until the development of sonar in the early 1900s. Sound waves emitted by sonar allow marine researchers to detect objects thousands of feet under water. Other tools are also used. Satellites, global positioning systems, radar, and echo-sounder systems are among the most important remote-sensing tools. These tools have been used to map areas several parts of the ocean, the Mid-Atlantic Ridge being one of the most prominent mapped features.

Core samples of sediment from deep areas of the ocean floor have been a boon to the theory that revolves around plate tectonics. The top layer of Earth's crust is made up of tectonic plates in constant, albeit slow, movement. Beginning 200 million years ago, the supercontinent Pangea—a land-mass made up of all of Earth's continents—began to break apart, eventually fragmenting into the present-day conti-nents separated by the oceans. Even today, spreading plates at the bottom of Earth's oceans spew molten rock from the mantle, creating new floor. The theory of plate tectonics explains the relative "newness" of the ocean floor compared to the age of the planet; the floor is constantly recycling itself.

The composition of oceanic water was established by about 1.5 billion years ago. The primary mixture is 96.5 percent water, 2.5 percent salts, and a small percentage of substances that include dissolved inorganic and organic materials, other particles, and atmospheric gases. The amount of salt lost through oceanic processes is equal to returns from continental drainage.

The composition of ocean water is ideal for the count-less organisms that, over hundreds of millions of years, have adapted to the mix of water and salt. Inorganic chem-icals, such as phosphorus, nitrogen, and zinc, provide further nourishment, as does sediment from continental shelves. In return, marine life breaks down much of the material that finds its way into the ocean. Photosynthesis, the essential process that brings energy to marine food chains, occurs just below the water's surface, where the ingredients of solar energy, carbon dioxide, and nutrient salts are all available. The byproduct of photosynthesis is oxygen, and Earth's waters are large producers of oxygen.

Complex circulation patterns influence the chemical composition of oceans. Not surprisingly, wind is a major factor in circulating ocean waters. As wind blows across the water, the ocean responds with surface waves. Vertical movements of water in the oceans, referred to as upwelling, cycle waters up into the surface layer. Downwelling occurs when water is carried vertically down from the surface. These motions exchange the cold, deeper layers of the ocean, which are rich in nutrients and carbon dioxide, with the warmer surface waters, rich in oxygen.

Several other forces govern the direction and formation of oceanic currents. The most significant are horizontal gradients of pressure, Coriolis forces, friction, and gravity. Horizontal pressure causes water molecules to move horizontally from regions of high pressure to regions of low pressure. Surface waters warm as they absorb solar radiation and become less dense. The Coriolis forces refer to the effects of Earth's rotation on the movement of oceanic waters. Spinning out of vast circular systems called gyres, currents move clockwise in the Northern Hemisphere and counterclockwise in the Southern.

Once water is set in motion, it won't stop until it meets a stronger, opposing force. It can be slowed, however, by friction from contact with slower currents and waves, as well as with essentially nonmoving volumes of water near the ocean floor. Currents also decelerate as gravity pulls them down. The region of the ocean affected by wind is the Ekman layer, which extends about 100 metres (330 feet) below the surface of the ocean. Below this layer, the circulation of currents is much slower.

Two properties of ocean water contribute enable circulation at great depths: temperature and salinity. When water cools, it becomes denser and sinks, displacing the water below. The more saline the water, the denser it is. Together, these properties create a process called thermohaline circulation, first discovered in 1960. Thermohaline circulation is constant in polar regions, where water at the surface cools, sinks, and is replaced with more water. The current is created and travels at depth until it finally upwells again in a return current to polar regions. Thermohaline circulation is responsible for slowly moving a huge volume of water all over the world. Carrying nutrients obtained from the ocean floor, the upwelling process brings these nutrients to the surface, replenishing the needs of ocean plant and animal life.

Oceanic water also interacts with the atmosphere, exchanging enormous quantities of oxygen and carbon dioxide. The ocean absorbs much of the sun's radiation as heat is delivered downward into the ocean's depths. Warmwater currents carry heat. When this heat is transferred to the atmosphere, air rises, creating regions of low pressure. In contrast, cold-water currents cause high pressure systems. Both warm and cold currents affect the climate, but the reverse is also true. Some scientists believe that global warming could shut down or weaken parts of the thermohaline ocean current system. Some scientists speculate that an influx of freshwater from ice sheets and glaciers running into the North Atlantic could "freshen," and thus disrupt the sections of the thermohaline circulation. Since freshwater is less dense than salt water, significant amounts of freshwater entering the North Atlantic may lower the density of surface waters and stop the sinking motion that drives thermohaline circulation.

Several well-documented current systems greatly impact climates. The Gulf Stream is a warm current flowing northeastward in the North Atlantic off the North American coast. It is part of a clockwise-rotating gyre that begins with the westward-moving North Equatorial Current. Some consider the Florida current sweeping warm water up the Florida and Carolina coasts part of this system as well. The Gulf Stream tends to change over time, at times even seeming to disappear and then reappear. Its winds carry warm, moist air to northwestern Europe. In winter, the air over the North Atlantic west of Norway is more than 22 °C (40 °F) warmer than the average for that latitude. The Gulf Stream is one of several western boundary currents. The Kuroshio in the northwestern Pacific is an example of another.

Although these currents bring moderate and warm weather to the coasts, occasionally irregular events cause shifts in the currents and dramatic changes in weather. El Niño is the name for unusually warm weather conditions that occur periodically along the Pacific coast of South America, near the Equator. El Niño occurs when trade winds (persistent winds blowing from the west) weaken, which reduces the upwelling of cool, nutrient-rich water, replacing warm surface water. The warming of the water kills plankton, a major food source for fish, and results in a temporary but major disruption of the region's marine ecosystem. El Niño also causes an atypical increase in precipitation in many areas, some thousands of miles away from the Equator. It is unclear why the trade winds weaken, so El Niño is hard to predict. However, the ecological and climatic effects may be felt for about a year.

These and other facts about the world's seas are known are mainly due to advances in oceanography, which is the study of all things related to the ocean. The science of oceanography is divided into four main components: marine geology, chemical oceanography, physical oceanography, and marine ecology. Marine geology focuses on the features and evolution of the oceans. Physical oceanography, chemical oceanography, and marine ecology are all closely related fields with overlapping concerns. In addition to tangible properties such as temperature, physical oceanography studies include the movement of ocean waters and their interactions with Earth's atmosphere. In contrast, chemical oceanography focuses on the composition of seawater and its chemical relationships with marine organisms, while marine ecology, which is also called biological oceanography, is the study of those organisms.

Modern oceanic exploration is conducted from platforms above water: ships, buoys, aircraft, or satellites. Modern investigations began during the Age of Sail, but newer vessels designed to withstand the actions of weather and waves are more accurate in their underwater measurements. Perhaps tomorrow's vessels will be stationed on the ocean floor—a location that is increasingly being viewed as an area to harvest. Ocean basins are rich in minerals such as iron and manganese. Amazingly, the ocean contains very nearly every element found on Earth. Deep-submergence research vehicles have located mineral deposits, as well as never-before-seen biological communities, at seafloor spreading centres.

The ocean is a trove of significant resources. It is a source of food for humans and many organisms that live in marine ecosystems. After desalinization, ocean water is made useful for agricultural purposes, irrigating fields in places with little access to freshwater. Additionally, the oceans figure prominently in trade and transportation. Companies pump oil from hundreds of offshore wells in their quest to supply a world full of consumers hungry for petroleum. Offshore drilling is not without its danger to marine ecosystems, as evidenced by 2010's Deepwater Horizon disaster in the Gulf of Mexico. Thankfully, there also is clean energy to be had from the sea, as tides and waves are converted to electricity.

However, human activities are exerting an ever-increasing influence over the world's oceans. Atmospheric carbon dioxide, which is often transferred to the oceans, continues to increase. Phytoplankton and other organisms in the oceans, along with chemical processes in the water, absorb tremendous amounts of carbon dioxide. As carbon emissions from human activities increase, there is a question of whether the ocean will be able to absorb more in the future. Additionally, man-made pollutants alter oceanic processes by blocking light from reaching photosynthetic organisms and those that rely on vision, change the chemical composition of seawater in coastal and runoff areas, and introduce potentially harmful compounds to marine life.

Despite centuries of research, the ocean remains one of the few places on Earth that has not been completely explored and described. Oceanographers continue to provide insight into formerly unknown aspects of oceanography. Perhaps no oceanographer was so famous as Jacques-Yves Cousteau, whose name has become synonymous with deep-sea exploration. In addition, Robert Ballard's discovery of the Titanic in 1985 sparked a curiosity in deep-sea archaeology. Additional knowledge of the oceans would enable scientists to accurately predict phenomena such as the timing and intensity of El Niño and the behaviour of earthquake-predicated tsunamis. Having a greater understanding of marine ecology would enable humans to harvest the resources they need from the oceans in sustainable ways.

The oceans have played a crucial roles in the origin and development of life on Earth, and they continue to be essential for maintaining life. Whether they continue to provide these critical services, remaining a crucial resource for the future of this big "Blue Planet," is largely up to the actions of human beings in the coming decades.

CHAPTER 1

THE OCEAN

T he ocean is a continuous body of salt water that is contained in enormous basins on Earth's surface. When viewed from space, the predominance of the oceans on Earth is readily apparent. The oceans and their marginal seas cover nearly 71 percent of Earth's surface, with an average depth of 3,795 metres (12,450 feet). The exposed land occupies the remaining 29 percent of the planetary surface and has a mean elevation of only 840 metres (2,756 feet). Actually, all the elevated land could be hidden under the oceans and Earth reduced to a smooth sphere that would be completely covered by a continuous layer of seawater 2,686 metres (8,812 feet) deep. This is known as the sphere depth of the oceans and serves to underscore the abundance of water on Earth's surface.

Earth is unique in the solar system because of its distance from the Sun and its period of rotation. These combine to subject Earth to a solar radiation level that maintains the planet at a mean surface temperature of 17 °C (62.6 °F), which varies little over annual and night-day cycles. This mean temperature allows water to exist on Earth in all three of its phases—solid, liquid, and gaseous. No other planet in the solar system has this feature. The liquid phase predominates on Earth. By volume, 97.957 percent of the water on the planet exists as oceanic water and associated sea ice. The gaseous phase and droplet water in the atmosphere constitute 0.001 percent. Fresh water in lakes and streams makes up 0.036 percent, while groundwater is 10 times more abundant at 0.365 percent. Glaciers and ice caps constitute 1.641 percent of Earth's total water volume.

Each of the above is considered to be a reservoir of water. Water continuously circulates between these reservoirs in what is called the hydrologic cycle, which is driven by energy from the Sun. Evaporation, precipitation, movement of the atmosphere, and the downhill flow of river water, glaciers, and groundwater keep water in motion between the reservoirs and maintain the hydrologic cycle.

The large range of volumes in these reservoirs and the rates at which water cycles between them combine to create important conditions on Earth. If small changes occur in the rate at which water is cycled into or out of a reservoir, the volume of a reservoir changes. These volume changes may be relatively large and rapid in a small reservoir or small and slow in a large reservoir. A small percentage change in the volume of the oceans may produce a large proportional change in the land-ice reservoir, thereby promoting glacial and interglacial stages. The rate at which water enters or leaves a reservoir divided into the reservoir volume determines the residence time of water in the reservoir. The residence time of water in a reservoir, in turn, governs many of the properties of that reservoir.

RELATIVE DISTRIBUTION OF THE OCEANS

Those conducting oceanic research generally recognize the existence of three major oceans, the Pacific, Atlantic, and Indian. (The Arctic Ocean is considered an extension of the Atlantic.) Arbitrary boundaries separate these three bodies of water in the Southern Hemisphere. One boundary extends southward to Antarctica from the Cape of Good Hope, while another stretches southward from Cape Horn. The last one passes through

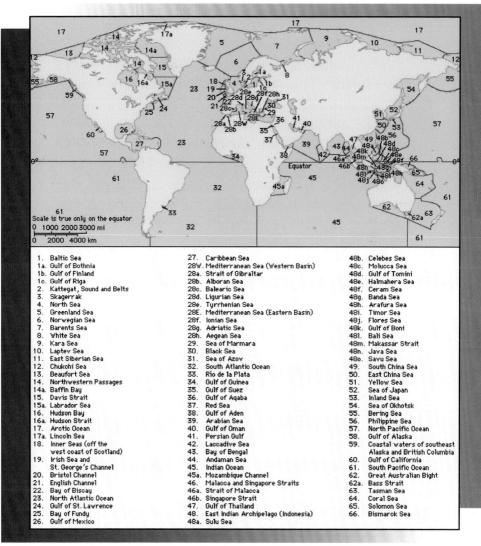

Boundaries of the world's oceans and seas. Encyclopædia Britannica, Inc.

1. Baltic Sea	27. Caribbean Sea	48b. Celebes Sea
1a. Gulf of Bothnia	28W. Mediterranean Sea (Western Basin)	48c. Molucca Sea
1b. Gulf of Finland	28a. Strait of Gibraltar	48d. Gulf of Tomini
1c. Gulf of Riga	28b. Alboran Sea	48e. Halmahera Sea
2. Kattegat, Sound and Belts	28c. Balearic Sea	48f. Ceram Sea
3. Skagerrak	28d. Ligurian Sea	48g. Banda Sea
4. North Sea	28e. Tyrrhenian Sea	48h. Arafura Sea
5. Greenland Sea	28E. Mediterranean Sea (Eastern Basin)	48i. Timor Sea
6. Norwegian Sea	28f. Ionian Sea	48j. Flores Sea
7. Barents Sea	28g. Adriatic Sea	48k. Gulf of Boni
8. White Sea	28h. Aegean Sea	48l. Bali Sea
9. Kara Sea	29. Sea of Marmara	48m. Makassar Strait
10. Laptev Sea	30. Black Sea	48n. Java Sea
11. East Siberian Sea	31. Sea of Azov	48o. Savu Sea
12. Chukchi Sea	32. South Atlantic Ocean	49. South China Sea
13. Beaufort Sea	33. Río de la Plata	50. East China Sea
14. Northwestern Passages	34. Gulf of Guinea	51. Yellow Sea
14a. Baffin Bay	35. Gulf of Suez	52. Sea of Japan
15. Davis Strait	36. Gulf of Aqaba	53. Inland Sea
15a. Labrador Sea	37. Red Sea	54. Sea of Okhotsk
16. Hudson Bay	38. Gulf of Aden	55. Bering Sea
16a. Hudson Strait	39. Arabian Sea	56. Philippine Sea
17. Arctic Ocean	40. Gulf of Oman	57. North Pacific Ocean
17a. Lincoln Sea	41. Persian Gulf	58. Gulf of Alaska
18. Inner Seas (off the	42. Laccadive Sea	59. Coastal waters of southeast
west coast of Scotland)	43. Bay of Bengal	Alaska and British Columbia
19. Irish Sea and	44. Andaman Sea	60. Gulf of California
St. George's Channel	45. Indian Ocean	61. South Pacific Ocean
20. Bristol Channel	45a. Mozambique Channel	62. Great Australian Bight
21. English Channel	46. Malacca and Singapore Straits	62a. Bass Strait
22. Bay of Biscay	46a. Strait of Malacca	63. Tasman Sea
23. North Atlantic Ocean	46b. Singapore Strait	64. Coral Sea
24. Gulf of St. Lawrence	47. Gulf of Thailand	65. Solomon Sea
25. Bay of Fundy	48. East Indian Archipelago (Indonesia)	66. Bismarck Sea
26. Gulf of Mexico	48a. Sulu Sea	

Malaysia and Indonesia to Australia, and then on to Antarctica. Many subdivisions can be made to distinguish the limits of seas and gulfs that have historical, political, and sometimes ecological significance. However, water properties, ocean currents, and biological populations do not necessarily recognize these boundaries. Indeed, many researchers do not either. The oceanic area surrounding the Antarctic is considered by some to be the Southern Ocean.

If area-volume analyses of the oceans are to be made, then boundaries must be established to separate individual regions. In 1921 Erwin Kossina, a German geographer, published tables giving the distribution of oceanic water with depth for the oceans and adjacent seas. This work was updated in 1966 by H.W. Menard and S.M. Smith. The latter only slightly changed the numbers derived by Kossina. This was remarkable, since the original effort relied entirely on the sparse depth measurements accumulated by individual wire soundings, while the more recent work had the benefit of acoustic depth soundings collected since the 1920s. This type of analysis, called hypsometry, allows quantification of the surface area distribution of the oceans and their marginal seas with depth.

The distribution of oceanic surface area with 5° increments of latitude shows that the distribution of land and water on Earth's surface is markedly different in the Northern and Southern hemispheres. The Southern Hemisphere may be called the water hemisphere, while the Northern Hemisphere is the land hemisphere. This is especially true in the temperate latitudes.

This asymmetry of land and water distribution between the Northern and Southern hemispheres makes the two hemispheres behave very differently in response to the annual variation in solar radiation received by Earth. The Southern Hemisphere shows only a small change in surface temperature from summer to winter at temperate latitudes. This variation is controlled primarily by the ocean's response to seasonal changes in heating and cooling. The Northern Hemisphere has one change in surface temperature controlled by its oceanic area and

HYPSOMETRY

Hypsometry is the science of measuring the elevation and depth of features on Earth's surface with respect to sea level. Data collected using hypsometers, wire sounders, echo sounders, and satellite-based altimeters is used to quantify the distribution of land at different elevations across a given area and the surface-area distribution of the oceans and their marginal seas with depth. Scientists can show how the areas of oceans, marginal seas, and terrestrial basins change with elevation and depth using a special curve known as a hypsometric, or hypsographic, curve.

another controlled by its land area. In the temperate latitudes of the Northern Hemisphere, the land is much warmer than the oceanic area in summer and much colder in winter. This situation creates large-scale seasonal changes in atmospheric circulation and climate in the Northern Hemisphere that are not found in the Southern Hemisphere.

MAJOR SUBDIVISIONS OF THE OCEANS

If the volume of an ocean is divided by its surface area, the mean depth is obtained. With or without marginal seas, the Pacific is the largest ocean in both surface area and volume, the Atlantic is next, and the Indian is the smallest. The Atlantic exhibits the largest change in surface area and volume when its marginal seas are subtracted. This indicates that the Atlantic has the greatest area of bordering seas, many of which are shallow.

Hypsometry can show how the area of each ocean or marginal sea changes as depth changes. A special curve known as a hypsometric, or hypsographic, curve can be drawn that portrays how the surface area of Earth is

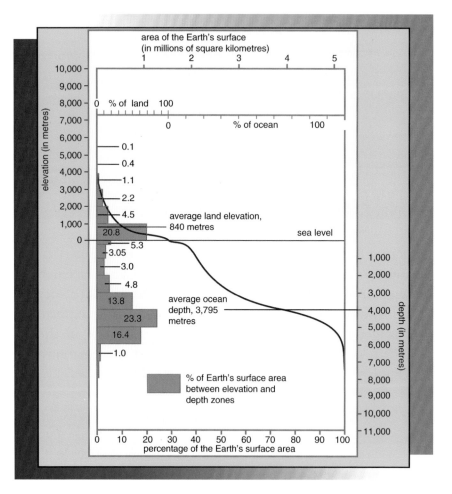

Hypsographic curve showing how the surface area of Earth is distributed with elevation and depth. Copyright Encyclopædia Britannica, Inc.; rendering for this edition by Rosen Educational Services

distributed with elevation and depth. This curve has been drawn to represent the total Earth and all of its oceans; likewise, curves can be constructed for each individual ocean and sea. The average depth of the world's oceans, 3,795 metres (12,451 feet), and the average elevation of the land, 840 metres (2,756 feet), are indicated. The highest point on land, Mount Everest (8,850 metres [29,035 feet]), and the deepest point in the ocean, located in the Mariana Trench (11,034 metres [36,201 feet]), mark the upper and lower limits of the curve, respectively. Since this curve is drawn on a grid of elevation versus Earth's area, the area under the curve covering the 29.2 percent of Earth's surface that is above sea level is the volume of land above sea level. Similarly, the area between sea level and the curve depicting the remaining 70.8 percent of Earth's surface below sea level represents the volume of water contained in the oceans.

Portions of this curve describe the area of Earth's surface that exists between elevation or depth increments. On land, little of Earth's total area—only about 4 percent—is at elevations above 2,000 metres (6,562 feet). Most of the land, 25.3 percent of the total Earth, is between 0 and 2,000 metres. About 13.6 percent of the total land area is at higher elevations, with 86.4 percent between 0 and 2,000 metres when the areas are determined relative to land area only. In the oceans, the percentages of the area devoted to depth increments yield information about the typical structure and shape of the oceanic basins. The small depth increment of 0–200 metres (0–660 feet) occupies about 5.4 percent of Earth's total area or 7.6 percent of the oceans' area. This approximates the world's area of continental shelves, the shallow flat borderlands of the continents that have been alternately covered by the oceans during interglacial stages and uncovered during glacial periods.

At depths between 200 and 1,000 metres (about 660 and 3,300 feet) and between 1,000 and 2,000 metres (about 3,300 and 6,600 feet), an area only slightly larger—6.02 percent of Earth's total area or 8.5 percent of the oceans' area—is found. These depths are related to the regions of the oceans that have very steep slopes where depth increases rapidly. These are the continental slope regions that mark the true edge of the continental landmasses. Marginal seas of moderate depths and the tops of sea-mounts, however, add their area to these depth zones when all the oceans are considered. The majority of the oceanic area lies between 4,000 and 5,000 metres (about 13,100 and 16,400 feet).

The continental shelf region varies immensely from place to place. The seaward boundary of the continental shelf historically is determined by the 100-fathom, or 200-metre, depth contour. However, 85 fathoms, or 170 metres (about 560 feet), is a closer approximation. The true boundary at any given location is marked by a rapid change in slope of the seafloor known as the shelf break. This change in slope may be nearly at the coastline in areas where crustal plates converge, as along the west coast of North and South America, or it may be located more than 1,000 km (620 miles) seaward of the coast, as off the north coast of Siberia. The average width of the shelf is about 75 km (47 miles), and the shelf has an average slope of about 0.01°, a slope that is barely discernible to the human eye. Seaward of the shelf break, the continental slope is inclined by about 4°.

ORIGIN OF OCEAN WATERS

The huge volume of water contained in the oceans (and seas), 137×10^7 cubic km (about 33×10^7 cubic miles), has been produced during the geologic history of Earth. There is little information on the early history of Earth's waters. However, fossils dated from the Precambrian some 3.3 billion years ago show that bacteria and cyano-bacteria (blue-green algae) existed, indicating the presence of water during this period. Carbonate sedimentary rocks, obviously laid down in an aquatic environment, have been dated to 1 billion years ago. Also, there is fossil evidence of primitive marine algae and invertebrates from the outset of the Cambrian Period some 542 million years ago.

The presence of water on Earth at even earlier times is not documented by physical evidence. It has been suggested, however, that the early hydrosphere formed in response to condensation from the early atmosphere. The ratios of certain elements on Earth indicate that the planet formed by the accumulation of cosmic dust and was slowly warmed by radioactive and compressional heating. This heating led to the gradual separation and migration of materials to form Earth's core, mantle, and crust. The early atmosphere is thought to have been highly reducing and rich in gases, notably in hydrogen, and to include water vapour.

Earth's surface temperature and the partial pressures of the individual gases in the early atmosphere affected the atmosphere's equilibration with the terrestrial surface. As time progressed and the planetary interior continued to warm, the composition of the gases escaping from within Earth gradually changed the properties of its atmosphere, producing a gaseous mixture rich in carbon dioxide (CO_2), carbon monoxide (CO), and molecular nitrogen (N_2). Photodissociation (i.e., separation due to the energy of light) of water vapour into molecular hydrogen (H_2) and molecular oxygen (O_2) in the upper atmosphere allowed the hydrogen to escape and led to a progressive increase of the partial pressure of oxygen at Earth's surface. The reaction of this oxygen with the materials of the surface gradually caused the vapour pressure of water vapour to increase to a level at which liquid water could form. This water in liquid form accumulated in isolated depressions of Earth's surface, forming the nascent oceans.

The high carbon dioxide content of the atmosphere at this time would have allowed a buildup of dissolved carbon dioxide in the water and made these early oceans acidic and capable of dissolving surface rocks that would add to the water's salt content. Water must have evaporated and condensed rapidly and accumulated slowly at first. The required buildup of atmospheric oxygen was slow because much of this gas was used to oxidize methane, ammonia, and exposed rocks high in iron. Gradually, the partial pressure of the oxygen gas in the atmosphere rose as photosynthesis by bacteria and photodissociation continued to supply oxygen. Biological processes involving algae increased, and they gradually decreased the carbon dioxide content and increased the oxygen content of the atmosphere until the oxygen produced by biological processes outweighed that produced by photodissociation. This, in turn, accelerated the formation of surface water and the development of the oceans.

COMPOSITION OF SEAWATER

The chemical composition of seawater is influenced by a wide variety of chemical transport mechanisms. Rivers add dissolved and particulate chemicals to the oceanic margins. Wind-borne particulates are carried to mid-ocean regions thousands of kilometres from their continental source areas. Hydrothermal solutions that have circulated through crustal materials beneath the seafloor add both dissolved and particulate materials to the deep ocean. Organisms in the upper ocean convert dissolved materials to solids, which eventually settle to greater oceanic depths. Particulates in transit to the sea-floor, as well as materials both on and within the seafloor, undergo chemical exchange with surrounding solutions. Through these local and regional chemical input and removal mechanisms, each element in the oceans tends to exhibit spatial and temporal concentration variations. Physical mixing in the oceans (thermohaline and wind-driven circulation) tends to homogenize the chemical composition of seawater. The opposing influences of physical mixing and of biogeochemical input and removal mechanisms result in a substantial variety of chemical distributions in the oceans.

DISSOLVED INORGANIC SUBSTANCES

In contrast to the behaviour of most oceanic substances, the concentrations of the principal inorganic constituents of the oceans are remarkably constant. Calculations indicate that, for the main constituents of seawater, the time required for thorough oceanic mixing is quite short compared with the time that would be required for input or removal processes to significantly change a constituent's concentration. The concentrations of the principal constituents of the oceans vary primarily in response to a comparatively rapid exchange of water (precipitation and evaporation), with relative concentrations remaining nearly constant.

Salinity is used by oceanographers as a measure of the total salt content of seawater. Practical salinity, symbol S, is determined through measurements of a ratio between the electrical conductivity of seawater and the electrical conductivity of a standard solution. Practical salinity can be used to calculate precisely the density of seawater samples. Because of the constant relative

PRINCIPAL CONSTITUENTS OF SEAWATER*

IONIC CONSTITUENT	G/KG OF SEAWATER	MOLES/ KG**	RELATIVE CONCENTRATION
chloride	19.162	0.5405	1.0000
sodium	10.679	0.4645	0.8593
magnesium	1.278	0.0526	0.0974
sulfate	2.680	0.0279	0.0517
calcium	0.4096	0.01022	0.0189
potassium	0.3953	0.01011	0.0187
carbon (inorganic)	0.0276	0.0023	0.0043
bromide	0.0663	0.00083	0.00154
boron	0.0044	0.00041	0.00075
strontium	0.0079	0.00009	0.000165
fluoride	0.0013	0.00007	0.000125

*Concentrations at salinity equal to 34.7.
**Ionic concentrations are conventionally expressed in molecular units. One mole per kilogram is equivalent to $6.023(10^{23})$ ions or molecules per kilogram of seawater. The relative concentrations in column 4 provide the number of ions of each constituent in one kilogram of seawater as compared to the number of chloride ions in one kilogram of seawater.

proportions of the principal constituents, salinity can also be used to directly calculate the concentrations of the major ions in seawater. The measure of practical salinity was originally developed to provide an approximate measure of the total mass of salt in 1 kg (2.2 pounds) of seawater. Seawater with S equal to 35 contains approximately 35 grams (1.2 ounces) of salt and 965 grams (34 ounces) of water.

Many other constituents are of great importance to the biogeochemistry of the oceans. Such chemicals as inorganic phosphorus (HPO_4^{2-} and PO_4^{3-}) and inorganic nitrogen (NO_3^-, NO_2^-, and NH_4^+) are essential to the growth of marine organisms. Nitrogen and phosphorus are incorporated into the tissues of marine organisms in approximately a 16:1 ratio and are eventually returned to solution in approximately the same proportion. As a consequence, in much of the oceanic waters dissolved inorganic phosphorus and nitrogen exhibit a close covariance. Dissolved inorganic phosphorus distributions in the Pacific Ocean strongly bear the imprint of phosphorus incorporation by organisms in the surface waters of the ocean and of the return of the phosphorus to solution via a rain of biological debris remineralized in the deep ocean. Inorganic phosphate concentrations in the western Pacific range from somewhat less than 0.1 micromole per kg (1×10^{-7} mole per kg) at the surface to approximately 3 micromoles/kg (3×10^{-6} mole/kg) at depth. Inorganic nitrogen ranges between somewhat less than 1 micromole/kg and 45 micromoles/kg along the same section of ocean and exhibits a striking covariance with phosphate.

A variety of elements essential to the growth of marine organisms, as well as some elements that have no known biological function, exhibit nutrient-like behaviour broadly similar to nitrate and phosphate. Silicate is incorporated into the hard structural parts of certain types of marine organisms (diatoms and radiolarians) that are abundant in the upper ocean. Dissolved silicate concentrations range between less than 1 micromole/kg (1×10^{-6} mole/kg) in surface waters to approximately 180 micromoles/kg (1.8×10^{-4} mole/kg) in the deep North Pacific. The concentration of zinc, a metal essential to a variety of biological functions, ranges between approximately 0.05 nanomole/kg (5×10^{-11} mole/kg) in the surface ocean to as much as 6 nanomoles/kg (6×10^{-9} mole/kg) in the deep Pacific. The distribution of zinc in the oceans is observed to generally parallel silicate distributions. Cadmium, though having no known biological function, generally exhibits distributions that are covariant with phosphate and concentrations that are even lower than those of zinc.

Many elements, including the essential trace metals iron, cobalt, and copper, show surface depletions but in general exhibit behaviour more complex than that of phosphate, nitrate, and silicate. Some of the complexities observed in elemental oceanic distributions are attributable to the adsorption of elements on the surface of sinking particles. Adsorptive processes, either exclusive of or in addition to biological uptake, serve to remove elements from the upper ocean and deliver them to greater depths. The distribution patterns of a number of trace elements are complicated by their participation in oxidation-reduction (electron-exchange) reactions. In general, electron-exchange reactions lead to profound changes in the solubility and reactivity of trace metals in seawater. Such reactions are important to the oceanic behaviour of a variety of elements, including iron, manganese, copper, cobalt, chromium, and cerium.

The processes that deliver dissolved, particulate, and gaseous materials to the oceans ensure that they contain, at some concentration, very nearly every element that is found in Earth's crust and atmosphere. The principal components of the atmosphere, nitrogen (78.1 percent), oxygen (21.0 percent), argon (0.93 percent), and carbon dioxide (0.035 percent), occur in seawater in variable proportions, depending on their solubilities and oceanic chemical reactions. In equilibrium with the atmosphere, the concentrations of the unreactive gases, nitrogen and argon, in seawater (0 °C [32 °F], salinity 35) are 616 micromoles/kg and 17 micromoles/kg, respectively. For seawater at 35 °C (95 °F), these concentrations would decrease by approximately a factor of two. The solubility behaviours of argon and oxygen are quite similar. For seawater in equilibrium with the atmosphere, the ratio of oxygen and argon concentrations is approximately 20.45. Since oxygen is a reactive gas essential to life, oxygen concentrations in seawater that are not in direct equilibrium with the atmosphere are quite variable. Although oxygen is produced by photosynthetic organisms at shallow, sunlit ocean depths, oxygen concentrations in near-surface waters are established primarily by exchange with the atmosphere. Oxygen concentrations in the oceans generally exhibit minimum values at intermediate depths and relatively high values in deep waters. This distribution pattern results from a combination of biological oxygen utilization and physical mixing of the ocean waters. Estimates of the extent of oxygen utilization in the oceans can be obtained by comparing concentrations of oxygen with those of argon, since the latter are only influenced by physical processes. The physical processes that influence oxygen distributions include, in particular, the large-scale replenishment of oceanic bottom waters with cold, dense, oxygen-rich waters sinking toward the bottom from high latitudes. Due to the release of nutrients that accompanies the consumption of oxygen by biological debris, dissolved oxygen concentrations generally appear as a mirror image of dissolved nutrient concentrations.

While the atmosphere is a vast repository of oxygen compared with the oceans, the total carbon dioxide content of the oceans is very large compared with that of the atmosphere. Carbon dioxide reacts with water in seawater to form carbonic acid (H_2CO_3), bicarbonate ions (HCO_3^-), and carbonate ions (CO_3^{2-}). Approximately 90 percent of the total organic carbon in seawater is present as bicarbonate ions. The formation of bicarbonate and carbonate ions from carbon dioxide is accompanied by the liberation of hydrogen ions (H^+). Reactions between hydrogen ions and the various forms of inorganic carbon buffer the acidity of seawater. The relatively high concentrations of both total inorganic carbon and boron—as $B(OH)_3$ and $B(OH)_4^-$—in seawater are sufficient to maintain the pH of seawater between 7.4 and 8.3. (The term pH is defined as the negative logarithm of the hydrogen ion concentration in moles per kg. Thus, a pH equal to 8 is equivalent to 1×10^{-8} mole of H^+ ions per kg of seawater.) This is quite important because the extent and rate of many reactions in seawater are highly pH-dependent. Carbon dioxide produced by the combination of oxygen and organic carbon generally produces an acidity maximum (pH minimum) near the depth of the oxygen minimum in seawater. In addition to exchange with the atmosphere and, through respiration, with the biosphere, dissolved inorganic carbon concentrations in seawater are influenced by the formation and dissolution of the calcareous shells ($CaCO_3$) of organisms (foraminiferans, coccolithophores, and pteropods) abundant in the upper ocean.

DISSOLVED ORGANIC SUBSTANCES

Processes involving dissolved and particulate organic carbon are of central importance in shaping the chemical character of seawater. Marine organic carbon principally originates in the uppermost 100 metres (330 feet) of the oceans where dissolved inorganic carbon is photosynthetically converted to organic materials. The "rain" of organic-rich particulate materials, resulting directly and indirectly from photosynthetic production, is a principal factor behind the distributions of many organic and inorganic substances in the oceans. A large fraction of the vertical flux of materials in the uppermost waters is converted to dissolved substances within the upper 400 metres (about 1,300 feet) of the oceans. Dissolved organic carbon (DOC) accounts for at least 90 percent of the total organic carbon in the oceans. Estimates of DOC appropriate to the surface of the open ocean range between roughly 100 and 500 micromoles of carbon per kg of seawater. DOC concentrations in the deep ocean are 5 to 10 times lower than surface values.

DOC occurs in an extraordinary variety of forms, and, in general, its composition is controversial and poorly understood. Conventional techniques have indicated that, in surface waters, about 15 percent of DOC can be identified as carbohydrates and combined amino acids. At least 1–2 percent of DOC in surface waters occurs as lipids and 20–25 percent as relatively unreactive humic substances. The relative abundances of reactive organic substances, such as amino acids and carbohydrates, are considerably reduced in deep ocean waters. Dissolved and particulate organic carbon in the surface ocean participates in diel cycles (i.e., those of a 24-hour period) related to photosynthetic production and photochemical transformations. The influence of dissolved organic matter on ocean chemistry is often out of proportion to its oceanic abundance. Photochemical reactions involving DOC can influence the chemistry of vital trace nutrients such as iron, and, even at dissolved concentrations on the order of one nanomole/kg (1×10^{-9} mole/kg), dissolved organic substances in the upper ocean waters are capable of greatly altering the

A drainpipe spews untreated sewage near Gaza, releasing harmful chemicals into the Mediterranean Sea. Human activity is a prime source of such toxins. Warrick Page/Getty Images

bioavailability of essential trace nutrients, as, for example, copper and zinc.

Effects of Human Activities

Although the oceans constitute an enormous reservoir, human activities have begun to influence their composition on both a local and a global scale. The addition of nutrients (through the discharge of untreated sewage or the seepage of soluble mineral fertilizers, for example) to coastal waters results in increased phytoplankton growth, high levels of dissolved and particulate organic materials, decreased penetration of light through seawater, and alteration of the community structure of bottom-dwelling organisms. Through industrial and automotive emissions, lead concentrations in the surface ocean have increased dramatically on a global scale compared with preindustrial levels. Certain toxic organic compounds, such as polychlorinated biphenyls (PCBs), are found in seawater and marine organisms and are attributable solely to the activities of humankind.

Although most radioactivity in seawater is natural (approximately 90 percent as potassium-40 and less than 1 percent each as rubidium-87 and uranium-238), strontium-90 and certain other artificial radioisotopes have unique environmental pathways and potential for bioaccumulation. Among the most dramatic influences of human activities on a global scale is the remarkable increase of carbon dioxide levels in the atmosphere. Atmospheric carbon dioxide levels are expected to double by the middle of the 21st century, with potentially profound consequences for global climate and agricultural patterns. It is thought that the oceans, as a great reservoir of carbon dioxide, will ameliorate this consequence of human activities to some degree.

THE PHYSICAL PROPERTIES OF SEAWATER

Water is a unique substance. Not only is water the most abundant substance at Earth's surface, but it also has the most naturally occurring physical states of any Earth material or substance (solid, liquid, and gas) and the greatest capacity to do things without being altered significantly. It is essential for sustaining life on Earth and affects the physical environment in a myriad of ways, as evidenced by the sculpting of landscape features by moving water, the maintaining of Earth's radiation balance by atmospheric water vapour transfer, and the transporting of inorganic and organic materials about the planet's surface by the oceans. The addition of salt to water changes the behaviour of water only slightly.

SALINITY DISTRIBUTION

A discussion of salinity, the salt content of the oceans, requires an understanding of two important concepts: (1) the present-day oceans are considered to be in steady state, receiving as much salt as they lose, and (2) the oceans have been mixed over such a long time period that the composition of sea salt is everywhere the same in the open ocean. This uniformity of salt content results in oceans in which the salinity varies little over space or time.

The range of salinity observed in the open ocean is from 33 to 37 grams (1.2 to 1.3 ounces) of salt per kg of seawater or parts per thousand (‰). For the most part, the observed departure from a mean value of approximately

35‰ is caused by processes at Earth's surface that locally add or remove fresh water. Regions of high evaporation have elevated surface salinities, while regions of high precipitation have depressed surface salinities. In near-shore regions close to large freshwater sources, the salinity may be lowered by dilution. This is especially true in areas where the region of the ocean receiving the fresh water is isolated from the open ocean by the geography of the land.

Areas of the Baltic Sea may have salinity values depressed to 10‰ or less. Increased salinity by evaporation is accentuated where isolation of the water occurs. This effect is found in the Red Sea, where the surface salinity rises to 41‰. Coastal lagoon salinities in areas of high evaporation may be much higher. The removal of fresh water by evaporation or the addition of fresh water by precipitation does not affect the constancy of composition of the sea salt in the open sea. A river draining a particular soil type, however, may bring to the oceans only certain salts that will locally alter the salt composition. In areas of high evaporation where the salinity is driven to very high values, precipitation of particular salts may alter the composition too. At high latitudes where sea ice forms seasonally, the salinity of the seawater is elevated during ice formation and reduced when the ice melts.

At depth in the oceans, salinity may be altered as seawater percolates into fissures associated with deep-ocean ridges and crustal rifts involving volcanism. This water then returns to the ocean as superheated water carrying dissolved salts from the magmatic material within the crust. It may lose much of its dissolved load to precipitates on the seafloor and gradually blend in with the surrounding seawater, sharing its remaining dissolved substances.

Salt concentrations as high as 256‰ have been found in hot but dense pools of brine trapped in depressions at the bottom of the Red Sea. The composition of the salts in these pools is not the same as the sea salt of the open oceans.

The salinities of the open oceans found at the greater depths are quite uniform in both time and space with average values of 34.5 to 35‰. These salinities are determined by surface processes such as those described above when the water, now at depth, was last in contact with the surface.

The intertropical convergence, with its high precipitation centred about 5° N, supports the tropical rainforests of the world and leaves its imprint on the oceans as a latitudinal depression of surface salinity. At approximately 30°–35° N and 30°–35° S, the subtropical zones called the horse latitudes are belts of high evaporation that produce major deserts and grasslands on the continents and cause the surface salinity to rise. At 50°–60° N and 50°–60° S, precipitation again increases.

HORSE LATITUDES

The horse latitudes are two subtropical atmospheric high-pressure belts that encircle Earth around latitudes 30°–35° N and 30°–35° S and that generate light winds and clear skies. Because they contain dry, subsiding air, they produce arid climates in the areas below them. The Sahara, for example, is situated in a horse latitude. The Southern Hemisphere, which has more water area than the Northern, has the more continuous belt of subsiding air. The belts contain several separate high-pressure centres and shift a few degrees away from the equator in summer.

The horse latitudes were named by the crews of sailing ships, who sometimes threw horses overboard to conserve water when their ships were becalmed in the high-pressure belts.

TEMPERATURE DISTRIBUTION

Mid-ocean surface temperatures vary with latitude in response to the balance between incoming solar radiation and outgoing long-wave radiation. There is an excess of incoming solar radiation at latitudes less than approximately 45° and an excess of radiation loss at latitudes higher than approximately 45°. Superimposed on this radiation balance are seasonal changes in the intensity of solar radiation and the duration of daylight hours due to the tilt of Earth's axis to the plane of the ecliptic and the rotation of the planet about this axis. The combined effect of these variables is that average ocean surface temperatures are higher at low latitudes than at high latitudes. Because the Sun, with respect to Earth, migrates annually between the Tropic of Cancer and the Tropic of Capricorn, the yearly change in heating of Earth's surface is small at low latitudes and large at mid- and higher latitudes.

Water has an extremely high heat capacity, and heat is mixed downward during summer surface-heating conditions and upward during winter surface cooling. This heat transfer reduces the actual change in ocean surface temperatures over the annual cycle. In the tropics the ocean surface is warm year-round, varying seasonally about 1 to 2 °C (1.8 to 3.6 °F). At mid-latitudes the mid-ocean temperatures vary about 8 °C (14.4 °F) over the year. At the polar latitudes the surface temperature remains near the ice point of seawater—about -1.9 °C (28.6 °F).

Land temperatures have a large annual range at high latitudes because of the low heat capacity of the land surface. Proximity to land, isolation of water from the open ocean, and processes that control stability of the surface water combine to increase the annual range of nearshore ocean surface temperature.

In winter, prevailing winds carry cold air masses off the continents in temperate and subarctic latitudes, cooling the adjacent surface seawater below that of the mid-ocean level. In summer, the opposite effect occurs, as warm continental air masses move out over the adjacent sea. This creates a greater annual range in sea surface temperatures at mid-latitudes on the western sides of the oceans of the Northern Hemisphere but has only a small effect in the Southern Hemisphere as there is little land present. Instead, the oceans of the Southern Hemisphere act to control the air temperature, which in turn influences the land temperatures of the temperate zone and reduces the annual temperature range over the land.

Currents carry water having the characteristics of one latitudinal zone to another zone. The northward displacement of warm water to higher latitudes by the Gulf Stream of the North Atlantic and the Kuroshio (Japan Current) of the North Pacific creates sharp changes in temperature along the current boundaries or thermal fronts, where these northward-moving flows meet colder water flowing southward from higher latitudes. Cold water currents flowing from higher to lower latitudes also displace surface isotherms from near constant latitudinal positions. At low latitudes the trade winds act to move water away from the lee coasts of the landmasses to produce areas of coastal upwelling of water from depth and reduce surface temperatures.

Temperatures in the oceans decrease with increasing depth. There are no seasonal changes at the greater depths. The temperature range extends from 30 °C (86 °F) at the sea surface to -1 °C (30.2 °F) at the seabed. Like salinity, the temperature at depth is determined by the conditions that the water encountered when it was last at the surface. In the low latitudes the temperature change from top to bottom in the oceans is large. In high temperate and Arctic regions, the formation of dense water at the surface that sinks to depth produces nearly isothermal conditions with depth.

Areas of the oceans that experience an annual change in surface heating have a shallow wind-mixed layer of elevated temperature in the summer. Below this nearly isothermal layer 10 to 20 metres (about 33 to 66 feet) thick, the temperature decreases rapidly with depth, forming a shallow seasonal thermocline (i.e., layer of sharp vertical temperature change). During winter cooling and increased wind mixing at the ocean surface, convective overturning and mixing erase this shallow thermocline and deepen the isothermal layer. The seasonal thermocline re-forms when summer returns. At greater depths, a weaker nonseasonal thermocline is found separating water from temperate and subpolar sources.

Below this permanent thermocline, temperatures decrease slowly. In the very deep ocean basins, the temperature may be observed to increase slightly with depth. This occurs when the deepest parts of the oceans are filled by water with a single temperature from a common source. This water experiences an adiabatic temperature rise as it sinks. Such a temperature rise does not make the water column unstable because the increased temperature is caused by compression, which increases the density of the water. For example, surface seawater of 2 °C (35.6 °F) sinking to a depth of 10,000 metres (32,800 feet) increases its temperature by about 1.3 °C (2.3 °F). When measuring deep-sea temperatures, the adiabatic temperature rise, which is a function of salinity, initial temperature, and pressure change, is calculated and subtracted from the

observed temperature to obtain the potential temperature. Potential temperatures are used to identify a
common type of water and to trace this water back to
its source.

Thermal Properties

The unit of heat called the gram calorie is defined as the
amount of heat required to raise the temperature of
1 gram (0.04 ounce) of water 1 °C (1.8 °F). The kilocalorie,
or food calorie, is the amount of heat required to raise 1 kg
(2.2 pounds) of water 1 °C. Heat capacity is the amount of
heat required to raise 1 gram of material 1 °C under constant pressure. In the International System of Units (SI),
the heat capacity of water is 1 kilocalorie per kg per degree
Celsius. Water has the highest heat capacity of all common Earth materials; therefore, water on Earth acts as a
thermal buffer, resisting temperature change as it gains or
loses heat energy.

The heat capacity of any material can be divided by
the heat capacity of water to give a ratio known as the
specific heat of the material. Specific heat is numeri-
cally equal to heat capacity but has no units. In other
words, it is a ratio without units. When salt is present,
the heat capacity of water decreases slightly. Seawater
of 35‰ has a specific heat of 0.932 compared to 1.000
for pure water.

Pure water freezes at 0 °C (32 °F) and boils at 100 °C (212
°F) under normal pressure conditions. When salt is added,
the freezing point is lowered and the boiling point is raised.
The addition of salt also lowers the temperature of maximum density below that of pure water (4 °C
[39.2 °F]). The temperature of maximum density decreases
faster than the freezing point as salt is added.

At 30‰ salinity, the temperature of maximum density is lower than the initial freezing point of saltwater. Therefore, a maximum density is never achieved, as seawater of this salinity is cooled because freezing occurs first. At 24.70‰ salinity, the freezing point and the temperature of maximum density coincide at -1.332 °C (29.6 °F). At salinities typical of the open oceans, which are greater than 24.7‰ , the freezing point is always higher than the temperature of maximum density.

When water changes its state, hydrogen bonds between molecules are either formed or broken. Energy is required to break the hydrogen bonds, which allows water to pass from a solid to a liquid state or from a liquid to a gaseous state. When hydrogen bonds are formed, permitting water to change from a liquid to a solid or from a gas to a liquid, energy is liberated. The heat energy input required to change water from a solid at 0 °C to a liquid at 0 °C is the latent heat of fusion and is 80 calories per gram of ice. Water's latent heat of fusion is the highest of all common materials. Because of this, heat is released when ice forms and is absorbed during melting, which tends to buffer air temperatures as land and sea ice form and melt seasonally.

When water converts from a liquid to a gas, a quantity of heat energy known as the latent heat of vaporization is required to break the hydrogen bonds. At 100 °C, 540 calories per gram of water are needed to convert 1 gram of liquid water to 1 gram of water vapour under normal pressure. Water can evaporate at temperatures below the boiling point, and ice can evaporate into a gas without first melting in a process called sublimation. Evaporation below 100 °C and sublimation require more energy per gram than 540 calories. At 20 °C (68 °F) about 585 calories are required to vaporize 1 gram of water. When water vapour condenses back to liquid water, the latent heat of vaporization is liberated. The evaporation of water from the surface of Earth and its condensation in the atmosphere constitute the single most important way that heat from Earth's surface is transferred to the atmosphere. This process is the source of the power that drives hurricanes and a principal mechanism for cooling the surface of the oceans. The latent heat of vaporization of water is the highest of all common substances.

DENSITY OF SEAWATER AND PRESSURE

The density of a material is given in units of mass per unit volume and expressed in kilograms per cubic metre in the SI system of units. In oceanography the density of seawater has been expressed historically in grams per

DENSITY VALUES OF SEAWATER*					
SALINITY	5	10	20	30	35
TEMPERATURE (°C)					
0	3.97	8.01	16.07	24.10	28.13
5	4.01	7.97	15.86	23.74	27.70
10	3.67	7.56	15.32	23.08	26.97
15	3.01	6.85	14.50	22.15	25.99
20	2.07	5.86	13.42	20.98	24.78
25	0.87	4.62	12.10	19.60	23.36
30	−0.57	3.15	10.57	18.01	21.75
*See text for density unit designation.					

cubic centimetre. The density of seawater is a function of temperature, salinity, and pressure. Because oceanographers require density measurements to be accurate to the fifth decimal place, manipulation of the data requires writing many numbers to record each measurement. Also, the pressure effect can be neglected in many instances by using potential temperature. These two factors led oceanographers to adopt a density unit called sigma-*t* (σ_t). This value is obtained by subtracting 1.0 from the density and multiplying the remainder by 1,000. The σ_t has no units and is an abbreviated density of seawater controlled by salinity and temperature only. The σ_t of seawater increases with increasing salinity and decreasing temperature.

The relationship between pressure and density is demonstrated by observing the effect of pressure on the density of seawater at 35‰ and 0 °C (32 °F). Because a 1-metre (3.3-foot) column of seawater produces a pressure of about 1 decibar (0.1 atmosphere), the pressure in decibars is approximately equal to the depth in metres. (One decibar is one-tenth of a bar, which in turn is equal to 10^5 newtons per square metre.)

Increasing density values demonstrate the compressibility of seawater under the tremendous pressures present in the deep ocean. If the average pressure over 4,000 metres (13,100 feet: the approximate mean depth of the ocean) is calculated, it is found to be approximated by that at 2,000 metres (about 6,600 feet). The average volume change due to pressure for each gram of water in the entire water column is $(1/1.02813 – 1/1.03747)$ cm³/g, or 0.00876 cm³/g. Because the number of grams of water in a column of seawater 4×10^5 cm in length is equal to the number of centimetres times the average density of the water, 1.03747 g/cm³, the expansion of the entire water

DENSITY CHANGES WITH DEPTH (seawater 35 parts per thousand and 0 °C)		
DEPTH (M)	PRESSURE (DECIBARS)	DENSITY (G/CM³)
0	0	1.02813
1,000	1,000	1.03285
2,000	2,000	1.03747
4,000	4,000	1.04640
6,000	6,000	1.05495
8,000	8,000	1.06315
10,000	10,000	1.07104

column is about 4×10^5 cm $\times$ 0.00876 cm³/g $\times$ 1.03747 g/cm³, or an average sea level rise of about 36 metres (118 feet) if the area of the oceans is considered constant.

The temperature of maximum density and the freezing point of water decrease as salt is added to water, and the temperature of maximum density decreases more rapidly than the freezing point. At salinities less than 24.7‰ the density maximum is reached before the ice point, while at the higher salinities more typical of the open oceans the maximum density is never achieved naturally. This ability of low-salinity water and, of course, fresh water to pass through a density maximum makes them both behave differently from marine systems when water is cooled at the surface and density-driven overturn occurs.

During the fall a lake is cooled at its surface, the surface water sinks, and convective overturn proceeds as the density of the surface water increases with the decreasing temperature. By the time the surface water reaches 4 °C (39.2 °F), the temperature of maximum density for fresh water, the density-driven convective overturn has reached the bottom of the lake, and overturn ceases. Further cooling of the surface produces less dense water, and the lake becomes stably stratified with regard to temperature-controlled density. Only a relatively shallow surface layer is cooled below 4 °C. When this surface layer is cooled to the ice point, 0 °C, ice is formed as the latent heat of fusion is extracted. In a deep lake the temperature at depth remains at 4 °C. In the spring the surface water warms up and the ice melts. A shallow convective overturn resumes until the lake is once more isothermal at 4 °C. Continued warming of the surface produces a stable water column.

In seawater in which the salinity exceeds 24.7‰ , convective overturn also occurs during the cooling cycle and penetrates to a depth determined by the salinity and temperature-controlled density of the cooled water. Since no density maximum is passed, the thermally driven convective overturn is continuous until the ice point is reached where sea ice forms with the extraction of the latent heat of fusion. Since salt is largely excluded from the ice in most cases, the salinity of the water beneath the ice increases slightly and a convective overturn that is both salt- and temperature-driven continues as sea ice forms.

The continuing overturn requires that a large volume of water be cooled to a new ice point dictated by the salinity increase before additional ice forms. In this manner, very dense seawater that is both cold and of elevated salinity is formed. Such areas as the Weddell Sea in Antarctica produce the densest water of the oceans. This water, known as Antarctic Bottom Water, sinks to the deepest depths of the oceans. The continuing overturn slows the rate at which the sea ice forms, limiting the seasonal thickness of the ice. Other factors that control the thickness of ice are the rate at which heat is conducted through the ice layer and the insulation provided by snow on the ice. Seasonal sea ice seldom exceeds about 2 metres (6.6 feet) in thickness. During the warmer season, melting sea ice supplies a freshwater layer to the sea surface and thereby stabilizes the water column.

Surface processes that alter the temperature and salinity of seawater drive the vertical circulation of the oceans. Known as thermohaline circulation, it continually replaces seawater at depth with water from the surface and slowly replaces surface water elsewhere with water rising from deeper depths.

OPTICAL PROPERTIES

Water is transparent to the wavelengths of electromagnetic radiation that fall within the visible spectrum and is opaque to wavelengths above and below this band. However, once in the water, visible light is subject to both refraction and attenuation.

Light rays that enter the water at any angle other than a right angle are refracted (i.e., bent) because the light waves travel at a slower speed in water than they do in air. The amount of refraction, referred to as the refractive index, is affected by both the salinity and temperature of the water. The refractive index increases with increasing salinity and decreasing temperature. This relationship allows the refractive index of a sample of seawater at a constant temperature to be used to determine the salinity of the sample.

Some of the Sun's radiant energy is reflected at the ocean surface and does not enter the ocean. That which penetrates the water's surface is attenuated by absorption and conversion to other forms of energy, such as heat that warms or evaporates water, or is used by plants to fuel photosynthesis. Sunlight that is not absorbed can be scattered by molecules and particulates suspended in the water. Scattered light is deflected into new directional paths and may wander randomly to eventually be either absorbed or directed upward and out of the water. It is this upward scattered light and the light reflected from particles that determine the colour of the oceans, as seen from above.

Water molecules, dissolved salts, organic substances, and suspended particulates combine to cause the intensity of available solar radiation to decrease with depth. Observations of light attenuation in ocean waters indicate that not only does the intensity of solar radiation decrease with depth but also the wavelengths present in the solar spectrum are not attenuated at the same rates. Both short wavelengths (ultraviolet) and long wavelengths (infrared) are absorbed rapidly and are not available for scattering. Only blue-green wavelengths penetrate to any depth, and because the blue-green light is most available for scattering, the oceans appear blue to the human eye. Changes in the colour of the ocean waters are caused either by the colour of the particulates in suspension and dissolved substances or by the changing quality of the solar radiation at the ocean surface as determined by the angle of the Sun and atmospheric conditions. In the clearest ocean waters only about 1 percent of the surface radiation remains at a depth of 150 metres (about 500 feet). No sunlight penetrates below 1,000 metres (3,300 feet).

There are many ways of measuring light attenuation in the oceans. A common method involves the use of a Secchi disk, a weighted round white disk about 30 cm (11.8 inches) in diameter. The Secchi disk is lowered into the ocean to the depth where it disappears from view; its reflectance equals the intensity of light backscattered from the water. This depth in metres divided into 1.7 yields an attenuation, or extinction, coefficient for available light as averaged over the Secchi disk depth. The light extinction coefficient, x, may then be used in a form of Beer's law, $I_z = I_o e^{xz}$, to estimate I_z, the intensity of light at depth z from I_o, the intensity of light at the ocean surface. This method gives no indication of the attenuation

LOSS OF LIGHT (PERCENT) IN ONE METRE OF SEAWATER*								
	VIOLET		BLUE–GREEN			YEL–LOW	ORANGE	RED
wavelength (micrometre)	0.30	0.40	0.46	0.50	0.54	0.58	0.64	0.70
oceanic water, most transparent	16%	4%	2%	3%	5%	9%	29%	42%
oceanic water, least transparent	57%	16%	11%	10%	13%	19%	36%	55%
coastal water, average		63%	37%	29%	28%	30%	45%	74%

*According to Jerlov.

change with depth or the attenuation of specific wavelengths of light.

A photocell may be lowered into the ocean to measure light intensity at discrete depths and to determine light reduction from the surface value or from the previous depth value. The photocell may sense all available wavelengths or may be equipped with filters that pass only certain wavelengths of light. Since I^z and I_o are known, changing light intensity values may be used in Beer's law to determine how the attenuation coefficient changes with depth and quality of light. Measurements of this type are used to determine the level of photosynthesis as a function of radiant energy level with depth and to measure changes in the turbidity of the water caused by particulate distribution with depth.

Different areas of the oceans tend to have different optical properties. Near rivers, silt increases the suspended particle effect. Where nutrients and sunlight are abundant, phytoplankton (unicellular plants) increase the opacity of the water and lend it their colour. Organic substances from excretion and decomposition also have colour and absorb light.

Solar radiation received at the ocean surface is constantly changing in time and space. Cloud cover, atmospheric dust, atmospheric gas composition, roughness of the ocean surface, and elevation angle of the Sun combine to change both the quality and quantity of light

SUNLIGHT REFLECTANCE							
Sun's elevation angle (in degrees)	90	50	40	30	20	10	5
reflectance (percent)	3	3	4	6	12	27	42

that enters the ocean. When the Sun's rays are perpendicular to a smooth ocean surface, reflectance is low. When the solar rays are oblique to the ocean surface, reflectance is increased. If the ocean is rough with waves, reflectance is increased when the Sun is at high elevation and decreased when it is at low elevation. Since latitude plays a role in the elevation of the Sun above the horizon, light penetration is always less at the higher latitudes. Cloud cover, density layering, fog, and dust cause refraction and atmospheric scattering of sunlight. When strongly scattered, the Sun's rays are not unidirectional and there are no shadows. Light enters the ocean from all angles under this condition, and the elevation angle of the Sun loses its importance in controlling surface reflectance. The solar energy available to penetrate the ocean is 100 percent minus the tabulated reflectance value.

These data indicate that water is a good absorber of solar radiation.

ACOUSTIC PROPERTIES

Water is an excellent conductor of sound, considerably better than air. The attenuation of sound by absorption and conversion to other energy forms is a function of sound frequency and the properties of water.

The attenuation coefficient, x, in Beer's law, as applied to sound, where I_z and I_o are now sound intensity values, is dependent on the viscosity of water and inversely proportional to the frequency of the sound and the density of the water. High-pitched sounds are absorbed and converted to heat faster than low-pitched sounds. Sound velocity in water is determined by the square root of elasticity divided by the water's density. Because water is only slightly compressible, it has a large value of elasticity and therefore conducts sound rapidly. Since both the elasticity and density of seawater change with temperature, salinity, and pressure, so does the velocity of sound.

In the oceans the speed of sound varies between 1,450 and 1,570 metres (4,757 and 5,151 feet) per second. It increases about 4.5 metres (14.8 feet) per second per each degree C (1.8 °F) increase and 1.3 metres (4.3 feet) per second per each 1‰ increase in salinity. Increasing pressure also increases the speed of sound at the rate of about 1.7 metres (5.6 feet) per second for an increase in pressure of 100 metres (about 330 feet) in depth, which is equal to approximately 10 bars, or 10 atmospheres.

The greatest changes in temperature and salinity with depth that affect the speed of sound are found near the surface. Changes of sound speed in the horizontal are usually slight except in areas where abrupt boundaries exist between waters of different properties. The effects of salinity and temperature on sound speed are more important than the effect of pressure in the upper layers. Deeper in the ocean, salinity and temperature change less with depth, and pressure becomes the important controlling factor.

In regions of surface dilution, salinity increases with depth near the surface, while in areas of high evaporation salinity decreases with depth. Temperature usually decreases with depth and normally exerts a greater influence on sound speed than does the salinity in the surface layer of the open oceans. In the case of surface dilution, salinity and temperature effects on the speed of sound oppose each other, while in the case of evaporation they reinforce each other, causing the speed of sound to decrease with depth. Beneath the upper oceanic layers the speed of sound increases with depth.

If a sound wave (sonic pulse) travels at a right angle to these layers, as in depth sounding, no refraction occurs; however, the speed changes continuously with depth, and an average sound speed for the entire water column must be used to determine the depth of water. Variations in the speed of sound cause sound waves to refract when they travel obliquely through layers of water that have different properties of salinity and temperature. Sound waves traveling downward and moving obliquely to the water layers will bend upward when the speed of sound increases with depth and downward when the speed decreases with depth. This refraction of the sound is important in the sonar detection of submarines because the actual path of a sound wave must be known to determine a submarine's position relative to the transmitter of the sound. Refraction also produces shadow zones that sound waves do not penetrate because of their curvature.

At depths of approximately 1,000 metres (about 3,300 feet), pressure becomes the important factor: it combines with temperature and salinity to produce a zone of minimum sound speed. This zone has been named the SOFAR (sound fixing and ranging) channel. If a sound is generated by a point source in the SOFAR zone, it becomes trapped by refraction. Dispersed horizontally rather than in three directions, the sound is able to travel for great distances. Hydrophones lowered to this depth many kilometres from the origin of the sound are able to detect the sound pulse. The difference in arrival time of the pulse at separate listening posts may be used to triangulate the position of the pulse source.

Hearing is an important sensory mechanism for marine animals because seawater is more transparent to sound than to light. Animals communicate with each other over long distances and also locate objects by sending directional sound signals that reflect from targets and are received as echoes. Information about the size of a target is gained by varying the frequency of the sound; high-frequency (or short-wavelength) sound waves reflect better from small targets than low-frequency sound waves. The intensity and quality of the returning signal also provide information about the properties of the reflecting target.

CHEMICAL EVOLUTION OF THE OCEANS

The chemical history of the oceans has been divided into three stages. The first is an early stage in which the Earth's crust was cooling and reacting with volatile or highly reactive gases of an acidic, reducing nature to produce the oceans and an initial sedimentary rock mass. This stage lasted until about 3.5 billion years ago. The second stage was a period of transition from the initial to essentially modern conditions, and it is estimated to have ended 2 to 1.5 billion years ago. Since that time it is likely that there has been little change in seawater composition.

THE EARLY OCEANS

The initial accretion of Earth by agglomeration of solid particles occurred about 4.6 billion years ago. Heating of this initially cool, unsorted conglomerate by the decay of radioactive elements and the conversion of kinetic and potential energy to heat resulted in the development of a liquid iron core and the gross internal zonation of Earth. It has been concluded that formation of Earth's core took about 500 million years. It is likely that core formation resulted in the escape of an original primitive atmosphere and its replacement by one derived from loss of volatile substances from Earth's interior. Whether most of this degassing took place during core formation or soon afterward or whether there has been significant degassing of Earth's interior throughout geologic time is uncertain. Recent models of Earth formation, however, suggest early differentiation of Earth into three major zones (core, mantle, and crust) and attendant early loss of volatile substances from the interior. It is also likely that Earth, after initial cold agglomeration, reached temperatures such that the whole Earth approached the molten state. As the initial crust of Earth solidified, volatile gases would be released to form an atmosphere that would contain water, later to become the hydrosphere; carbon gases, such as carbon dioxide, methane, and carbon monoxide; sulfur gases, mostly hydrogen sulfide; and halogen compounds, such as hydrochloric acid. Nitrogen also may have been present, along with minor amounts of other gases. Gases of low atomic number, such as hydrogen and helium, would escape Earth's gravitational field. Substances degassed from the planetary interior have been called excess volatiles because their masses cannot be accounted for simply by rock weathering.

At an initial crustal temperature of about 600 °C (1,100 °F), almost all these compounds, including water (H_2O), would be in the atmosphere. The sequence of events that occurred as the crust cooled is difficult to construct. Below 100 °C (212 °F) all the H_2O would have condensed, and the acid gases would have reacted with the original igneous crustal minerals to form sediments and an initial ocean. There are at least two possible

ESTIMATE OF "EXCESS VOLATILES" (units of 10^{20} grams)	
water	16,600
total carbon as carbon dioxide	910
sulfur	22
nitrogen	42
chlorine	300
hydrogen	10
boron, bromine, argon, fluorine, etc.	4

Source: W. W. Rubey (1951).

pathways by which these initial steps could have been accomplished.

One pathway assumes that the 600 °C (1,100 °F) atmosphere contains, together with other compounds, water (as vapour), carbon dioxide, and hydrochloric acid in the ratio of 20:3:1 and would cool to the critical temperature of water. The water vapour therefore would have condensed into an early hot ocean. At this stage, the hydrochloric acid would be dissolved in the ocean (about 1 mole per litre), but most of the carbon dioxide would still be in the atmosphere with about 0.5 mole per litre in the ocean water. This early acid ocean would react vigorously with crustal minerals, dissolving out silica and cations and creating a residue that consisted principally of aluminous clay minerals that would form the sediments of the early ocean basins. This pathway of reaction assumes that reaction rates are slow relative to cooling. A second pathway of reaction, which assumes that cooling is slow, is also possible. In this case, at a temperature of about 400 °C (750 °F) most of the water vapour would be removed from the atmosphere by hydration reactions with pyroxenes and olivines. Under these conditions, water vapour would not condense until some unknown temperature was reached, and Earth might have had at an early stage in its history an atmosphere rich in carbon dioxide and no ocean: the surface would have been much like that of present-day Venus.

The pathways described are two of several possibilities for the early surface environment of Earth. In either case, after Earth's surface had cooled to 100 °C (212 °F), it would have taken only a short time geologically for the acid gases to be used up in reactions involving igneous rock minerals. The presence of bacteria and possibly algae in the fossil record of rocks older than 3 billion years attests to the fact that Earth's surface had cooled to temperatures lower than 100 °C (212 °F) by this time and that the neutralization of the original acid gases had taken place. If most of the degassing of primary volatile substances from Earth's interior occurred early, the chloride released by reaction of hydrochloric acid with rock minerals would be found in the oceans and seas or in evaporite deposits, and the oceans would have a salinity and volume comparable to those that they have today.

This conclusion is based on the assumption that there has been no drastic change in the ratios of volatiles released through geologic time. The overall generalized reaction indicative of the chemistry leading to formation of the early oceans can be written in the form: primary igneous rock minerals + acid volatiles + $H_2O \rightarrow$ sedimentary rocks + oceans + atmosphere. Notice from this equation that if all the acid volatiles and H_2O were released early in the history of Earth and in the proportions found today, then the total original sedimentary rock mass produced would be equal to that of the present time, and ocean salinity and volume would be near what they are now. If, on the other hand, degassing were linear with time, then the sedimentary rock mass would have accumulated at a linear rate, as would oceanic volume. However, the salinity of the oceans would remain nearly the same if the ratios of volatiles degassed did not change with time. The most likely situation is that presented here—namely, that major degassing occurred early in Earth history, after which minor amounts of volatiles were released episodically or continuously for the remainder of geologic time. The salt content of the oceans based on the constant proportions of volatiles released would depend primarily on the ratio of sodium chloride (NaCl) locked up in evaporites to that dissolved in the oceans. If all the sodium chloride in evaporites were added to the oceans today, the salinity would be roughly doubled. This value gives a sense of the maximum salinity the oceans could have attained throughout geologic time.

One component missing from the early terrestrial surface was free oxygen because it would not have been a constituent released from the cooling crust. As noted earlier, early production of oxygen was by photodissociation of water in the atmosphere as a result of absorption of ultraviolet light. The reaction is $2H_2O + hv \rightarrow O_2 + 2H_2$, in which hv represents a photon of ultraviolet light. The hydrogen produced would escape into space, and the O_2 would react with the early reduced gases by reactions such as $2H_2S + 3O_2 \rightarrow 2SO_2 + 2H_2O$. Oxygen production by photodissociation gave the early reduced atmosphere a start toward present-day conditions, but it was not until the appearance of photosynthetic organisms approximately 3.3 billion years ago that it was possible for the accumulation of oxygen in the atmosphere to proceed at a rate sufficient to lead to today's oxygenated environment. The photosynthetic reaction leading to oxygen production may be written $6CO_2 + 6H_2O + hv \rightarrow C_6H_{12}O_6 + 6O_2$, in which $C_6H_{12}O_6$ represents sugar.

THE TRANSITION STAGE

The nature of the rock record from the time of the first sedimentary rocks (about 3.5 billion years ago) to approximately 2 to 1.5 billion years ago suggests that the amount of oxygen in the atmosphere was significantly lower than today and that there were continuous chemical trends in the sedimentary rocks formed and, more subtly, in oceanic composition. The source rocks of sediments during this time were likely to be more basaltic than would later ones; sedimentary detritus was formed by the alteration of these rocks in an oxygen-deficient atmosphere and accumulated primarily under anaerobic marine conditions. The chief difference between reactions involving mineral-ocean equilibriums at this time and at the present time was the role played by ferrous iron. The concentration of dissolved iron in the present-day oceans is low because of the insolubility of oxidized iron oxides. During the period 3.5 to 1.5 billion years ago, oxygen-deficient environments were prevalent; these favoured the formation of minerals containing ferrous iron (reduced state of iron) from the alteration of basaltic rocks. Indeed, the iron carbonate siderite and the iron silicate greenalite, in close association with chert and the iron sulfide pyrite, are characteristic minerals that occur in middle Precambrian iron formations (those about 1.5 to 2.4 billion years old). The chert originally was deposited as amorphous silica; equilibrium between amorphous silica, siderite, and greenalite at 25 °C (77 °F) and 1 atmosphere of total pressure requires a carbon dioxide pressure of about $10^{-2.5}$ atmosphere, or 10 times the present-day value.

The oceans at this time can be thought of as the solution resulting from an acid leach of basaltic rocks, and because the neutralization of the volatile acid gases was not restricted primarily to land areas as it is presently, much of this alteration may have occurred by submarine processes. The atmosphere at the time was oxygen-deficient; anaerobic depositional environments with internal carbon dioxide pressures of about $10^{-2.5}$ atmosphere were prevalent, and the atmosphere itself may have had a carbon dioxide pressure near $10^{-2.5}$ atmosphere. If so, the pH of early ocean water was lower than that of modern seawater, the calcium concentration was higher, and the early ocean water was probably saturated with respect to amorphous silica (about 120 parts per million [ppm]).

To simulate what might have occurred, it is helpful to imagine emptying the Pacific basin, throwing in great masses of broken basaltic material, filling it with hydrochloric acid so that the acid becomes neutralized, and then carbonating the solution by bubbling carbon dioxide through it. Oxygen would not be permitted into the system. The hydrochloric acid would leach the rocks, resulting in the release and precipitation of silica and the production of a chloride ocean containing sodium, potassium, calcium, magnesium, aluminum, iron, and reduced sulfur species in the proportions present in the rocks. As complete neutralization was approached, aluminum could begin to precipitate as hydroxides and then combine with precipitated silica to form cation-deficient aluminosilicates. The aluminosilicates, as the end of the neutralization process was reached, would combine with more silica and with cations to form minerals like chlorite, and ferrous iron would combine with silica and sulfur to make greenalite and pyrite. In the final solution, chlorine would be balanced by sodium and calcium in roughly equal proportions, with subordinate potassium and magnesium; aluminum would be quantitatively removed, and silicon would be at saturation with amorphous silica. If this solution were then carbonated, calcium would be removed as calcium carbonate, and the chlorine balance would be maintained by abstraction of more sodium from the primary rock. The sediments produced in this system would contain chiefly silica, ferrous iron silicates, chloritic minerals, calcium carbonate, calcium magnesium carbonates, and minor pyrite.

If the hydrochloric acid added were in excess of the carbon dioxide, the resultant ocean would have a high content of calcium chloride, but the pH would still be near neutrality. If the carbon dioxide added were in excess of the chlorine, calcium would be precipitated as the carbonate until it reached a level approximately that of the present oceans—namely, a few hundred parts per million.

If this newly created ocean were left undisturbed for a few hundred million years, its waters would evaporate and be transported onto the continents (in the form of precipitation); streams would transport their loads into it. The sediment created in this ocean would be uplifted and incorporated into the continents. Gradually, the influence of the continental debris would be felt, and the pH might shift slightly. Iron would be oxidized out of the ferrous silicates to produce iron oxides, but the water composition would not vary a great deal.

The primary minerals of igneous rocks are all mildly basic compounds. When they react in excess with acids such as hydrochloric acid and carbon dioxide, they produce neutral or mildly alkaline solutions plus a set of altered aluminosilicate and carbonate reaction products.

It is highly unlikely that ocean water has changed through time from a solution approximately in equilibrium with these reaction products, which are clay minerals and carbonates.

THE MODERN OCEANS

The oceans probably achieved their modern characteristics 2 to 1.5 billion years ago. The chemical and mineralogical compositions and the relative proportions of sedimentary rocks of this age differ little from their Paleozoic counterparts (those dating from about 570 million to 245 million years ago). The fact that the acid sulfur gases had been neutralized to sulfate by this time is borne out by calcium sulfate deposits of late Precambrian age (roughly 570 million to 1.6 billion years old). Chemically precipitated ferric oxides in late Precambrian sedimentary rocks indicate available free oxygen, whatever its percentage. The chemistry and mineralogy of middle and late Precambrian shales is similar to that of Paleozoic shales. Thus, it appears that continuous cycling of sediments like those of the present time has occurred for 1.5 to 2 billion years and that these sediments have controlled oceanic composition.

It was once thought that the saltiness of the modern oceans simply represents the storage of salts derived from rock weathering and transported to the oceans by fluvial processes. With increasing knowledge of the age of Earth, however, it was realized that, at the present-day rate of delivery of salts to the oceans or even at much reduced rates, the total salt content and the mass of individual salts in the oceans could be attained in geologically short-time intervals compared to Earth's age. The total mass of salt in the oceans can be accounted for at present-day rates of stream delivery in about 12 million years. The mass of dissolved silica in ocean water can be doubled in only 20,000 years by addition of stream-derived silica; to double sodium would take 70 million years. It then became apparent that the oceans were not simply an accumulator of salts, but as water evaporated from the oceans, along with some salt, the introduced salts must be removed in the form of minerals. Thus, the concept of the oceans as a chemical system changed from that of a simple accumulator to that of a steady-state system in which rates of inflow of materials into the oceans equal rates of outflow. The steady-state concept permits influx to vary with time, but it would be matched by nearly simultaneous and equal variation of efflux. Calculations of rates of addition of elements to the oceanic system and removal from it show that for at least 100 million years the oceanic system has been in a steady state with approximately fixed rates of major element inflow and outflow and, thus, fixed chemical composition.

CHAPTER 2

OCEAN BASINS

Ocean basins constitute any of several vast submarine regions that collectively cover nearly three-quarters of Earth's surface. Together they contain the overwhelming majority of all water on the planet and have an average depth of almost 4 km (about 2.5 miles). A number of major features of the basins depart from this average—for example, the mountainous ocean ridges, deep-sea trenches, and jagged, linear fracture zones. Other significant features of the ocean floor include aseismic ridges, abyssal hills, and seamounts and guyots. The basins also contain a variable amount of sedimentary fill that is thinnest on the ocean ridges and usually thickest near the continental margins.

While the ocean basins lie much lower than sea level, the continents stand high—about 1 km (0.6 mile) above sea level. The physical explanation for this condition is that the continental crust is light and thick while the oceanic crust is dense and thin. Both the continental and

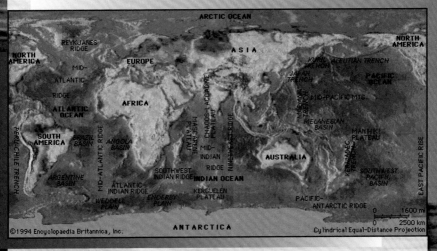

Major features of the ocean basins.

oceanic crusts lie over a more uniform layer called the mantle. As an analogy, one can think of a thick piece of styrofoam and a thin piece of wood floating in a tub of water. The styrofoam rises higher out of the water than the wood.

The ocean basins are transient features over geologic time, changing shape and depth while the process of plate tectonics occurs. The surface layer of Earth, the lithosphere, consists of a number of rigid plates that are in continual motion. The boundaries between the lithospheric plates form the principal relief features of the ocean basins: the crests of oceanic ridges are spreading centres where two plates move apart from each other at a rate of several centimetres per year. Molten rock material wells up from the underlying mantle into the gap between the diverging plates and solidifies into oceanic crust, thereby creating new ocean floor. At the deep-sea trenches, two plates converge, with one plate sliding down under the other into the mantle where it is melted. Thus, for each segment of new ocean floor created at the ridges, an

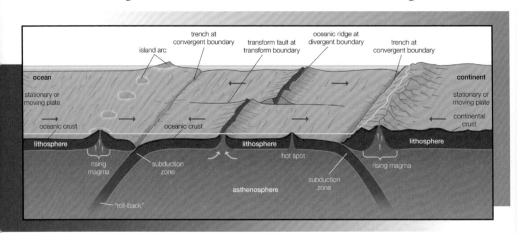

Three-dimensional diagram showing crustal generation and destruction according to the theory of plate tectonics; included are the three kinds of plate boundaries—divergent, convergent (or collision), and strike-slip (or transform). Encyclopædia Britannica, Inc.

equal amount of old oceanic crust is destroyed at the trenches, or so-called subduction zones. It is for this reason that the oldest segment of ocean floor, found in the far western Pacific, is apparently only about 200 million years old, even though the age of Earth is estimated to be at least 4.6 billion years.

The dominant factors that govern seafloor relief and topography are the thermal properties of the oceanic plates, tensional forces in the plates, volcanic activity, and sedimentation. In brief, the oceanic ridges rise about 2 km (1.2 miles) above the seafloor because the plates near these spreading centres are warm and thermally expanded. In contrast, plates in the subduction zones

SEA LEVEL

Sea level is the position of the air-sea interface on Earth's surface to which all terrestrial elevations and submarine depths are referred. The sea level constantly changes at every locality with the changes in tides, atmospheric pressure, and wind conditions. Longer-term changes in sea level are influenced by Earth's changing climates. Consequently, the level is better defined as mean sea level, the height of the sea surface averaged over all stages of the tide over a long period of time.

Global mean sea level rose at an average rate of about 1.2 mm (0.05 inch) per year over much of the 20th century, with shorter terms during which the rise was significantly faster (5.5 mm [0.2 inches] per year during the period from 1946 to 1956). This variable rise has been shown to have occurred for a very long time. The sea level appears to have been very close to its present position 35,000 years ago. It dropped 130 metres (426 feet) or more during the interval from 30,000 to 15,000 years ago and has been rising ever since. Fluctuations of equivalent magnitude probably have accompanied the alternate growth and melting of continental glaciers during the Pleistocene Epoch (from 2.6 million to 11,700 years ago) because the ocean's waters are the ultimate source of glacial ice. Slower changes in the shapes and sizes of the ocean basins have less effect.

are generally cooler. Tensional forces resulting in plate divergence at the spreading centres also create block-faulted mountains and abyssal hills, which trend parallel to the oceanic ridges. Seamounts and guyots, as well as abyssal hills and most aseismic ridges, are produced by volcanism. Continuing sedimentation throughout the ocean basin serves to blanket and bury many of the faulted mountains and abyssal hills with time. Erosion plays a relatively minor role in shaping the face of the deep seafloor, in contrast to the continents. This is because deep ocean currents are generally slow (they flow at less than 50 cm [20 inches] per second) and lack sufficient power.

EXPLORATION OF THE OCEAN BASINS

Mapping the characteristics of the ocean basin has been difficult for several reasons. First, the oceans are not easy to travel over; second, until recent times navigation has been extremely crude, so that individual observations have been only loosely correlated with one another; and, finally, the oceans are opaque to light—that is, the deep seafloor cannot be seen from the ocean surface. Modern technology has given rise to customized research vessels, satellite and electronic navigation, and sophisticated acoustic instruments that mitigate some of these problems.

The *Challenger* Expedition, mounted by the British in 1872–76, provided the first systematic view of a few of the major features of the seafloor. Scientists aboard the HMS *Challenger* determined ocean depths by means of wire-line soundings and discovered the Mid-Atlantic Ridge. Dredges brought up samples of rocks and sediments off the seafloor. The main advance in mapping, however, did not occur until sonar was developed in the early 20th century. This system for detecting the presence of objects underwater by acoustic echo provided marine researchers with a highly useful tool, since sound can be detected over several thousands of kilometers in the ocean (visible light, by comparison, can penetrate only 100 metres [about 330 feet] or so of water).

Modern sonar systems include the Seabeam multi-beam echo sounder and the GLORIA scanning sonar. They operate on the principle that the depth (or distance) of the seafloor can be determined by multiplying one-half the elapsed time between a downgoing acoustic pulse and its echo by the speed of sound in seawater (about 1,500 metres [4,900 feet] per second). Such multifrequency sonar systems permit the use of different pulse frequencies to meet different scientific objectives. Acoustic pulses of 12 kilohertz (kHz), for example, are normally employed to measure ocean depth, while lower frequencies—3.5 kHz to less than 100 hertz (Hz)—are used to map the thickness of sediments in the ocean basins. Very high frequencies of 100 kHz or more are employed in side-scanning sonar to measure the texture of the seafloor. The acoustic pulses are normally generated by piezoelectric transducers. For determining subbottom structure, low-frequency acoustic pulses are produced by explosives, compressed air, or water-jet implosion. Near-bottom sonar systems, such as the Deep Tow of the Scripps Institution of Oceanography (in La Jolla, Calif., U.S.), produce even more detailed images of the seafloor and subbottom structure. The Deep Tow package contains both echo sounders and side-scanning sonars, along with associated geophysical instruments, and is towed behind a ship at slow speed 10 to 100 metres (33 to 330 feet) above the seafloor. It yields very precise measurements of even finer-scale features than are resolvable with Seabeam and other comparable systems.

Another notable instrument system is ANGUS, a deep-towed camera sled that can take thousands of high-resolution photographs of the seafloor during a single day. It has been successfully used in the detection of hydrothermal vents at spreading centres. Overlapping photographic images make it possible to construct photomosaic strips about 10 to 20 metres (about 33 to 66 feet) wide that reveal details on the order of centimetres.

Three major navigation systems are in use in modern marine geology. These include electromagnetic systems such as Loran and Earth-orbiting satellites. Acoustic transponder arrays of two or more stations placed on the seafloor a few kilometres apart are used to navigate deeply towed instruments, submersibles, and occasionally surface research vessels when detailed mapping is conducted in small areas. These systems measure the distance between the instrument package and the transponder sites and, using simple geometry, compute fixes accurate to a few metres. Although the individual transponders can be used to determine positions relative to the array with great accuracy, the preciseness of the position of the array itself depends on which system is employed to locate it.

Earth-orbiting satellites such as Seasat and Geosat have uncovered some significant topographic features of the ocean basins. Scasat, launched in 1978, carried a radar altimeter into orbit. This device was used to measure the distance between the satellite path and the surfaces of the ocean and continents to 0.1 metre (0.3 foot). The measurements revealed that the shape of the ocean surface is warped by seafloor features: massive seamounts cause the surface to bulge over them because of gravitational attraction. Similarly, the ocean surface downwarps occur over deep-sea trenches. Using these satellite measurements of the ocean surface, William F. Haxby

SEASAT

Seasat is an experimental U.S. ocean surveillance satellite launched June 27, 1978. During its 99 days of operation, Seasat orbited Earth 14 times daily and monitored nearly 96 percent of its oceanic surface every 36 hours. Instruments on the unmanned spacecraft, engineered to penetrate cloud cover, provided data on a wide array of oceanographic conditions and features, including wave height, water temperature, currents, winds, icebergs, and coastal characteristics. Although Seasat ceased data transmission on Oct. 9, 1978, as a result of a power failure, it achieved its primary purpose: to demonstrate that much useful information about oceanographic phenomena could be obtained by means of satellite surveillance. Data transmitted by Seasat was made available to scientists representing 23 government and academic organizations. The information was also used to aid the crews of transoceanic vessels and aircraft.

computed the gravity field there. The resulting gravity map provides comprehensive coverage of the ocean surface on a 5'-by-5' grid that depicts 5 nautical miles on each side at the Equator. Coverage as complete as this is not available from echo soundings made from ships. Because the gravity field at the ocean surface is a highly sensitive indicator of marine topography, this map reveals various previously uncharted features, including seamounts, ridges, and fracture zones, while improving the detail on other known features. In addition, the gravity map shows a linear pattern of gravity anomalies that cut obliquely across the grain of the topography. These anomalies are most pronounced in the Pacific basin; they are apparently about 100 km (about 60 miles) across and some 1,000 km (about 600 miles) long. They have an amplitude of approximately 10 milligals (0.001 percent of Earth's gravity attraction) and are aligned west-northwest—very close to the direction in which the Pacific Plate moves over the mantle below.

DEEP-SEA SEDIMENTS

The ocean basin floor is everywhere covered by sediments of different types and origins. The only exception are the crests of the spreading centres where new ocean floor has not existed long enough to accumulate a sediment cover. Sediment thickness in the oceans averages about 450 metres (1,500 feet). The sediment cover in the Pacific basin ranges from 300 to 600 metres (about 1,000 to 2,000 feet) thick, and that in the Atlantic is about 1,000 metres (3,300 feet). Generally, the thickness of sediment on the oceanic crust increases with the age of the crust. Oceanic crust adjacent to the continents can be deeply buried by several kilometres of sediment. Deep-sea sediments can reveal much about the last 200 million years of Earth history, including seafloor spreading, the history of ocean life, the behaviour of Earth's magnetic field, and the changes in the ocean currents and climate.

The study of ocean sediments has been accomplished by several means. Bottom samplers, such as dredges and cores up to 30 metres (about 100 feet) long, have been lowered from ships by wire to retrieve samples of the upper sediment layers. Deep-sea drilling has retrieved core samples from the entire sediment layer in several hundred locations in the ocean basins. The seismic reflection method has been used to map the thickness of sediments in many parts of the oceans. Besides thickness, seismic reflection data can often reveal sediment type and the processes of sedimentation.

SEDIMENT TYPES

Deep-sea sediments can be classified as terrigenous, originating from land; as biogenic, consisting largely of the skeletal debris of microorganisms; or as authigenic, formed in place on the seafloor. Pelagic sediments, either terrigenous or biogenic, are those that are deposited very slowly in the open ocean either by settling through the volume of oceanic water or by precipitation. The sinking rates of pelagic sediment grains are extremely slow because they ordinarily are no larger than several micrometres. However, fine particles are normally bundled into fecal pellets by zooplankton, which allows sinking at a rate of 40 to 400 metres (130 to 1,300 feet) per day.

SEDIMENTATION PATTERNS

The patterns of sedimentation in the ocean basins have not been static over geologic time. The existing basins, no more than 200 million years old, contain a highly variable sedimentary record. The major factor behind the variations is plate movements and related changes in climate and ocean water circulation. Since about 200 million years ago, a single vast ocean basin has given way to five or six smaller ones. The Pacific Ocean basin has shrunk, while the North and South Atlantic basins have been created. The climate has changed from warm and mild to cool, stormy, and glacial. Plate movements have altered the course of surface and deep ocean currents and changed the patterns of upwelling, productivity, and biogenic sedimentation. Seaways have opened and closed. The Strait of Gibraltar, for example, was closed off about 6 million years ago, allowing the entire Mediterranean Sea to evaporate and leave thick salt deposits on its floor. Changes in seafloor spreading rates and glaciations have caused sea levels to rise and fall, greatly altering the deep-sea sedimentation pattern of both terrigenous and biogenic sediments. The calcite compensation depth (CCD), or the depth at which the rate of carbonate accumulation equals the rate of carbonate dissolution, has fluctuated more than 2,000 metres (about 6,600 feet) in response to changes in carbonate supply and the corrosive nature of ocean bottom waters. Bottom currents have changed, becoming erosive or nondepositional in some regions to produce geological unconformities (that is, gaps in the geological record) and redistribute enormous volumes of sediment to other locations. The Pacific Plate has been steadily moving northward, so that biogenic sediments of the equatorial regions are found in core samples taken in the barren North Pacific.

EVOLUTION OF THE OCEAN BASINS THROUGH PLATE MOVEMENTS

Through most of geologic time, probably extending back 2 billion years, the ocean basins have both grown and been consumed as plate tectonics continued on Earth. The latest phase of ocean basin growth began just less than 200 million years ago with the breakup of the supercontinent Pangea, the enormous landmass composed of nearly all the present-day continents. Since that time the major developments have included a shrinking of the Pacific basin at the expense of the growing Atlantic and Arctic basins, the opening of the Tethys seaway circling the globe in tropical latitudes and its subsequent closing, and the opening of the Southern Ocean as the southern continents moved north away from Antarctica.

The oldest known oceanic crust (estimated to be about 200 million years old) is located in the far western equatorial Pacific, east of the Mariana Island arc. The Pacific ocean floor at this site was generated during seafloor spreading from a pattern of ridges and plates that had existed for some unknown period of time. At least five different seafloor spreading centres were involved. In the Indian Ocean the oldest segment of seafloor was formed about 165 million to 145 million years ago by the rifting away of Africa and South America from Gondwana, a supercontinent consisting largely of the present-day continents of the Southern Hemisphere. At this time Africa was joined to South America, Eurasia, and North America. Today this old seafloor is found along the east coast of Africa from the Somali Basin to the east coast of South Africa and adjacent to Queen Maud Land and Enderby Land in East Antarctica.

Close to 180 million years ago (but before 165 million years ago), North America and Eurasia, which together made up most of the large northern continent of Laurasia, began drifting away from Africa and South America, creating the first seafloor in the central region of the North Atlantic and opening the Gulf of Mexico. The Tethys seaway also opened during this rifting phase as Europe pulled away from Africa. Shortly after this time continental fragments, including possibly Tibet, Myanmar (Burma), and Malaya, rifted away from the northwest coast of Australia and moved northward, thereby creating the oldest seafloor in the Timor Sea. During this period spreading continued in the Pacific basin with the growth of the Pacific Plate and the consumption by subduction of its bordering plates, including the Izanagi, Farallon, and Phoenix. The Pacific Plate moved northward during this phase and continues to do so today.

India and Madagascar, as a unit, rifted away from Australia and Antarctica prior to 130 million years ago and began drifting northward, creating seafloor adjacent to Western Australia and East Antarctica. Possibly simultaneously or shortly after this rifting began, South America started to separate from Africa, initiating the formation of seafloor in the South Atlantic Ocean.

Between 90 million and 80 million years ago, Madagascar and India separated, and the spreading ridges in the Indian Ocean were reorganized. India began drifting northward directly toward Asia. During this same period, Europe, joined to Greenland, began drifting away from North America, which resulted in the emergence of the seafloor in the Labrador Sea and the northernmost Atlantic Ocean. This spreading phase affected the passages in the Tethys seaway between Europe (Iberia) and northwest Africa, intermittently opening and closing it. In the southwest Pacific, New Zealand, along with the Lord Howe Rise and the Norfolk Ridge, rifted away from Australia and Antarctica between 80 million and 60 million years ago, opening the Tasman Sea.

About 60 million years ago a new rift and oceanic ridge formed between Greenland and Europe, separating them and initiating the formation of oceanic crust in the Norwegian Sea and the Eurasian basin in the eastern Arctic Ocean. The Amerasian basin in the western Arctic Ocean had formed during an earlier spreading phase from about 130 million to 110 million years ago. Between 60 million and 50 million years ago, significant events occurred in the Indian Ocean and southwest Pacific. Australia began drifting northward, away from East Antarctica, creating seafloor there. The northward movement of Australia resulted in the emergence of several subduction zones and island arcs in the southwest and equatorial Pacific. The Indian subcontinent first touched against the Asian continent about 53 million years ago, developing structures that preceded the main Himalayan orogeny (mountain-building event), which began in earnest some 40 million years ago.

ISLAND ARCS

Island arcs are long, curved chains of oceanic islands associated with intense volcanic and seismic activity and orogenic (mountain-building) processes. Prime examples of this form of geologic feature include the Aleutian-Alaska Arc and the Kuril-Kamchatka Arc.

Most island arcs consist of two parallel, arcuate rows of islands. The inner row of such a double arc is composed of a string of explosive volcanoes, while the outer row is made up of nonvolcanic islands. In the case of single arcs, many of the constituent islands are volcanically active.

An island arc typically has a landmass or a partially enclosed, unusually shallow sea on its concave side. Along the convex side there almost invariably exists a long, narrow deep-sea trench. The greatest ocean depths are found in these depressions of the seafloor, as in the case of the Mariana and Tonga trenches.

Destructive earthquakes occur frequently at the site of island arcs. Unlike the shallow earthquakes that are recorded in other areas of the world, these are deep-focus seismic events emanating from as much as 370 miles (600 km) below the base of an arc. The quakes tend to have foci of progressively greater depth toward the arc's concave side.

The majority of island arcs occur along the western margin of the Pacific Basin. The few exceptions are the East Indian and the West Indian arcs and the Scotia Arc in the South Atlantic. According to prevailing theory, island arcs are formed where two lithospheric plates (enormous rigid slabs that constitute segments of Earth's surface) converge. Upon colliding, one of the plates—that bearing heavy, oceanic crust—buckles downward and is forced into the partially molten lower mantle beneath the second plate with lighter, continental crust. An island arc is built up from the surface of the overriding plate by the extrusion of basalts and andesites. The basalts are thought to be derived from the semimolten mantle, whereas the andesites are probably generated by the partial melting of the descending plate and the sediments that have accumulated on its surface.

Less than 30 million years ago, seafloor spreading ceased in the Labrador Sea. Along the west coast of North America, the Pacific Plate and the North American Plate converged along what is now California shortly after 30 million years ago. This resulted in the cessation of a long history of subduction in the area and the gradual conversion of this continental margin to a transform fault zone. Continued closure between Africa and Europe, which began about 100 million years ago, caused the isolation of the Mediterranean Sea, so that by 6 million years ago this water body had completely evaporated.

The present-day Mediterranean seafloor was formed during a complex sequence of rifting between small plates in this region, beginning with the separation of North America and Europe from Africa about 200 million years ago. In the eastern Mediterranean the seafloor is no older than about 100 million years. West of Italy it was created during subsequent spreading between 30 million and 20 million years ago.

The Caribbean Sea and the Gulf of Mexico formed as a result of the relative movement between North America and South America. The seafloor of the Gulf of Mexico began forming some 160 million to 150 million years ago. A proto- or ancient Caribbean seafloor also was formed during this period but was later subducted. The present Caribbean seafloor consists of a captured piece of the Farallon Plate (from the Pacific basin) and is estimated to be for the most part of Cretaceous age (i.e., about 120 million to 85 million years old).

The seafloor in the western portion of the Philippine Sea developed between 60 million and 35 million years ago. In the east it was formed by backarc spreading from 30 million years ago. The origin of the older crust is not completely clear. It either was created by spreading in the Pacific basin and subsequent capture by the formation of the Bonin and Mariana arcs, or it resulted from backarc spreading behind trenches to the south.

OCEAN BASIN FEATURES

Ocean basins contain a number of physical features. Some of these, such as abyssal hills and deep-sea trenches, are analogous to topographic features on land. Although most of the ocean floor is made up of oceanic crust, some features of ocean basins (such as continental shelves and continental slopes) are made of continental crust.

ABYSSAL HILLS

Abyssal hills are small, topographically well-defined submarine hills that may rise from several metres to several hundred metres above the abyssal seafloor. (Abyssal hills appear some 3,000 to 6,000 metres [10,000 to 20,000 feet] below the surface of the ocean.) Typical abyssal hills have diameters of several to several hundred metres. They elongate parallel to spreading centres or to marine magnetic anomalies and cover the entire flanks and crests of oceanic ridges. Abyssal hill provinces, areas of abyssal seafloor occupied exclusively by such hills, characteristically occur seaward of the smooth abyssal plains at the bases of continental rises. Isolated hills and groups of hills also protrude from abyssal plain surfaces, and the base of an abyssal plain accumulation of marine sediment, as revealed by sub-bottom seismic profiling, generally matches the undulating topography and relief of abyssal hill provinces.

Apparently, the hills are constructed by two processes: volcanism and block faulting. The relative contribution of each may depend on the spreading rate. At slower rates, faulting of the oceanic crust is a dominant factor in forming the relief, and the relief of the hills is greater as the rate is slower. At the crest of a spreading centre, volcanism in the neovolcanic zone initiates the construction of volcanic hills. The zone of active faulting is where they form or are modified by block faulting. The existence of discrete and separate volcanic hills indicates that volcanism at a spreading centre is episodic.

Abyssal hills, although generally covered with marine sediments, probably are identical in composition and origin to the extrusive basaltic prominences on the upper flanks of mid-ocean ridges and rises. Thus, it is believed that abyssal hills underlie most of the ocean floor, locally buried by accumulations of abyssal sediment. In the Atlantic Ocean, long abyssal hill provinces parallel both flanks of the Mid-Atlantic Ridge along most of its length. The Pacific Ocean has a smaller supply of continental sediment than the Atlantic Ocean, and numerous trenches and local rises separate the main ocean floor from the continents, preventing the seaward transport of sediment. Consequently, between 80 and 85 percent of the Pacific abyssal floor is occupied by abyssal hills.

CONTINENTAL MARGINS

Continental margins make up the submarine edge of the continental crust. They are distinguished by relatively light and isostatically high-floating material in comparison with the adjacent oceanic crust. It is the name for the collective area that encompasses the continental shelf, continental slope, and continental rise.

The characteristics of the various continental margins are shaped by a number of factors. Chief among these are tectonics, fluctuations of sea level, the size of the rivers that empty onto a margin as determined by the amount of sediment they carry, and the energy conditions or strength of the ocean waves and currents along the margin.

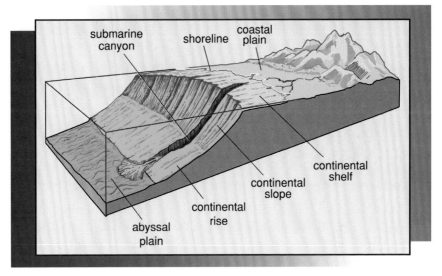

The broad, gentle pitch of the continental shelf gives way to the relatively steep continental slope. The more gradual transition to the abyssal plain is a sediment-filled region called the continental rise. The continental shelf, slope, and rise are collectively called the continental margin. Depth is exaggerated here for effect. Encyclopædia Britannica, Inc.

MARGIN TYPES

Continental margins on the leading edges of tectonic plates, like those around the rim of the Pacific Ocean, are usually narrow and have steep continental slopes and either poorly developed continental rises or none at all. The continental slope is often steep and falls away directly into a deep-sea trench. In many cases, the leading-edge margins are backed by mountain ranges. Continental margins on the trailing side of tectonic plates, like those around the Atlantic Ocean, are broad, with gentle continental slopes and well-developed continental rises. The adjacent land area is commonly a broad coastal plain that, depending on the state of sea level, may become submerged from time to time and hence part of the continental margin.

Since continental margins are the shallowest parts of the world's oceans, they are most affected by changes in sea level. Worldwide changes in sea level, called eustatic sea-level changes, have occurred throughout geologic history. The most common causes of such sea-level changes are global climatic fluctuations that lead to major glacial advances and retreats—that is, ice ages and inter-glacial periods. Other causes that are not as well understood may include major mountain-building events and isostatic changes in crustal plates. When continental glaciers advance, as they did several times during the Pleistocene Epoch (which extended from about 2.6 million to 11,700 years ago), water that would normally be in the oceans is locked up as ice on land, resulting in a drop in sea level. As the glaciers retreat, more water is fed to the ocean basins and the sea level rises. Fluctuations from highstand to lowstand have totaled 250 metres (about 800 feet) or more during Cenozoic time (roughly the last 65.5 million years), with concomitant fluctuations in exposure and flooding of the continental margins. (During a highstand the sea level is above the edge of the continental shelf, while during a lowstand it is below the shelf edge.)

Rivers bring a variety of sediments to the coast. These are classified by their mineralogy and by particle size and include sand, silt, and clay. To sedimentologists, sand is a grain of any composition from 63 to 2,000 micrometres (0.002 to 0.08 inch) in its largest diameter. Silt is 4 to 62 micrometres (0.0002 to 0.002 inch), and clay is any particle less than 4 micrometres. Most of the detrital minerals brought to the continental margins by rivers in sand and silt sizes are quartz, feldspars, and mica; those of clay size are a suite of clay minerals that most commonly include smectite, kaolinite, and illite. (Clay can, in other words, refer either to particle size or to a group of minerals.)

These, then, are the mineral constituents that together with calcium carbonates produced in the oceans by biogenic activity as shells and the hard parts of plants and animals, go to make up the sedimentary packages that are deposited on and constitute a fundamental part of continental margins.

A constant battle is being waged between the rivers that bring sediments eroded from the land to the sea and the waves and currents of the receiving body of water. This dynamic struggle goes on year after year, century after century, sometimes for millions of years. Take, for example, the north coast of the Gulf of Mexico, into which the Mississippi River flows. The continental margin at this site is subject to relatively low wave and current energy, and so the river filled up most of the adjacent continental shelf with a delta and typically dumps over 200 million tons of sediment each year directly at the top of the continental slope. By contrast, the Columbia River in the Pacific Northwest of the United States carries 131 million tons to the coast, where the sediments are attacked by the large waves and currents normal for that margin. As a result, sediments are widely dispersed, and the shelf is not filled with a large subaerial delta.

The effects of this battle are easily seen where human activities have interfered with the transport of sediments to the sea by major rivers. For example, the Nile River delta is retreating rapidly, widening the submerged portion of the continental margin, because the Aswan High Dam has trapped much of the sediment normally fed to the delta front. The lower Mississippi River has been artificially maintained in a channel by high man-made levees. These have stopped the floods that fed much of the western delta margin. Because of this, coupled with a slow rise in sea level and the effects of canals dug in the delta wetlands, the coast has begun to retreat significantly.

When rivers carrying sediment from the interiors of continents reach the sea, several things happen. Velocity in the river jet decreases rapidly, and the sand particles drop out to be picked up by the waves and currents along the coast, where they feed beaches or barrier island systems. If the river has a large enough discharge, the finer-than-sand-sized materials may be carried for kilometres onto the margin in a fresh- or brackish-water plume. The surf system then acts as a wave filter, trapping the sand in the coastal zone but allowing the finer materials to be carried out onto the margin. When estuaries are the receiving bodies of water on the coastal boundaries of continental margins, as in the case of the east coast of North America, virtually all the sediments brought down by the rivers are trapped within the confines of the estuaries.

In addition to the two primary types of continental margins, there also are special types that do not readily fit either category. One of the most intensely studied margins of the world is the Borderland, the continental margin of southern California and northern Baja California. It consists of a series of offshore basins and ridges, some of which are exposed as islands. This system of basins and ridges formed as the result of faulting associated with the movement of the Pacific Plate past the North American Plate. It remains tectonically active today and is related to the San Andreas Fault system of California. A second special type is the marginal plateau. The Blake Plateau off the east coast of Florida is a good example. Such a plateau constitutes a portion of a continental margin that has many of the features of a normal system but is found at much greater depth—1,000 metres (about 3,300 feet) in the case of the Blake Plateau.

Continental margins can be either constructional or erosional over varying periods of geologic time, depending on the combination of factors discussed above. When deposition exceeds erosion, the margin grows seaward, a process of progradation that builds out as well as up. When the erosive forces are predominant, the margin remains static or actually retreats over time. Some geologists think that the continental margin of the eastern United States has retreated as much as 5–30 km (3–19 miles) since the end of the Cretaceous Period some 65.5 million years ago.

ECONOMIC IMPORTANCE OF CONTINENTAL MARGINS

Continental margins are very significant economically. Most of the major fisheries of the world are located on them. Of these, sport fisheries and related tourist industries are becoming increasingly important to the economies of developed nations. Paradoxically, continental margins also are one of the world's biggest dump sites. All kinds of wastes are disposed of along the margins, and the effects of pollution have become a major global concern.

Continental margins are the only parts of the world's oceans to be effectively exploited for mineral resources. Millions of tons of sand are mined by dredges each year off the U.S. coasts alone for beach renourishment projects. From time to time placer deposits also have been worked. Examples include tin off Indonesia, gold off Alaska, and diamonds off Namibia. By far and away the largest mineral resources to be exploited from continental margins are oil and natural gas. Exploration of the continental margins by major oil companies has intensified and is expected to continue for the foreseeable future because the margins are the most likely sites of giant undiscovered petroleum deposits. Continental margins are made of thick accumulations of sedimentary rock, the type of rock in which oil and gas generally occur. In fact, most of the sedimentary rocks exposed on the continents were originally deposited on continental margins; thus, even the hydrocarbon deposits found on land were formed for the most part on ancient continental margins.

CONTINENTAL RISES

Continental rises are major depositional regimes in oceans made up of thick sequences of continental material that accumulate between the continental slope and the abyssal plain. Continental rises form as a result of three sedimentary processes: mass wasting, the deposition from contour currents, and the vertical settling of clastic and biogenic particles.

The first such process is a downslope movement of sediments by mass wasting, a set of gravity-deposition events, including submarine landslides, slumps, debris flows, and high-velocity sediment-laden density flows known as turbidity currents. Several phenomena may initiate gravity events. In tectonically active areas, earthquakes are important triggering mechanisms. Even in the Atlantic they play a significant role. One of the few documented major gravity events took place on the Grand Banks of Newfoundland in 1929, when an earthquake triggered a gravity flow that possibly attained velocities of more than 90 km (56 miles) per hour and was traced for hundreds of kilometres as it successively broke transatlantic cables. Other triggering events may be oversteepening of deposits on the sharply inclined portions of the continental slope, breaking internal waves that have been shown to affect the upper slope, and storm waves and storm-induced currents.

A second process that may be equally important, although its overall significance is subject to considerable scientific debate, is deposition from bottom currents that flow parallel to the slope of the continental rise—namely, contour currents. Resulting sediment accumulations are called contourites. The major points of contention concerning the efficacy of contour currents are (1) whether or not they are strong enough—they flow at a speed of about 20 cm (8 inches) per second—to build the huge thicknesses of sediment that make up the rises and (2) how the sediments get into the contour currents in the first place. It is probable that most of the mass of rise material is originally brought downslope by gravity events and then redistributed by contour currents.

Vertical settling through the water column of both clastic and biogenic particles is the third contributor of slope and rise sediments. These pelagic sediments are composed of clay minerals and fine-grained particles (chiefly quartz, mica, and carbonate) swept off the continental shelf, wind-blown dust, organic detritus, and the tests of plankton. Chief among the last group are the tests of foraminiferans, pteropods, and coccolithophores that are composed of calcium carbonate and those of diatoms and radiolarians that are made of silicon dioxide.

CONTINENTAL SHELVES

Continental shelves are broad, relatively shallow submarine terraces of continental crust that form the edge of a continental landmass. The geology of continental shelves is often similar to that of the adjacent exposed portion of the continent, and most shelves have a gently rolling topography called ridge and swale. Continental shelves make up about 8 percent of the entire area covered by oceans.

STRUCTURE

A continental shelf typically extends from the coast to depths of 100–200 metres (about 330–660 feet). It is gently inclined seaward at an average slope of about 0.1°. In nearly all instances, it ends at its seaward edge with an abrupt drop called the shelf break. Below this lies the continental slope, a much steeper zone that usually merges with a section of the ocean floor called the continental rise at a depth of roughly 4,000 to 5,000 metres (13,000 to 16,500 feet). A few continental margins—such as those off the Mediterranean coast of France and at Porcupine Bank, off the western coast of Ireland—do not have a sharply defined break in slope but rather maintain a generally convex shape to the seafloor.

The average width of continental shelves is about 65 km (40 miles). Almost everywhere the shelves represent simply a continuation of the continental landmass beneath the ocean margins. Accordingly, they are narrow, rough, and steep off mountainous coasts but broad and comparatively level offshore from plains. The shelf along the mountainous western coast of the United States, for example, is narrow, measuring only about 32 km (20 miles) wide, whereas that fringing the eastern coast extends more than 120 km (75 miles) in width. Exceptionally broad shelves occur off northern Australia and Argentina.

Continental shelves are usually covered with a layer of sand, silts, and silty muds. Their surfaces exhibit some relief, featuring small hills and ridges that alternate with shallow depressions and valleylike troughs. In a few cases, steep-walled V-shaped submarine canyons cut deeply into both the shelf and the slope below.

Origin

American oceanographer Donald J.P. Swift has called continental shelves "palimpsests," parchment writing tablets upon which stories are written after each previous writing has been erased. Each new stand of sea level "writes" a new story of sedimentation on the shelf after the previous episode has been erased by the rise or fall that preceded it, but with some traces of the previous environment of deposition or last erosional event remaining. The "eraser" is the surf, a high-energy force that erodes and reworks everything as it passes over, winnowing out the finer-than-sand-sized sediment and leaving the coarser material behind. An interpreted seismic line shows the complicated array of channels (eroded and then filled), old deltaic deposits, ancient erosional surfaces, and winnowed sand bodies that make up the continental shelf southwest of Cape San Blas on the panhandle of Florida.

How the above processes affect any particular margin depends on its tectonic setting and the size of the rivers that drain into it. On continental shelves backed by high mountain ranges, such as the Pacific coast of North and South America, the difference between high and low sea-level stands may be difficult to detect, being one of degree perhaps noticeable only by marginally increased sedimentation rates during lowstands, or intervals of decreased sea level. In many ways, continental shelves on tectonically active margins at present sea levels approximate lowstands on trailing-edge, or passive, margins.

When sea level is lowered on a trailing-edge shelf that has no adjacent high mountains, such as the Atlantic coast of North America, rivers are rejuvenated. In other words, their base level is lowered and they begin to erode their beds, carrying sediment from the continent across the former continental shelf that is now exposed and depositing it at the new coast. When sea level falls below the shelf break, the coast lies on the continental slope. As sea level rises again on tectonically stable or sinking shelves, small and medium-sized river mouths drown and estuaries form, trapping the sediment within them and starving the shelves. In these cases, sediment for the shelf is primarily produced by erosion of the coastline as the surf zone advances landward with rising sea level. Fine-grained material is winnowed out, to be either deposited back in the estuaries or carried in steps by advective processes across the shelf to the deeper water beyond. As a result, continental shelf surfaces on trailing-edge margins into which no large rivers flow are veneered with a sand sheet lying over a complex of older deposits, some of which peek through the surface as outcrops—vestiges of an earlier story written on the palimpsest. Large rivers that drain a large, high continent, such as the Mississippi, are able to keep pace with rising sea level and deliver enough sediment to keep an estuary from forming, and, at a high stillstand like that of the present, even fill their entire shelf area.

For many years after World War II, the period when many of the world's continental shelves were first described in detail, it was thought that the sand deposits on continental shelves were "relict," deposits left stranded by a higher sea level from the higher-energy regime of the surf zone that passed over them perhaps as much as a few thousand years before. Geophysical investigations of the shelf area since the mid-1970s have revealed the presence of many types of sand waves and ripple marks in seafloor sediments that show submerged continental shelf sediments to be constantly undergoing reworking and erosion. As scientific understanding of the physical processes that affect continental shelves increased, it was found that currents set up by large winter storms, monsoons, and hurricanes and typhoons are reworking the bottom by winnowing out the fine-grained materials and carrying them either back into the estuaries or beyond the shelf break, where they are lost from the system.

In short, the kind of sediment that covers the surface of a continental shelf is determined by the interplay among the tectonic setting, the size of the rivers that empty into it (size based on how much sediment they carry), and the wave energy that affects it, just as is the case with continental margins in general. Shelves such as that of western Florida that have been cut off from clastic input (that is, sediments composed chiefly of quartz and clay minerals derived from erosion of the continent) may be covered with carbonate sediments. In some cases, as in the islands of the Bahamas, the carbonate shelf, called a bank, is cut off from a continental source by deep water. Continental shelves with rivers that carry sediments from the continents to the shelf and beyond only at low-stands of sea level and those that drain mountainous areas on high-energy coasts are dominated by quartz sands. In addition, shelves with rivers that drain large continental areas and carry enough sediment to keep abreast of sea-level rise or dominate ambient wave-energy conditions will accumulate muddy sediment deposits out across their surfaces.

Since the 1970s an increasing number of investigators have sought to explain the origin of continental shelves and their related structures in terms of plate tectonics. According to this theory, the shelves of the Pacific Ocean, for example, formed as the leading edges of continental margins on lithospheric plates that terminate either at fracture zones (sites where two such plates slide past each other) or at subduction zones (sites where one of the colliding plates plunges into the underlying partially molten asthenosphere). Shelves of such origin tend to be steep, deformed, and covered by a thin layer of erosional debris. The Atlantic continental shelves, on the other hand, show little or no tectonic deformation and bear a thick veneer of sedimentary material. They are thought to be remnants of the trailing edges of the enormous plates that split apart and receded many millions of years ago to form the Atlantic basin. As the edges of the plates gradually contracted and subsided, large amounts of sand, silts, and mud from the continents settled and accumulated along their seaward side.

Continental Slopes

Continental slopes form the seaward borders of continental shelves. The world's combined continental slope has a total length of approximately 300,000 km (200,000 miles) and descends at an average angle in excess of 4 °From the shelf break at the edge of the continental shelf to the beginning of the ocean basins at depths of 100 to 3,200 metres (330 to 10,500 feet).

The gradient of the slope is lowest off stable coasts without major rivers and highest off coasts with young mountain ranges and narrow continental shelves. Most Pacific slopes are steeper than Atlantic slopes. Gradients are flattest in the Indian Ocean. About one-half of all continental slopes descend into deep-sea trenches or shallower depressions, and most of the remainder terminate in fans of marine sediment or in continental rises. The transition from continental crust to oceanic crust usually occurs below the continental slope.

About 8.5 percent of the ocean floor is covered by the continental slope-rise system. This system is an expression of the edge of the continental crustal block. Beyond the shelf-slope break, the continental crust thins quickly, and the rise lies partly on the continental crust and partly on the oceanic crust of the deep sea. Although the continental slope averages about 4°, it can approach vertical on carbonate margins, on faulted margins, or on leading-edge, tectonically active margins. Steep slopes usually have either a very poorly developed continental rise or none at all and are called escarpments.

Continental slopes are indented by numerous submarine canyons and mounds. The Blake Plateau off the southeastern United States and the continental borderland off southern California are examples of continental slopes separated from continental shelves by plateaus of intermediate depth. Slopes off mountainous coastlines and narrow shelves often have outcrops of rock.

The predominant sediments of continental slopes are muds; there are smaller amounts of sediments of sand or gravel. Over geologic time, the continental slopes are temporary depositional sites for sediments. During lowstands of sea level, rivers may dump their sedimentary burden directly on them. Sediments build up until the mass becomes unstable and sloughs off to the lower slope and the continental rise. During highstands of sea level, these processes slow down as the coastline retreats landward across the continental shelf, and more of the sediments delivered to the coast are trapped in estuaries and lagoons. Still the process continues, albeit slowly, as sediments are brought across the shelf break by winnowing of the shelf surface and by advection. Slopes are sometimes scoured by such major ocean currents as the Florida Current that work to erode their surfaces. Off active major deposition centres, such as the Mississippi delta, slope sequences may accumulate through progradation, while the active slope front is continuously shedding sediments downslope by gravity processes.

DEEP-SEA TRENCHES

These structures, which are also called oceanic trenches, are long, narrow, steep-sided depressions in the ocean bottom. Deep-sea trenches are locations in which the maximum oceanic depths, approximately 7,300 to more than 11,000 metres (24,000 to 36,000 feet), occur. They typically form in locations where one tectonic plate subducts under another. The deepest known depression of this kind is the Mariana Trench, which lies east of the Mariana Islands in the western North Pacific Ocean; it reaches 11,034 metres (36,200 feet) at its deepest point.

TYPES

Deep-sea trenches generally lie seaward of and parallel to adjacent island arcs or mountain ranges of the continental margins. They are closely associated with and found in subduction zones—that is, locations where a lithospheric plate bearing oceanic crust slides down into the upper mantle under the force of gravity. The result is a topographic depression where the oceanic plate comes in contact with the overriding plate, which may be either oceanic or continental. If the overriding plate is oceanic, an island arc develops. The trench forms an arc in plan view, and islands with explosive volcanoes develop on the overriding plate. If the overriding plate is continental, a marginal trench forms where the topographic depression appears to follow the outline of the continental margin. Explosive volcanoes are found there too.

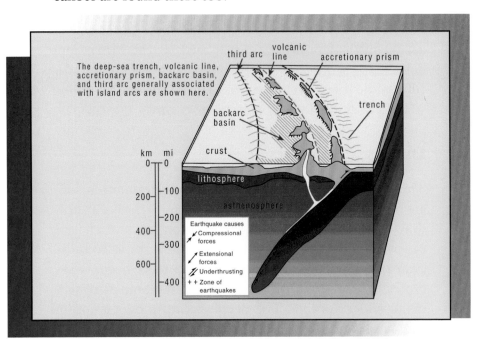

Features of a typical island arc. Copyright Encyclopædia Britannica, Inc.; rendering for this edition by Rosen Educational Services

Both types of subduction zones are associated with large earthquakes that originate at a depth of as much as 700 km (435 miles). The deep earthquakes below subduction zones occur in a plane that dips 30° or more under the overriding plate. Typical trench depths are 8 to 10 km (5 to 6 miles). The longest trench is the Peru-Chile Trench, which extends some 5,900 km (about 3,700 miles) along the west coast of South America. Trenches are relatively narrow, usually less than 100 km (about 60 miles) wide.

Of Earth's 20 major trenches, 17 are found in the Pacific basin, a vast area rimmed by trenches of both marginal and island arc varieties. Marginal trenches bound the west coast of Central and South America from the Gulf of California to southern Chile. Although they are deeply buried in sediment, trenches are found along the western North American continental margin from Cape Mendocino (in northern California) to the Canadian border. The Aleutian Trench extends from the northernmost point in the Gulf of Alaska west to the Kamchatka Peninsula in far eastern Russia. It can be classified as a marginal trench in the east but is more properly termed an island arc west of Alaska.

In the western Pacific the trenches are associated with island arcs. These include the Kuril, Japan, Bonin, Mariana, Ryukyu, and Philippine trenches that extend from Kamchatka to near the Equator. A complex pattern of island arcs is found in Indonesia. The major island arc here is the Java Trench, extending from northern Australia to the northwestern end of Sumatra in the northeast Indian Ocean. The region of New Guinea and the Solomon Islands includes the New Britain and Solomon trenches, the latter of which joins the New Hebrides Trench directly to the south. East of this area the Tonga and Kermadec trenches extend south from the Fiji Islands to New Zealand.

Two island arcs occur in the Atlantic Ocean. The South Sandwich Trench is located west of the Mid-Atlantic

Ridge between South America and Antarctica. The Puerto Rico Trench joins the Lesser Antilles Island arc in the eastern Caribbean.

A few trenches are partially filled with sediments derived from the bordering continents. The Aleutian Trench is effectively buried east of Kodiak Island in the Gulf of Alaska. There the ocean floor is smooth and flat. To the west, farther from the sediment supply of Alaska, the trench reaches depths of more than 7 km (about 4 miles). The Lesser Antilles trench in the eastern Caribbean is buried by sediments originating from South America.

STRUCTURE

Deep-sea trenches and their approaches are striking features on the ocean floor. In general, the cross sections of deep-sea trenches are V-shaped with steeper landward sides. Typical slopes range between 4° and 16°, although slopes as steep as 45° have been measured in the Tonga Trench of the equatorial South Pacific. Narrow, flat abyssal plains of ponded sediment generally occupy trench axes; however, in most deep-sea trenches the accumulated material is relatively shallow since the bottom of the trench subducts into Earth's interior.

Oceanward of trenches the seafloor is usually bulged upward in an outer ridge or rise of up to 1,000 metres (about 3,300 feet) in relief. This condition is thought to be the elastic response of the oceanic plate bending down into a subduction zone. The landward or island-arc slope of the trench is often interrupted by a submarine ridge, which sometimes breaks the ocean surface, as in the case of the Java Trench. Such a ridge is constructed from deformed sediments scraped off the top of the descending oceanic plate and is termed an accretionary prism. A line of explosive volcanoes, extruding (erupting) a lava that forms the volcanic rock andesite, is found on the overriding plate usually 100 km (about 60 miles) or so from the trench. In marginal trenches these volcanoes form mountain chains, such as the Cascades in the Pacific Northwest or the great volcanoes of the Andes. In island arcs they form active volcanic island chains, such as the Mariana Islands.

Behind the volcanic line of island arcs are sometimes found young, narrow ocean basins. These basins are bounded on the opposite side by submarine ridges. Such interarc, or backarc, basins are sites of seafloor spreading directly caused by the dynamics of subduction. They originate at the volcanic line, so that the outer bounding submarine ridge, or third arc, represents an older portion of the volcanic line that has spread away. These backarc basins bear many of the features characteristic of oceanic spreading centres. Well-studied examples of these features are found in the Lau Basin of the Tonga arc and also west of the Mariana Islands. The Sea of Japan originated from backarc spreading behind the Japanese arc that began some 30 million years ago. At least two backarc basins have opened behind the Mariana arc, creating seafloor in two phases from about 30 to 17 million years ago in the western Parece Vela Basin and from 5 million years ago in the Mariana Trough next to the islands. The Mariana Trough is a back-arc basin occurring due east of the Mariana arc.

It is important to note that some seafloor features bear the name *trench* and are deep linear troughs; however, they do not occur in subduction zones. The Vema Trench on the Mid-Indian Ridge is a fracture zone. The Vityaz Trench northwest of Fiji is an aseismic (inactive) feature of unknown origin. The Diamantina trench (Diamantina Fracture Zone) extends westward from the southwest coast of Australia. It is a rift valley that was formed when Australia separated from Antarctica between 60 million and 50 million years ago.

Origin of Deep-Sea Trenches

Geophysical data provide important clues concerning the origin of trenches. No abnormalities in the flow of internal Earth heat or variations in Earth's magnetic field occur at trenches. Precision measurements reveal that the force of gravity generally is lower than normal, however. These negative gravity anomalies are interpreted to mean that the segments of the lithosphere (that is, the crust and upper mantle comprising the rigid, outermost shell of Earth) that underlie trenches are being forced down against buoyant isostatic forces.

This interpretation of gravity data is substantiated by seismological studies. All trenches are associated with zones of earthquake foci. Along the periphery of the Pacific Ocean, earthquakes occur close to and landward of the trenches, at depths within Earth of 55 km (34 miles) or less. With increased landward distance away from the trenches, earthquakes occur at greater and greater depths—500 km (310 miles) or more. Seismic foci thus define tabular zones approximately 20 km (12 miles) thick that dip landward at about 45° beneath the continents. Analyses of these seismic zones and of individual earthquakes suggest that the seismicity results from the descent of a lithospheric plate with its associated crust into the asthenosphere (that is, the partially molten layer beneath the lithosphere); oceanic trenches are topographic expressions of this movement.

The sinking of oceanic lithosphere helps to explain the relative scarcity of sediment that has accumulated within the trenches. Small quantities of brown or red clay, siliceous organic remains, volcanic ash and lapilli, and coarse, graded layers that result from turbidity currents and from the slumping of the trench walls occur at trench axes. Sediments on trench walls shallower than 4,500 metres (about 14,800 feet) are predominantly calcareous foraminiferal oozes. Large quantities of sediment cannot accumulate because they either are dragged into Earth's interior by the plunging oceanic lithosphere or are distorted into folded masses and molded into new material of the continental periphery.

OCEANIC CRUST

The oceanic crust is the outermost layer of Earth's lithosphere that is found under the oceans. The oceanic crust is formed at spreading centres on oceanic ridges, and it is about 6 km (4 miles) thick. It is composed of several layers, not including the overlying sediment. The topmost layer, about 500 metres (1,650 feet) thick, includes lavas made of basalt (that is, rock material consisting largely of plagioclase [feldspar] and pyroxene). Oceanic crust differs from continental crust in several ways: it is thinner, denser, younger, of different chemical composition, and formed above the subduction zones.

The lavas are generally of two types: pillow lavas and sheet flows. Pillow lavas appear to be shaped exactly as the name implies—like large overstuffed pillows about 1 metre (3 feet) in cross section and 1 to several metres long. They commonly form small hills tens of metres high at the spreading centres. Sheet flows have the appearance of wrinkled bed sheets. They commonly are thin (only about 10 cm [4 inches] thick) and cover a broader area than pillow lavas. There is evidence that sheet flows are erupted at higher temperatures than those of the pillow variety. On the East Pacific Rise at 8° S latitude, a series of sheet flow eruptions (possibly since the mid-1960s) have covered more than 220 square km (85 square miles) of seafloor to an average depth of 70 metres (230 feet).

Below the lava is a layer composed of feeder, or sheeted, dikes that measures more than 1 km (0.6 mile) thick. Dikes are fractures that serve as the plumbing system for transporting magmas (molten rock material) to the seafloor to produce lavas. They are about 1 metre (3 feet) wide, subvertical, and elongate along the trend of the spreading centre where they formed, and they abut one another's sides—hence the term *sheeted*. These dikes also are of basaltic composition. There are two layers

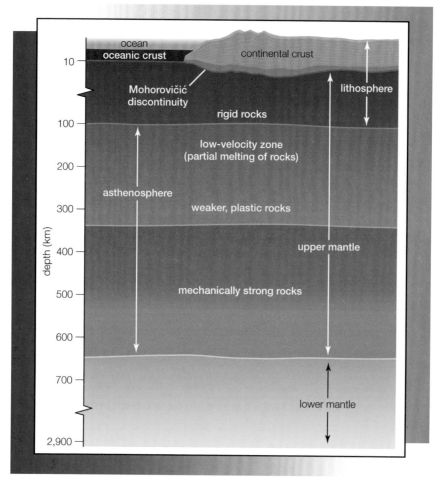

A cross section of Earth's outer layers, from the crust through the lower mantle. Encyclopædia Britannica, Inc.

below the dikes totaling about 4.5 km (3 miles) in thickness. Both of these include gabbros, which are essentially basalts with coarser mineral grains. These gabbro layers are thought to represent the magma chambers, or pockets of lava, that ultimately erupt on the seafloor. The upper gabbro layer is isotropic (uniform) in structure. In some places this layer includes pods of plagiogranite, a differentiated rock richer in silica than gabbro. The lower gabbro layer has a stratified structure and evidently represents the floor or sides of the magma chamber. This layered structure is called cumulate, meaning that the layers (which measure up to several metres thick) result from the sedimentation of minerals out of the liquid magma. The layers in the cumulate gabbro have less silica but are richer in iron and magnesium than the upper portions of the crust. Olivine, an iron-magnesium silicate, is a common mineral in the lower gabbro layer.

The oceanic crust lies atop Earth's mantle, as does the continental crust. Mantle rock is composed mostly of peridotite, which consists primarily of the mineral olivine with small amounts of pyroxene and amphibole.

INVESTIGATIONS OF THE OCEANIC CRUST

Knowledge of the structure and composition of the oceanic crust comes from several sources. Bottom sampling during early exploration brought up all varieties of the above-mentioned rocks, but the structure of the crust and the abundance of the constituent rocks were unclear. Simultaneously, seismic refraction experiments enabled researchers to determine the layered nature of the oceanic crust. These experiments involved measuring the travel times of seismic waves generated by explosions (such as dynamite blasts) set off over distances of several tens of kilometres. The results of early refraction experiments revealed the existence of two layers beneath the sediment cover. More sophisticated experiments and analyses led to dividing these layers into two parts, each with a different seismic wave velocity, which increases with depth. The seismic velocity is a kind of fingerprint that can be attributed to a limited number of rock types. Sampled rock data and seismic results were combined to yield a model for the structure and composition of the crust.

STUDY OF OPHIOLITES

Great strides in understanding the oceanic crust were made by the study of ophiolites. These are slices of the ocean floor that have been thrust above sea level by the action of plate tectonics. In various places in the world, the entire sequence of oceanic crust and upper mantle is exposed. These areas include, among others, Newfoundland and the Pacific Coast Ranges of California, the island of Cyprus in the Mediterranean Sea, and the mountains in Oman on the southeastern tip of the Arabian Peninsula. Ophiolites reveal the structure and composition of the oceanic crust in astonishing detail. Also, the process of crustal formation and hydrothermal circulation, as well as the origin of marine magnetic anomalies, can be studied with comparative clarity. Although it is clear that ophiolites are of marine origin, there is some controversy as to whether they represent typical oceanic crust or crust formed in settings other than an oceanic spreading centre—behind island arcs, for example.

The age of the oceanic crust does not go back farther than about 200 million years. Such crust is being formed today at oceanic spreading centres. Many ophiolites are much older than the oldest oceanic crust, demonstrating continuity of the formation processes over hundreds of millions of years. Methods that may be used to determine the age of the crustal material include direct dating of rock samples by radiometric dating (measuring the relative abundances of a particular radioactive isotope and its daughter isotopes in the samples) or by the analyses of fossil evidence, marine magnetic anomalies, or ocean depth. Of these, magnetic anomalies deserve special attention.

A marine magnetic anomaly is a variation in strength of Earth's magnetic field caused by magnetism in rocks of the ocean floor. Marine magnetic anomalies typically represent 1 percent of the total geomagnetic field strength. They can be stronger ("positive") or weaker ("negative") than the average total field. Also, the magnetic anomalies occur in long bands that run parallel to spreading centres for hundreds of kilometres and may reach up to a few tens of kilometres in width.

MARINE MAGNETIC ANOMALIES

Marine magnetic anomalies were first discovered off the coast of the western United States in the late 1950s and completely baffled scientists. The anomalies were charted from southern California to northern Washington and out several hundred kilometres. Russian-born American geophysicist Victor Vacquier noticed that these linear anomalies ended at the fracture zones mapped in this area. In addition, he noticed that they had unique shapes, occurred in a predictable sequence across their trends, and could be correlated across the fracture zones. Soon thereafter, linear magnetic anomalies were mapped over the Reykjanes Ridge south of Iceland. They were found to occur on both sides of the ridge crest and parallel to it. Simultaneously, Alan Cox and several other American geophysicists documented evidence that Earth's magnetic field had reversed in the past: the north magnetic pole had been the south magnetic pole about 700,000 years ago, and there were reasons to believe older reversals existed. Also at this time, American geophysicist Robert S. Dietz and American geologist Harry H. Hess were formulating the theory of seafloor spreading—the hypothesis that oceanic crust is created at the crests of the oceanic ridges and consumed in the deep-sea trenches.

It remained for English geologists Frederick J. Vine and Drummond H. Matthews and Canadian geophysicist Lawrence W. Morley to put these observations together in a theory that explained marine magnetic anomalies. The theory rests on three assumptions: (1) that Earth's magnetic field periodically reverses polarity, (2) that seafloor spreading occurs, and (3) that the oceanic crust is permanently magnetized as it forms and cools at spreading centres. The theory expresses the assumptions—namely, that the oceanic crust records reversals of Earth's field as it is formed during seafloor spreading. Positive anomalies result when the crust is magnetized in a "normal" polarity parallel to the ambient field of Earth, and negative anomalies result when the crust is "reversely" magnetized in an opposite sense. As the magnetized crust moves down the flanks of a ridge away from the spreading centre, it remains permanently magnetized and "carries" the magnetic anomalies along with it.

A brilliant leap in understanding was now possible. If the age of the field reversals were known, the age of the ocean crust could be predicted by mapping the corresponding anomaly. By the mid-1960s, Cox and his colleagues had put together a schedule of reversals for the last four or five million years by studying the ages and magnetic polarities of lava flows found on land. Vine and the Canadian geologist J. Tuzo Wilson applied the time scale to marine magnetic anomalies mapped over the Juan de Fuca Ridge, a spreading centre off the northwest United States. They thus dated the crust there and also computed the first seafloor spreading rate of about 30 mm (1.2 inches) per year. The rate is computed by dividing the distance of an anomaly from the ridge crest by the age of the anomaly twice. Thus the oceanic crust at the Juan de Fuca Ridge is moving at about 15 mm (0.6 inch) per year away from the ridge crest and at about 60 mm (2.4 inches) per year away from the crustal segment on the opposite side of the crest.

During the 1960s and '70s marine magnetic anomalies were mapped over wide areas of the ocean basins. By using estimates of the ages of oceanic crust obtained from core samples by deep-sea drilling, a magnetic anomaly time scale was constructed, and at the same time the spreading history for the ocean basins covering the last 200 million years or so was proposed.

It is thought that the most important contributor to marine magnetic anomalies is the layer of lavas in the upper oceanic crust. A secondary contribution originates in the upper layer of gabbros. The dike layer is essentially demagnetized by the action of hydrothermal waters at the spreading centres. The dominant mechanism of permanent magnetization is the thermoremanent magnetization (or TRM) of iron-titanium oxide minerals. These minerals lock in a TRM as they cool below 200–300 °C (392–572 °F) in the presence of Earth's magnetic field. Although several processes are capable of altering the TRM, including reheating and oxidation at the seafloor, it is remarkably robust, as is evidenced by magnetic anomalies as old as 165 million years in the far western equatorial Pacific.

OCEANIC PLATEAUS

Oceanic plateaus, which are also called submarine plateaus, are large regions of submarine elevation that rise sharply at least 200 metres (about 660 feet) above the surrounding deep-sea floor. Oceanic plateaus are characterized principally by extensive, relatively flat or gently tilted summits. Most oceanic plateaus were named early in the 20th century prior to the invention of sonic sounding, and many of these features have been shown by modern bathymetric data to be portions of the oceanic ridges. Thus, the Albatross Plateau of the eastern equatorial Pacific now is recognized as belonging to the East Pacific Rise and has been shown to possess a much more irregular summit than early data indicated.

Most plateaus are steplike interruptions of the continental slopes and appear to be downwarped or downfaulted blocks of former continental shelves. These marginal plateaus are exemplified by the Blake Plateau off the southeastern United States. This plateau's flat surface lies between 700 and 1,000 m (2,300 and 3,300 feet) below sea level, is more than 300 km (185 miles) wide, and covers approximately 130,000 square km (50,000 square miles) of seafloor. The crust underlying the plateau, although relatively thin and veneered by flat-lying marine sediments, is otherwise continental in character.

Other plateaus, such as the coral-capped plateaus of the South China Sea, occur in the ocean well beyond the continental margins. They stand above the surrounding deep-sea floor as isolated topographic highs and are believed to be composed of continental rock cores

Crew members aboard a drilling ship inspect a rock core during a scientific expedition that succeeded for the first time in drilling through the upper oceanic crust. JOI Alliance/IODP

overlain by flat-lying marine sediments. Presumably, these mid-ocean plateaus are minor fragments of continent that have been isolated during continental drift and seafloorspreading.

Oceanic Ridges

Oceanic ridges are continuous submarine mountain chains that extend approximately 80,000 km (50,000 miles) through all the world's oceans. Individually, ocean ridges are the largest features in ocean basins. Collectively, the oceanic ridge system is the most prominent feature on Earth's surface after the continents and the ocean basins themselves. In the past these features were referred to as mid-ocean ridges, but, as will be seen, the largest oceanic ridge, the East Pacific Rise, is far from a mid-ocean location, and the nomenclature is thus inaccurate. Oceanic

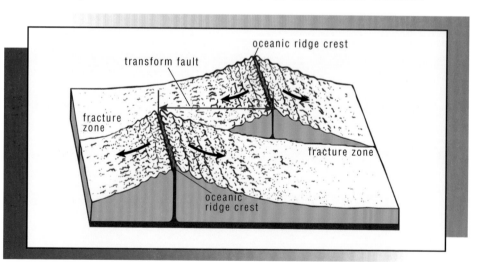

Oceanic ridges offset by transform faults and fracture zones. The arrows show the direction of movement across the transform faults. Copyright Encyclopædia Britannica, Inc.; rendering for this edition by Rosen Educational Services

ridges are not to be confused with aseismic ridges, which have an entirely different origin.

PRINCIPAL CHARACTERISTICS

Oceanic ridges are found in every ocean basin and appear to girdle the planet. The ridges rise from depths near 5 km (3 miles) to an essentially uniform depth of about 2.6 km (1.6 miles) and are roughly symmetrical in cross section. They can be thousands of kilometres wide. In places, the crests of the ridges are offset across transform faults within fracture zones, and these faults can be followed down the flanks of the ridges. (Transform faults are those along which lateral movement occurs.) The flanks are marked by sets of mountains and hills that are elongate and parallel to the ridge trend.

New oceanic crust (and part of Earth's upper mantle, which, together with the crust, makes up the lithosphere) is formed at seafloor spreading centres at these crests of the oceanic ridges. Because of this, certain unique geologic features are found there. Fresh basaltic lavas are exposed on the seafloor at the ridge crests. These lavas are progressively buried by sediments as the seafloor spreads away from the site. The flow of heat out of the crust is many times greater at the crests than elsewhere in the world. Earthquakes are common along the crests and in the transform faults that join the offset ridge segments. Analysis of earthquakes occurring at the ridge crests indicates that the oceanic crust is under tension there. A high-amplitude magnetic anomaly is centred over the crests because fresh lavas at the crests are being magnetized in the direction of the present geomagnetic field.

The depths over the oceanic ridges are rather precisely correlated with the age of the ocean crust; specifically, it has been demonstrated that the ocean depth is proportional to the square root of crustal age. The theory explaining this relationship holds that the increase in depth with age is due to the thermal contraction of the oceanic crust and upper mantle as they are carried away from the seafloor spreading centre in an oceanic plate. Because such a tectonic plate is ultimately about 100 km (62 miles) thick, contraction of only a few percent predicts the entire relief of an oceanic ridge. It then follows that the width of a ridge can be defined as twice the distance from the crest to the point where the plate has cooled to a steady thermal state. Most of the cooling takes place within 70 or 80 million years, by which time the ocean depth is about 5 to 5.5 km (3.1 to 3.5 miles). Because this cooling is a function of age, slow-spreading ridges, such as the Mid-Atlantic Ridge, are narrower than faster-spreading ridges, such as the East Pacific Rise. Further, a correlation has been found between global spreading rates and the transgression and regression of ocean waters onto the continents. About 100 million years ago, during the early Cretaceous Period when global spreading rates were uniformly high, oceanic ridges occupied comparatively more of the ocean basins, causing the ocean waters to transgress (spill over) onto the continents, leaving marine sediments in areas now well away from coastlines.

Besides ridge width, other features appear to be a function of spreading rate. Global spreading rates range from 10 mm (0.4 inch) per year or less up to 160 mm (6.3 inches) per year. Oceanic ridges can be classified as slow (up to 50 mm [about 2 inches]) per year, intermediate (up to 90 mm [about 3.5 inches]) per year, and fast (up to 160 mm per year). Slow-spreading ridges are characterized by a rift valley at the crest. Such a valley is fault-controlled. It is typically 1.4 km (0.9 mile) deep and 20–40 km (about 12–25 miles) wide. Faster-spreading ridges lack rift valleys. At intermediate rates, the crest regions are broad highs with occasional fault-bounded valleys no deeper than 200 metres (about 660 feet). At fast rates, an axial high is present at the crest. The slow-spreading rifted ridges have rough faulted topography on their flanks, while the faster-spreading ridges have much smoother flanks.

DISTRIBUTION OF MAJOR RIDGES AND SPREADING CENTRES

Oceanic spreading centres are found in all the ocean basins. In the Arctic Ocean a slow-rate spreading centre is located near the eastern side in the Eurasian basin. It can be followed south, offset by transform faults, to Iceland. Iceland has been created by a hot spot located directly below an oceanic spreading centre. The ridge leading south from Iceland is named the Reykjanes Ridge, and, although it spreads at 20 mm (0.8 inch) per year or less, it lacks a rift valley. This is thought to be the result of the influence of the hot spot.

The Atlantic Ocean

The Mid-Atlantic Ridge extends from south of Iceland to the extreme South Atlantic Ocean near 60° S latitude. It bisects the Atlantic Ocean basin, which led to the earlier designation of mid-ocean ridge for features of this type. The Mid-Atlantic Ridge became known in a rudimentary fashion during the 19th century. In 1855 Matthew Fontaine Maury of the U.S. Navy prepared a chart of the Atlantic in which he identified it as a shallow "middle ground." During the 1950s the American oceanographers Bruce Heezen and Maurice Ewing proposed that it was a continuous mountain range.

In the North Atlantic the ridge spreads slowly and displays a rift valley and mountainous flanks. In the South

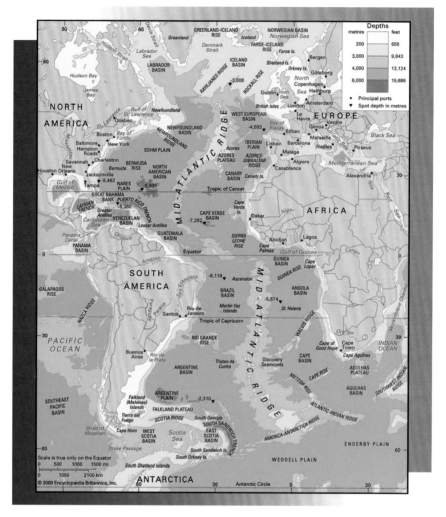

The Atlantic Ocean, with depth contours and submarine features.

Atlantic spreading rates are between slow and intermediate, and rift valleys are generally absent, as they occur only near transform faults.

The Indian Ocean

A very slow oceanic ridge, the Southwest Indian Ridge, bisects the ocean between Africa and Antarctica. It joins the Mid-Indian and Southeast Indian ridges east of

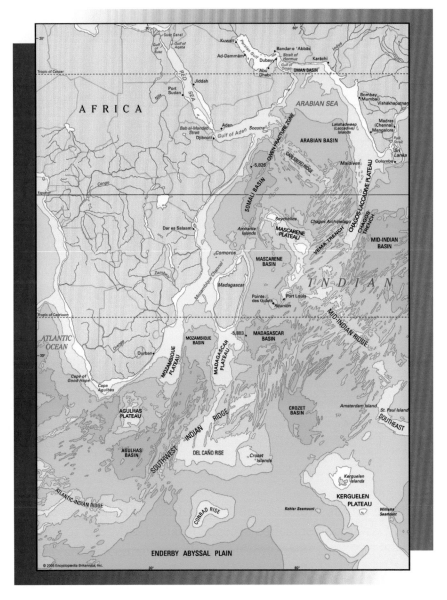

The Indian Ocean, with depth contours and undersea features.

Madagascar. The Carlsberg Ridge is found at the north end of the Mid-Indian Ridge. It continues north to join spreading centres in the Gulf of Aden and Red Sea. Spreading is very slow at this point but approaches

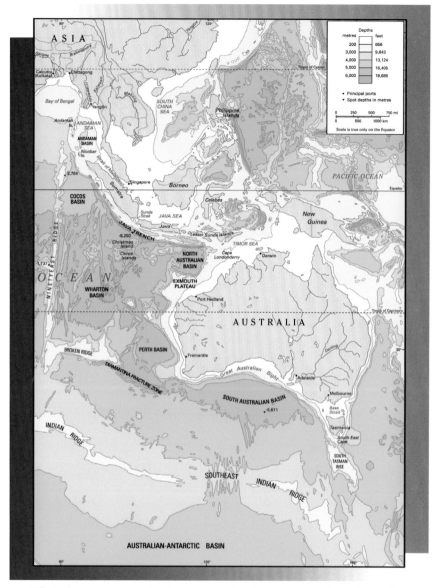

The Indian Ocean, with depth contours and undersea features. Encyclopaedia Britannica, Inc.

intermediate rates on the Carlsberg and Mid-Indian ridges. The Southeast Indian Ridge spreads at intermediate rates. This ridge continues from the western Indian Ocean in a southeasterly direction, bisecting the ocean between Australia and Antarctica. Rifted crests and rugged mountainous flanks are characteristic of the Southwest Indian Ridge. The Mid-Indian Ridge has fewer features of this kind, and the Southeast Indian Ridge has generally smoother topography. The latter also displays distinct asymmetric seafloor spreading south of Australia. Analysis of magnetic anomalies shows that rates on opposite sides of the spreading centre have been unequal at many times over the past 50 or 60 million years.

Pacific Ocean

The Pacific-Antarctic Ridge can be followed from a point midway between New Zealand and Antarctica northeast to where it joins the East Pacific Rise off the margin of South America. The former spreads at intermediate to fast rates.

The East Pacific Rise extends from this site northward to the Gulf of California, where it joins the transform zone of the Pacific-North American plate boundary. Offshore from Chile and Peru, the East Pacific Rise is currently spreading at fast rates of 159 mm (6.3 inches) per year or more. Rates decrease to about 60 mm (about 2.4 inches) per year at the mouth of the Gulf of California. The crest of the ridge displays a low topographic rise along its length rather than a rift valley. The East Pacific Rise was first detected during the Challenger Expedition of the 1870s. It was described in its gross form during the 1950s and '60s by oceanographers, including Heezen, Ewing, and Henry W. Menard. During the 1980s, Kenneth C. Macdonald, Paul J. Fox, and Peter F. Lonsdale discovered that the main spreading centre appears to be interrupted and offset a few kilometres to one side at various places along the crest of the East Pacific Rise. However, the ends of the offset spreading centres overlap each other by several kilometres. These were identified as a new type of geologic

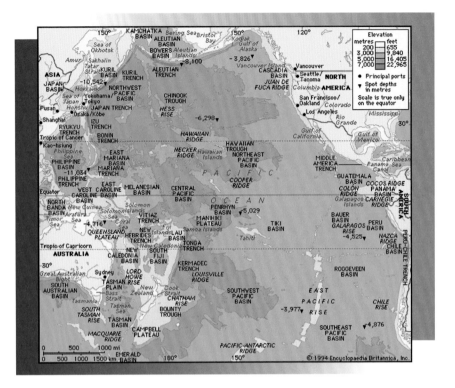

The Pacific Ocean, with depth contours and submarine features.

feature of oceanic spreading centres and were designated overlapping spreading centres. Such centres are thought to result from interruptions of the magma supply to the crest along its length and define a fundamental segmentation of the ridge on a scale of tens to hundreds of kilometres.

Many smaller spreading centres branch off the major ones or are found behind island arcs. In the western Pacific, spreading centres occur on the Fiji Plateau between the New Hebrides and Fiji Islands and in the Woodlark Basin between New Guinea and the Solomon Islands. A series of spreading centres and transform faults lie between the East Pacific Rise and South America near 40° to 50° S latitude. The Scotia Sea between South

America and the Antarctic Peninsula contains a spreading centre. The Galápagos spreading centre trends east-west between the East Pacific Rise and South America near the Equator. Three short spreading centres are found a few hundred kilometres off the shore of the Pacific Northwest. These are the Gorda Ridges off northern California, the Juan de Fuca Ridge off Oregon and Washington, and the Explorer Ridge off Vancouver Island.

In a careful study of the seafloor spreading history of the Galapagos and the Juan de Fuca spreading centres, the American geophysicist Richard N. Hey developed the idea of the propagating rift. In this phenomenon, one branch of a spreading centre ending in a transform fault lengthens at the expense of the spreading centre across the fault. The rift and fault propagate at one to five times the spreading rate and create chevron patterns in magnetic anomalies and the grain of the seafloor topography resembling the wake of a boat.

SPREADING CENTRES AND ASSOCIATED PHENOMENA

From the 1970s highly detailed studies of spreading centres using deeply towed instruments, photography, and manned submersibles have resulted in new revelations about the processes of seafloor spreading. The most profound discoveries have been of deep-sea hydrothermal vents and previously unknown biological communities.

Spreading Centre Zones

Spreading centres are divided into several geologic zones. The neovolcanic zone is at the very axis. It is 1–2 km (0.6–1.2 miles) wide and is the site of recent and active volcanism and of the hydrothermal vents. It is marked by chains of small volcanoes or volcanic ridges. Adjacent to the neovolcanic zone is one marked by fissures in the seafloor. This may be 1 to 2 km wide. Beyond this point occurs a zone of active faulting. Here, fissures develop into normal faults with vertical offsets. This zone may be 10 km (about 6 miles) or more wide. At slow spreading rates the faults have offsets of hundreds of metres, creating rift valleys and rift mountains. At faster rates the vertical offsets are 50 metres (about 160 feet) or less. A deep rift valley is not formed because the vertical uplifts are cancelled out by faults that downdrop uplifted blocks. This results in linear, fault-bounded abyssal hills and valleys trending parallel to the spreading centre.

Warm springs emanating from the seafloor in the neovolcanic zone were first found on the Galápagos spreading centre. These waters were measured to have temperatures about 20 °C (36 °F) above the ambient temperature. In 1979 hydrothermal vents with temperatures near 350 °C (662 °F) were discovered on the East Pacific Rise off Mexico. Since then similar vents have been found on the spreading centres off the Pacific Northwest coast of the United States, on the south end of the northern Mid-Atlantic Ridge, and at many locations on the East Pacific Rise.

Hydrothermal Vents

Hydrothermal vents are localized discharges of heated seawater. They result from cold seawater percolating down into the hot oceanic crust through the zone of fissures and returning to the seafloor in a pipelike flow at the axis of the neovolcanic zone. The heated waters often carry sulfide minerals of zinc, iron, and copper leached from the crust. Outflow of these heated waters probably accounts for 20 percent of Earth's heat loss. Exotic biological communities exist around the hydrothermal vents. These ecosystems are totally independent of energy from the Sun. They are not dependent on photosynthesis but rather on chemosynthesis by sulfur-fixing bacteria. The sulfide minerals precipitated in the neovolcanic zone can accumulate in substantial amounts and are sometimes buried by lava flows at a later time. Such deposits are mined as commercial ores in ophiolites on Cyprus and in Oman.

Magma Chambers

Magma chambers have been detected beneath the crest of the East Pacific Rise by seismic experiments. (The principle underlying the experiments is that partially molten or molten rock slows the travel of seismic waves and also strongly reflects them.) The depth to the top of the chambers is about 2 km (1.2 miles) below the seafloor. The width is more difficult to ascertain but is probably 1 to 4 km (0.6 to 2.5 miles). Their thickness seems to be about 2 to 6 km (1.2 to 3.7 miles), on the basis of studies of ophiolites. The chambers have been mapped along the trend of the crest between 9° and 13° N latitude. The top is relatively continuous, but is apparently interrupted by offsets of transform faults and overlapping spreading centres.

CHAPTER 3
CIRCULATION AND WAVES

S eawater is in constant motion. Water circulates around the globe through ocean currents, which are, generally speaking, propelled by winds affecting water at the ocean's surface above and by changes in the density of fluids below. Ocean circulation is also affected by pressure gradients, the Coriolis effect, friction, and other factors. Ocean waves are manifestations of energy transferred through a liquid medium. Waves (which occur as gravity waves and tides) are most apparent at the ocean's surface and in locations where the oceans border landmasses.

THE CIRCULATION OF THE OCEAN WATERS

The general circulation of the oceans defines the average movement of seawater, which, like the atmosphere, follows a specific pattern. Superimposed on this pattern are oscillations of tides and waves, which are not considered part of the general circulation. There also are meanders and eddies that represent temporal variations of the general circulation. The ocean circulation pattern exchanges water of varying characteristics, such as temperature and salinity, within the interconnected network of oceans and is an important part of the heat and freshwater fluxes of the global climate. Horizontal movements are called currents, which range in magnitude from a few centimetres per second to as much as 4 metres (13.1 feet) per second. A characteristic surface speed is about 5 to 50 cm (2 to 20 inches) per second. Currents diminish in intensity with increasing depth. Vertical movements, often referred to as upwelling and downwelling, exhibit much lower speeds, amounting to only a few metres per month. As seawater is nearly incompressible, vertical movements are associated with regions of convergence and divergence in the horizontal flow patterns.

Ocean circulation derives its energy at the sea surface from two sources that define two circulation types: (1) wind-driven circulation forced by wind stress on the sea surface, inducing a momentum exchange, and (2) thermohaline circulation driven by the variations in water density imposed at the sea surface by exchange of ocean heat and water with the atmosphere, inducing a buoyancy exchange. These two circulation types are not fully independent, since the sea-air buoyancy and momentum exchange are dependent on wind speed. The wind-driven circulation is the more vigorous of the two and is configured as large gyres that dominate an ocean region. The wind-driven circulation is strongest in the surface layer. The thermohaline circulation is more sluggish, with a typical speed of 1 cm (0.4 inch) per second, but this flow extends to the seafloor and forms circulation patterns that envelop the global ocean.

DISTRIBUTION OF OCEAN CURRENTS

Maps of the general circulation at the sea surface are constructed from a vast amount of data obtained from inspecting the residual drift of ships after course direction and speed are accounted for in a process called dead reckoning. This information is amplified by satellite-tracked drifters at sea. The pattern is nearly entirely that of wind-driven circulation.

Deep-ocean circulation consists mainly of thermohaline circulation. The currents are inferred from the distribution of seawater properties, which trace the

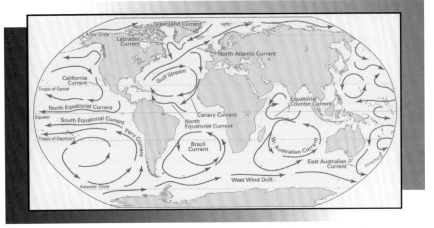

Major surface currents of the world's oceans. Subsurface currents also move vast amounts of water, but they are not known in such detail. Merriam-Webster, Inc.

spreading of specific water masses. The distribution of density or field of mass is also used to estimate the deep currents. Direct observations of subsurface currents are made by deploying current meters from bottom-anchored moorings and by setting out neutral buoyant instruments whose drift at depth is tracked acoustically.

CAUSES OF OCEAN CURRENTS

The general circulation is governed by the equation of motion, one of Sir Isaac Newton's fundamental laws of mechanics applied to a continuous volume of water. This equation states that the product of mass and current acceleration equals the vector sum of all forces that act on the mass. Besides gravity, the most important forces that cause and affect ocean currents are horizontal pressure-gradient forces, Coriolis forces, and frictional forces. Temporal and inertial terms are generally of secondary importance to the general flow, though they become important for transient features of meanders and eddies.

PRESSURE GRADIENTS

The hydrostatic pressure, p, at any depth below the sea surface is given by the equation $p = g\rho z$, where g is the acceleration of gravity, ρ is the density of seawater, which increases with depth, and z is the depth below the sea surface. This is called the hydrostatic equation, which is a good approximation for the equation of motion for forces acting along the vertical. Horizontal differences in density (due to variations of temperature and salinity) measured along a specific depth cause the hydrostatic pressure to vary along a horizontal plane or geopotential surface, a surface perpendicular to the direction of the gravity acceleration. Horizontal gradients of pressure, though much smaller than vertical changes in pressure, give rise to ocean currents.

In a homogeneous ocean, which would have a constant potential density, horizontal pressure differences are possible only if the sea surface is tilted. In this case, surfaces of equal pressure, called isobaric surfaces, are tilted in the deeper layers by the same amount as the sea surface. This is referred to as the barotropic field of mass. The unchanged pressure gradient gives rise to a current speed independent of depth. The oceans of the world, however, are not homogeneous. Horizontal variations in temperature and salinity cause the horizontal pressure gradient to vary with depth. This is the baroclinic field of mass, which leads to currents that vary with depth. The horizontal pressure gradient in the ocean is a combination of these two mass fields.

The tilt, or topographic relief, of the isobaric surface marking sea surface (defined as $p = 0$) can be constructed from a three-dimensional density distribution using the hydrostatic equation. Since the absolute value of pressure is not known at any depth in the ocean, the sea surface slope is presented relative to that of a deep isobaric surface; it is assumed that the deep isobaric surface is level. Since the wind-driven circulation attenuates with increasing depth, an associated decrease of isobaric tilt with increasing depth is expected. Representation of the sea surface relief relative to a deep reference surface is a good representation of the absolute shape of the sea surface. The total relief of the sea surface amounts to about 2 metres (6.6 feet), with "hills" in the subtropics and "valleys" in the polar regions. This pressure head drives the surface circulation.

CORIOLIS EFFECT

The rotation of Earth about its axis causes moving particles to behave in a way that can only be understood by adding a rotational dependent force. To an observer in space, a moving body would continue to move in a straight line unless the motion were acted upon by some other force. To an Earth-bound observer, however, this motion cannot be along a straight line because the reference frame is the rotating Earth. This is similar to the effect that would be experienced by an observer standing on a large turntable if an object moved over the turntable in a straight line relative to the "outside" world. An apparent deflection of the path of the moving object would be seen. If the turntable rotated counterclockwise, the apparent deflection would be to the right of the direction of the moving object, relative to the observer fixed on the turntable.

This remarkable effect is evident in the behaviour of ocean currents. It is called the Coriolis force, named after Gustave-Gaspard Coriolis, a 19th-century French engineer and mathematician. For Earth, horizontal deflections due to the rotational induced Coriolis force act on particles moving in any horizontal direction. There also are apparent vertical forces, but these are of minor importance to ocean currents. Because Earth rotates from west to east about its axis, an observer in the Northern Hemisphere would notice a deflection of a moving body toward the right. In the Southern Hemisphere, this deflection would be toward the left. At the equator there would be no apparent horizontal deflection.

It can be shown that the Coriolis force always acts perpendicular to motion. Its horizontal component, C_f, is proportional to the sine of the geographic latitude (θ, given as a positive value for the Northern Hemisphere and a negative value for the Southern Hemisphere) and the speed, c, of the moving body. It is given by $C_f = c\,(2\omega \sin \theta)$, where $\omega = 7.29 \times 10^{-5}$ radian per second is the angular velocity of Earth's rotation.

FRICTIONAL FORCES

Movement of water through the oceans is slowed by friction, with surrounding fluid moving at a different velocity. A faster-moving fluid layer tends to drag along a slower-moving layer, and a slower-moving layer will tend to reduce the speed of a faster-moving layer. This momentum transfer between the layers is referred to as frictional forces. The momentum transfer is a product of turbulence that moves kinetic energy to smaller scales until at the centimetre scale it is dissipated as heat. The wind blowing over the sea surface transfers momentum to the water. This frictional force at the sea surface (i.e., the wind stress) produces the wind-driven circulation. Currents moving along the ocean floor and the sides of the ocean also are subject to the influence of boundary-layer friction. The motionless ocean floor removes momentum from the circulation of the ocean waters.

GEOSTROPHIC CURRENTS

For most of the ocean volume away from the boundary layers, which have a characteristic thickness of 100 metres (about 330 feet), frictional forces are of minor importance, and the equation of motion for horizontal forces can be expressed as a simple balance of horizontal pressure gradient and Coriolis force. This is called geostrophic balance.

On a nonrotating Earth, water would be accelerated by a horizontal pressure gradient and would flow from high to low pressure. On the rotating Earth, however, the Coriolis force deflects the motion, and the acceleration ceases only when the speed, c, of the current is just fast enough to produce a Coriolis force that can exactly balance the horizontal pressure-gradient force. This geostrophic balance is given as $dp/dn = \rho c 2 \omega \sin \theta$, where dp/dn is the horizontal pressure gradient. From this balance, it follows that the current direction must be perpendicular to the pressure gradient because the Coriolis force always acts perpendicular to the motion. In the Northern Hemisphere this direction is such that the high pressure is to the right when looking in current direction, while in the Southern Hemisphere it is to the left. This type of current is called a geostrophic current. The simple equation given above provides the basis for an indirect method of computing ocean currents. The relief of the sea surface also defines the streamlines (paths) of the geostrophic current at the surface relative to the deep reference level. The hills represent high pressure, and the valleys stand for low pressure. Clockwise rotation in the Northern Hemisphere with higher pressure in the centre of rotation is called anticyclonic motion. Counterclockwise rotation with lower pressure in its centre is cyclonic motion. In the Southern Hemisphere the sense of rotation is the opposite, because the effect of the Coriolis force has changed its sign of deflection.

DENSITY CURRENTS IN THE OCEANS

Density currents are currents that are kept in motion by the force of gravity acting on a relatively small density difference caused by variations in salinity, temperature, or sediment concentration. Salinity and temperature variations produce stratification in oceans. Below the surface layer, which is disturbed by waves and is lighter than the deeper waters because it is warmer or less saline, the oceans are composed of layers of water that have distinctive chemical and physical characteristics, which move more or less independently of each other and which do not lose their individuality by mixing even after they have flowed for hundreds of kilometres from their point of origin.

An example of this type of density current, or stratified flow, is provided by the water of the Mediterranean Sea as it flows through the Strait of Gibraltar out into the Atlantic. Because the Mediterranean is enclosed in a basin that is relatively small compared with the ocean basins and because it is located in a relatively arid climate, evaporation exceeds the supply of fresh water from rivers. The result is that the Mediterranean contains water that is both warmer and more saline than normal deep-sea water, the temperature ranging from 12.7 to 14.5 °C (54.9 to 58.1 °F) and the salinity from 38.4 to 39.0 parts per thousand. Because of these characteristics, the Mediterranean water is considerably denser than the water in the upper parts of the North Atlantic, which has a salinity of about 36 parts per thousand and a temperature of about 13 °C (55.4 °F). The density contrast causes the lighter Atlantic water to flow into the Mediterranean in the upper part of the Strait of Gibraltar (down to a depth of about 200 metres [about 660 feet]) and the denser Mediterranean water to flow out into the Atlantic in the lower part of the strait (from about 200 metres to the top of the sill separating the Mediterranean from the Atlantic at a depth of 320 metres [1,050 feet]).

Because the strait is only about 20 km (12.4 miles) wide, both inflow and outflow achieve relatively high speeds. Near the surface the inflow may have speeds as high as 2 metres (6.6 feet) per second, and the outflow reaches speeds of more than 1 metre (3.3 feet) per second at a depth of about 275 metres (about 900 feet). One result of the high current speeds in the strait is that there is a considerable amount of mixing, which reduces the salinity of the outflowing Mediterranean water to about 37 parts per thousand. The outflowing water sinks to a depth of about 1,500 metres (about 4,920 feet) or more, where it encounters colder, denser Atlantic water. It then spreads out as a layer of more saline water between two Atlantic water masses.

EKMAN LAYER

The wind exerts stress on the ocean surface proportional to the square of the wind speed and in the direction of the wind, setting the surface water in motion. This motion extends to a depth of about 100 metres (330 feet) in what is called the Ekman layer, after the Swedish oceanographer V. Walfrid Ekman, who in 1902 deduced these results in a theoretical model constructed to help explain observations of wind drift in the Arctic. Within the oceanic Ekman layer the wind stress is balanced by the Coriolis force and frictional forces. The surface water is directed at an angle of 45° to the wind, to the right in the Northern Hemisphere and to the left in the Southern Hemisphere. With increasing depth in the boundary layer, the current speed is reduced, and the direction rotates farther away from the wind direction following a spiral form, becoming antiparallel to the surface flow at the base of the layer where the speed is $\frac{1}{23}$ of the surface speed. This so-called Ekman spiral may be the exception rather than the rule, as the specific conditions are not often met, though deflection of a wind-driven surface current at somewhat smaller than 45° is observed when the wind field blows with a steady force and direction for the better part of a day. The average water particle within the Ekman layer moves at an angle of 90° to the wind; this movement is to the right of the wind direction in the Northern Hemisphere and to its left in the Southern Hemisphere. This phenomenon is called Ekman transport, and its effects are widely observed in the oceans.

Since the wind varies from place to place, so does the Ekman transport, forming convergence and divergence zones of surface water. A region of convergence forces surface water downward in a process called downwelling, while a region of divergence draws water from below into the surface Ekman layer in a process known as upwelling. Upwelling and downwelling also occur where the wind blows parallel to a coastline. The principal upwelling regions of the world are along the eastern boundary of the subtropical ocean waters, as, for example, the coastal region of Peru and northwestern Africa. Upwelling in these regions cools the surface water and brings nutrient-rich subsurface water into the sunlit layer of the ocean, resulting in a biologically productive region. Upwelling and high productivity also are found along divergence zones at the equator and around Antarctica. The primary downwelling regions are in the subtropical ocean waters — e.g., the Sargasso Sea in the North Atlantic. Such areas are devoid of nutrients and are poor in marine life.

The vertical movements of ocean waters into or out of the base of the Ekman layer amount to less than 1 metre (3.3 feet) per day, but they are important since they extend the wind-driven effects into deeper waters. Within an upwelling region, the water column below the Ekman layer is drawn upward. This process, with conservation of angular momentum on the rotating Earth, induces the water column to drift toward the poles. Conversely, downwelling forces water into the water column below the

Ekman layer, inducing drift toward the equator. An additional consequence of upwelling and downwelling for stratified waters is to create a baroclinic field of mass. Surface water is less dense than deeper water. Ekman convergences have the effect of accumulating less dense surface water. This water floats above the surrounding water, forming a hill in sea level and driving an anticyclonic geostrophic current that extends well below the Ekman layer. Divergences do the opposite; they remove the less dense surface water, replacing it with denser, deeper water. This induces a depression in sea level with a cyclonic geostrophic current.

The ocean current pattern produced by the wind-induced Ekman transport is called the Sverdrup transport, after the Norwegian oceanographer H.U. Sverdrup, who formulated the basic theory in 1947. Several years later (1950), the American geophysicist and oceanographer Walter H. Munk and others expanded Sverdrup's work, explaining many of the major features of the wind-driven general circulation by using the mean climatological wind stress distribution at the sea surface as a driving force.

WIND-DRIVEN CIRCULATION

Wind stress induces a circulation pattern that is similar for each ocean. In each case, the wind-driven circulation is divided into large gyres that stretch across the entire ocean: subtropical gyres extend from the equatorial current system to the maximum westerlies in a wind field near 50° latitude, and subpolar gyres extend poleward of the maximum westerlies. The depth penetration of the wind-driven currents depends on the intensity of ocean stratification: for those regions of strong stratification, such as the tropics, the surface currents extend to a depth of less than 1,000 metres (about 3,300 feet). Within the low-stratification polar regions, the wind-driven circulation reaches all the way to the seafloor.

EQUATORIAL CURRENTS

At the equator the currents are for the most part directed toward the west, the North Equatorial Current in the Northern Hemisphere and the South Equatorial Current in the Southern Hemisphere. Near the thermal equator, where the warmest surface water is found, there occurs the eastward-flowing Equatorial Counter Current. This current is slightly north of the geographic equator, drawing the northern fringe of the South Equatorial Current to 5° N. The offset to the Northern Hemisphere matches a similar offset in the wind field. The east-to-west wind across the tropical ocean waters induces Ekman transport divergence at the equator, which cools the surface water there.

At the geographic equator a jetlike current is found just below the sea surface, flowing toward the east counter to the surface current. This is called the Equatorial Undercurrent. It attains speeds of more than 1 metre (3.3 feet) per second at a depth of nearly 100 metres (330 feet). It is driven by higher sea level in the western margins of the tropical ocean, producing a pressure gradient, which in the absence of a horizontal Coriolis force drives a west-to-east current along the equator. The wind field reverses the flow within the surface layer, inducing the Equatorial Undercurrent.

Equatorial circulation undergoes variations following the irregular periods of roughly three to eight years of the Southern Oscillation (i.e., fluctuations of atmospheric pressure over the tropical Indo-Pacific region). Weakening of the east-to-west wind during a phase of the Southern Oscillation allows warm water in the western margin to slip back to the east by increasing the flow of the Equatorial

Counter Current. Surface water temperatures and sea level decrease in the west and increase in the east. This event is called El Niño. The combined El Niño/Southern Oscillation effect has received much attention because it is associated with global-scale climatic variability. In the tropical Indian Ocean, the strong seasonal winds of the monsoons induce a similarly strong seasonal circulation pattern.

The Subtropical Gyres

These are anticyclonic circulation features. The Ekman transport within these gyres forces surface water to sink, giving rise to the subtropical convergence near 20°–30° latitude. The centre of the subtropical gyre is shifted to the west. This westward intensification of ocean currents was explained by the American meteorologist and oceanographer Henry M. Stommel (1948) as resulting from the fact that the horizontal Coriolis force increases with latitude. This causes the poleward-flowing western boundary current to be a jetlike current that attains speeds of 2 to 4 metres (6.6 to 13.1 feet) per second. This current transports the excess heat of the low latitudes to higher latitudes. The flow within the equatorward-flowing interior and eastern boundary of the subtropical gyres is quite different. It is more of a slow drift of cooler water that rarely exceeds 10 cm (3.9 inches) per second. Associated with these currents is coastal upwelling that results from offshore Ekman transport.

The strongest of the western boundary currents is the Gulf Stream in the North Atlantic Ocean. It carries about 30 million cubic metres (1.1 billion cubic feet) of ocean water per second through the Straits of Florida and roughly 80 million cubic metres (2.8 billion cubic feet) per second as it flows past Cape Hatteras off the coast of North Carolina, U.S. Responding to the large-scale wind field over the North Atlantic, the Gulf Stream separates from the continental margin at Cape Hatteras. After separation, it forms waves or meanders that eventually generate many eddies of warm and cold water. The warm eddies, composed of thermocline water normally found south of the Gulf Stream, are injected into the waters of the continental slope off the coast of the northeastern United States. They drift to the southeast at rates of approximately 5 to 8 cm (2 to 3.1 inches) per second, and after a year they rejoin the Gulf Stream north of Cape Hatteras. Cold eddies of slope water are injected into the region south of the Gulf Stream and drift to the southwest. After two years they reenter the Gulf Stream just north of the Antilles Islands. The path that they follow defines a clockwise-flowing recirculation gyre seaward of the Gulf Stream.

Among the other western boundary currents, the Kuroshio of the North Pacific is perhaps the most like the Gulf Stream, having a similar transport and array of eddies. The Brazil and East Australian currents are relatively weak. The Agulhas Current has a transport close to that of the Gulf Stream. It remains in contact with the margin of Africa around the southern rim of the continent. It then separates from the margin and curls back to the Indian Ocean in what is called the Agulhas Retroflection. Not all the water carried by the Agulhas returns to the east; about 10 to 20 percent is injected into the South Atlantic Ocean as large eddies that slowly migrate across it.

THE SUBPOLAR GYRES

The subpolar gyres are cyclonic circulation features. The Ekman transport within these features forces upwelling and surface water divergence. In the North Atlantic the subpolar gyre consists of the North Atlantic Current at its equatorward side and the Norwegian Current that carries relatively warm water northward along the coast of Norway. The heat released from the Norwegian Current into the atmosphere maintains a moderate climate in northern Europe. Along the east coast of Greenland is the southward-flowing cold East Greenland Current. It loops around the southern tip of Greenland and continues flowing into the Labrador Sea. The southward flow that continues off the coast of Canada is called the Labrador Current. This current separates for the most part from the coast near Newfoundland to complete the subpolar gyre of the North Atlantic. Some of the cold water of the Labrador Current, however, extends farther south.

In the North Pacific the subpolar gyre is composed of the northward-flowing Alaska Current, the Aleutian Current (also known as the Subarctic Current), and the southward-flowing cold Oyashio Current. The North Pacific Current forms the separation between the subpolar and subtropical gyres of the North Pacific.

In the Southern Hemisphere, the subpolar gyres are less defined. Large cyclonic flowing gyres lie poleward of the Antarctic Circumpolar Current and can be considered counterparts to the Northern Hemispheric subpolar gyres. The best-formed is the Weddell Gyre of the South Atlantic sector of the Southern Ocean. The Antarctic coastal current flows toward the west. The northward-flowing current off the east coast of the Antarctic Peninsula carries cold Antarctic coastal water into the circumpolar belt. Another cyclonic gyre occurs north of the Ross Sea.

ANTARCTIC CIRCUMPOLAR CURRENT

The Southern Ocean links the major oceans by a deep circumpolar belt in the 50°–60° S range. In this belt flows the Antarctic Circumpolar Current from west to east, encircling the globe at high latitudes. It transports 125 million cubic metres (4.4 billion cubic feet) of seawater per second over a path of about 24,000 km (14,900 miles) and is the most important factor in diminishing the differences between oceans. The Antarctic Circumpolar Current is not a well-defined single-axis current but rather consists of a series of individual filaments separated by frontal zones. It reaches the seafloor and is guided along its course by the irregular bottom topography. Large meanders and eddies develop in the current as it flows. These features induce poleward transfer of heat, which may be significant in balancing the oceanic heat loss to the atmosphere above the Antarctic region farther south.

THERMOHALINE CIRCULATION

The general circulation of the oceans consists primarily of the wind-driven currents. These, however, are superimposed on the much more sluggish circulation driven by horizontal differences in temperature and salinity—namely, the thermohaline circulation. The thermohaline circulation reaches down to the seafloor and is often referred to as the deep, or abyssal, ocean circulation. Measuring seawater temperature and salinity distribution is the chief method of studying the deep-flow patterns. Other properties also are examined; for example, the concentrations of oxygen, carbon-14, and such synthetically produced compounds as chlorofluorocarbons are measured to obtain resident times and spreading rates of deep water.

In some areas of the ocean, generally during the winter season, cooling or net evaporation causes surface water to become dense enough to sink. Convection penetrates to a level where the density of the sinking water matches that of the surrounding water. It then spreads slowly into the rest of the ocean. Other water must replace the surface

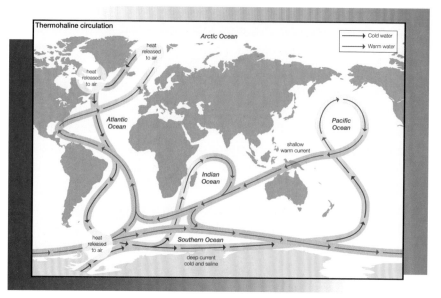

Thermohaline circulation transports and mixes the water of the oceans. In the process it transports heat, which influences regional climate patterns. The density of seawater is determined by the temperature and salinity of a volume of seawater at a particular location. The difference in density between one location and another drives the thermohaline circulation. Encyclopaedia Britannica, Inc.

water that sinks. This sets up the thermohaline circulation. The basic thermohaline circulation is one of sinking of cold water in the polar regions, chiefly in the northern North Atlantic and near Antarctica. These dense water masses spread into the full extent of the ocean and gradually upwell to feed a slow return flow to the sinking regions. A theory for the thermohaline circulation pattern was proposed by Stommel and Arnold Arons in 1960.

In the Northern Hemisphere, the primary region of deep water formation is the North Atlantic; minor amounts of deep water are formed in the Red Sea and Persian Gulf. A variety of water types contribute to the so-called North Atlantic Deep Water. Each one of them differs, though they share a common attribute of being relatively warm (greater than 2 °C [35.6 °F]) and salty (greater than 34.9 parts per thousand) compared with the other major producer of deep and bottom water, the Southern Ocean (0 °C [32 °F] and 34.7 parts per thousand). North Atlantic Deep Water is primarily formed in the Greenland and Norwegian seas, where cooling of the salty water introduced by the Norwegian Current induces sinking. This water spills over the rim of the ridge that stretches from Greenland to Scotland, extending to the seafloor to the south as a convective plume. It then flows southward, pressed against the western edge of the North Atlantic. Additional deep water is formed in the Labrador Sea. This water, somewhat less dense than the overflow water from the Greenland and Norwegian seas, has been observed sinking to a depth of 3,000 metres (about 9,800 feet) within convective features referred to as chimneys. Vertical velocities as high as 10 cm (3.9 inches) per second have been observed within these convective features.

A third variety of North Atlantic Deep Water is derived from net evaporation within the Mediterranean Sea. This draws surface water into the Mediterranean through the Strait of Gibraltar. The mass of salty water formed within the Mediterranean exits as a deeper stream. It descends to depths of 1,000 to 2,000 metres (3,300 to 6,600 feet) in the North Atlantic Ocean, forming the uppermost layer of North Atlantic Deep Water. The outflow in the Strait of Gibraltar reaches as high as 2 metres (about 7 feet) per second, but its total transport amounts to only 5 percent of the total North Atlantic Deep Water formed. The outflow of the Mediterranean plays a significant role in boosting the salinity of North Atlantic Deep Water.

The blend of North Atlantic Deep Water, with a total formation rate of 15 to 20×10^6 cubic metres (5.3 to 7.1×10^8 cubic feet) per second, quickly ventilates the Atlantic Ocean, resulting in a residence time of less than 200 years. The deep water spreads away from its source along the western side of the Atlantic Ocean and, on reaching the Antarctic Circumpolar Current, spreads into the Indian and Pacific oceans. The sinking of North Atlantic Deep Water is compensated for by the slow upwelling of deep water, mainly in the Southern Ocean, to replenish the upper stratum of water that has descended as North Atlantic Deep Water. North Atlantic Deep Water exported to the other oceans must be balanced by the inflow of upper-layer water into the Atlantic. Some water returns as cold, low-salinity Pacific water through the Drake Passage in the form of what is known as Antarctic Intermediate Water, and some returns as warm salty thermocline water from the Indian Ocean around the southern rim of Africa.

Remnants of North Atlantic Deep Water mix with Southern Ocean water to spread along the seafloor into the North Pacific Ocean. Here, it upwells to a level of 2,000–3,000 metres (6,600–9,800 feet) and returns to the south lower in salinity and oxygen but higher in nutrient concentrations as North Pacific Deep Water. This North Pacific Deep Water is eventually swept eastward with the Antarctic Circumpolar Current. Modification of deep water in the North Pacific is the direct consequence of vertical mixing, which carries into the deep ocean the low salinity properties of North Pacific Intermediate Water. The latter is formed in the northwestern Pacific Ocean. Because of the immenseness of the North Pacific and the extremely long residence time (more than 500 years) of the water, enormous quantities of North Pacific Deep Water can be produced by vertical mixing.

Considerable volumes of cold water generally of low salinity are formed in the Southern Ocean. Such water masses spread into the interior of the global ocean and to a large extent are responsible for the anomalous cold, low-salinity state of the modern oceans. The circumstances leading to this role for the Southern Ocean are related to the existence of a deep-ocean circumpolar belt around Antarctica that was established some 25 million years ago by the shifting lithospheric plates which make up Earth's surface. This belt establishes the Antarctic Circumpolar Current, which isolates Antarctica from the warm surface waters of the subtropics. The Antarctic Circumpolar Current does not completely sever contact with the lower latitudes. The Southern Ocean does have access to the waters of the north, but through deep- and bottom-water pathways. The basic dynamics of the Antarctic Circumpolar Current lifts dense deep water occurring north of the current to the ocean surface south of it. Once exposed to the cold Antarctic air masses, the upwelling deep water is converted to the cold Antarctic Bottom Water and Antarctic Intermediate Water. The southward and upwelling deep water, which carries heat injected into the deep ocean by processes farther north, is balanced by the northward spread of cooler, fresher, oxygenated water masses of the Southern Ocean. It is estimated that the overturning rate of water south of the Antarctic Circumpolar Current amounts to 35 to 45 million cubic metres (1.2 to 1.6 billion cubic feet) per second, most of which becomes Antarctic Bottom Water.

The primary site of Antarctic Bottom Water formation is within the continental margins of the Weddell Sea, though some is produced in other coastal regions, such as the Ross Sea. Also, there is evidence of deep convective overturning farther offshore. Antarctic Bottom Water, formed at a rate of 30 million cubic metres (1.1 billion cubic feet) per second, slips below the Antarctic Circumpolar Current and spreads to regions well north of the equator. Slowly upwelling and modified by mixing with less dense water, it returns to the Southern Ocean as deep water.

The remaining upwelling of deep water spreads near the surface to the north, where it forms Antarctic Intermediate Water within the Antarctic Circumpolar Current zone and spreads along the base of the thermoclines farther north. This water mass forms a sheet of low-salinity water that demarcates the lower boundary of the subtropical thermocline. It upwells into the thermocline, partly compensating for the sinking of North Atlantic Deep Water.

WAVES OF THE SEA

There are many types of ocean waves. Waves differ from each other in size and in terms of the forces that drive them. Waves represent an oscillatory motion of seawater at regular time intervals or periods. Some may be running, or progressive, waves in which the crests propagate, while others are stationary, or standing, waves. Two of the more common types of waves, gravity waves and tides, are considered here. For gravity waves, the stabilizing force—i.e.,

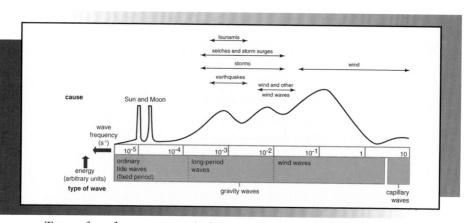

Types of surface waves and their relative energy levels. Copyright Encyclopædia Britannica, Inc.; rendering for this edition by Rosen Educational Services

the force that attempts to restore the crests and troughs of the waves to the average sea level—is Earth's gravity. The distance between the crests, or wavelength, of gravity waves range from a few centimetres to many kilometres. Tiny waves at the ocean surface with a wavelength of less than 1.7 cm (0.7 inch) are called capillary waves. Their restoring force is the surface tension of seawater. Capillary waves are direct products of the wind stress exerted on the sea surface and tend to feed wind energy into gravity waves, which characteristically have longer wavelengths.

Tides are essentially gravity waves that have long periods of oscillation. They may be called forced waves, because they have fixed, prescribed periods that are strictly determined by astronomical forces induced by the relative movements of the Moon, Earth, and Sun. Sometimes the term "tidal wave" is used incorrectly to include such phenomena as surges, which are called storm tides, or destructive waves known as tsunamis that are induced by undersea earthquakes. In the following discussion, the use of the words "tide" and "tidal" is restricted to tides of astronomical origin and the forces and phenomena associated with them.

SURFACE GRAVITY WAVES

Of the nontidal kinds of running surface waves, three types may be distinguished: wind waves and swell, wind surges, and sea waves of seismic origin (tsunamis).

WIND WAVES AND SWELL

Wind waves are the wind-generated gravity waves. After the wind has abated or shifted or the waves have migrated away from the wind field, such waves continue to propagate as swell.

The dependence of the sizes of the waves on the wind field is a complicated one. A general impression of this dependence is given by the descriptions of the various states of the sea corresponding to the scale of wind strengths known as the Beaufort scale, named after the British admiral Sir Francis Beaufort, who drafted it in 1808 using as his yardstick the surface of sail that a fully rigged warship of those days could carry in the various wind forces. When considering the descriptions of the sea surface, it must be remembered that the size of the waves depends not only on the strength of the wind but also on its duration and its fetch—i.e., the length of its path over the sea.

The theory of waves starts with the concept of simple waves, those forming a strictly periodic pattern with one wavelength and one wave period and propagating in one direction. Real waves, however, always have a more irregular appearance. They may be described as composite waves, in which a whole spectrum of wavelengths, or periods, is present and which have more or less diverging directions of propagation. In reporting observed wave heights and periods (or lengths) or in forecasting them, one height or one period is mentioned as the height or period, however, and some agreement is needed in order to guarantee uniformity of meaning. The height of simple waves means the elevation difference between the top of a crest and the bottom of a trough. The significant height, a characteristic height of irregular waves, is by convention the average of the highest one-third of the observed wave heights. Period, or wavelength, can be determined from the average of a number of observed time intervals between the passing of successive well-developed wave crests over a certain point, or of observed distances between them.

Wave period and wavelength are coupled by a simple relationship: wavelength equals wave period times wave speed, or $L = TC$, when L is wavelength, T is wave period, and C is wave speed.

The wave speed of surface gravity waves depends on the depth of water and on the wavelength, or period; the speed increases with increasing depth and increasing wavelength, or period. If the water is sufficiently deep, the wave speed is independent of water depth. This relationship of wave speed to wavelength and water depth (d) is given by the equations below. With g being the gravity acceleration (9.8 metres [32 feet] per second squared), $C^2 = gd$, when the wavelength is 20 times greater than the water depth (waves of this kind are called long gravity waves or shallow-water waves); and $C^2 = gL/2\pi$, when the wavelength is less than two times the water depth (such waves are called short waves or deep water waves). For waves with lengths between 2 and 20 times the water depth, the wave speed is governed by a more complicated equation combining these effects:

$$C^2 = \frac{gL}{2\pi} \tanh \left(2\pi \frac{d}{L}\right),$$

where tanh is the hyperbolic tangent.

A few examples are listed below for short waves, giving the period in seconds, the wavelength in metres, and wave speed in metres per second:

period T (sec)	1	2	4	8	16
wavelength L (m)	1.56	6.2	25.0	100	400
wave speed in deep water (m/sec)	1.56	3.1	6.2	12.5	25.0

Waves often appear in groups as the result of interference of wave trains of slightly differing wavelengths. A wave group as a whole has a group speed that generally is less than the speed of propagation of the individual waves; the two speeds are equal only for groups composed of long waves. For deepwater waves, the group velocity (V) is half the wave speed (C). In the physical sense, group velocity is the velocity of propagation of wave energy. From the dynamics of the waves, it follows that the wave energy per unit area of the sea surface is proportional to the square of the wave height, except for the very last stage of waves running into shallow water, shortly before they become breakers.

The height of wind waves increases with increasing wind speed and with increasing duration and fetch of the wind (i.e., the distance over which the wind blows). Together with height, the dominant wavelength also increases. Finally, however, the waves reach a state of saturation because they attain the maximum significant height to which the wind can raise them, even if duration and fetch are unlimited. For instance, winds of 5 metres (16 feet) per second, 15 metres (about 50 feet) per second, and 25 metres (about 80 feet) per second may raise waves with significant heights up to 0.5 metre (1.6 feet), 4.5 metres (15 feet), and 12.5 metres (about 40 feet), respectively, with corresponding wavelengths of 16 metres (about 52 feet), 140 metres (about 460 feet), and 400 metres (1,300 feet), respectively.

After becoming swell, the waves may travel thousands of kilometres over the ocean, particularly if the swell is from the large storms of moderate and high latitudes, whence it easily may travel into the subtropical and equatorial zones, and the swell of the trade winds, which runs into the equatorial calms. In traveling, the swell waves gradually become lower; energy is lost by internal friction and air resistance and by energy dissipation because of some divergence of the directions of propagation (fanning out). With respect to the energy loss, there is a selective damping of the composite waves, the shorter waves of the wave mixture suffering a stronger damping over a given distance than the longer ones. As a consequence, the dominant wavelength of the spectrum shifts toward the greater wavelengths. Therefore, an old swell must always be a long swell.

When waves run into shallow water, their speed of propagation and wavelength decrease, but the period remains the same. Eventually, the group velocity, the velocity of energy propagation, also decreases, and this decrease causes the height to increase. The latter effect may, however, be affected by refraction of the waves, a swerving of the wave crests toward the depth lines and a corresponding deviation of the direction of propagation. Refraction may cause a convergence or divergence of the energy stream and result in a raising or lowering of the waves, especially over nearshore elevations or depressions of the sea bottom.

In the final stage, the shape of the waves changes, and the crests become narrower and steeper until, finally, the waves become breakers (surf). Generally, this occurs where the depth is 1.3 times the wave height.

WIND SURGES

Running wind surges are long waves caused by a piling up of the water over a large area through the action of a traveling wind or pressure field. Examples include the surge in front of a traveling storm cyclone, particularly the devastating hurricane surge caused by a tropical cyclone, and the surge occasionally caused by a wind convergence line, such as a traveling front with a sharp wind shift.

WAVES OF SEISMIC ORIGIN

A tsunami (Japanese: *tsu*, "harbour," and *nami*, "sea") is a very long wave of seismic origin that is caused by a submarine or coastal earthquake, landslide, or volcanic eruption. Such a wave may have a length of hundreds of kilometres

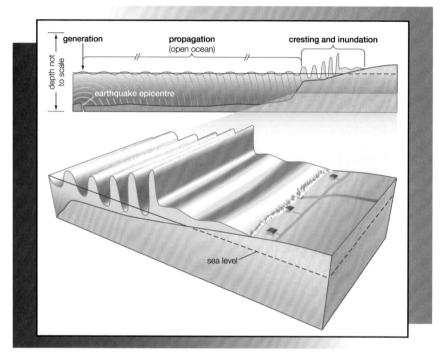

After being generated by an undersea earthquake or landslide, a tsunami may propagate unnoticed over vast reaches of open ocean before cresting in shallow water and inundating a coastline. Encyclopædia Britannica, Inc.

and a period on the order of a quarter of an hour. It travels across the ocean at a tremendous speed. (Tsunamis are long waves traveling at the wave speed given by $C^2 = gd$.) To a depth of 4,000 metres (about 13,100 feet), for instance, the corresponding wave speed is about 200 metres (about 660 feet) per second, or 800 km (about 500 miles) per hour. In the open ocean the height of tsunamis may be less than 1 metre (3.3 feet), and they pass unnoticed. As they approach a continental shelf, however, their speed is reduced and their height increases dramatically. Tsunamis have caused enormous destruction of life and property, piling up in coastal waters at places thousands of kilometres away from their point of origin, particularly in the Pacific Ocean.

TSUNAMIS

Tsunamis, which are also called seismic sea waves, are catastrophic ocean waves usually caused by submarine earthquakes, underwater or coastal landslides, or volcanic eruptions. The term *tsunami* is Japanese for "harbour wave." The term *tidal wave* is frequently used for such a wave, but it is a misnomer, for the wave has no connection with the tides.

After an earthquake or other generating impulse occurs, a train of simple, progressive oscillatory waves is propagated great distances over the ocean surface in ever-widening circles, much like the waves produced by a pebble falling into a shallow pool. In deep water a tsunami can travel as fast as 800 km (500 miles) per hour. The wavelengths are enormous, about 100 to 200 km (60 to 120 miles), but the wave amplitudes (heights) are very small, only about 30 to 60 cm (1 to 2 feet). The waves' periods (the lengths of time for successive crests or troughs to pass a single point) are very long, varying from five minutes to more than an hour. These long periods, coupled with the extremely low steepness of the waves, enables them to be completely obscured in deep water by normal wind waves and swell.

The aftermath of the December 2004 tsunami in Aceh, Indon. Philip A. McDaniel/U.S. Navy

As the waves approach the coast of a continent, however, friction with the rising sea bottom reduces the velocity of the waves. As the velocity lessens, the wavelengths become shortened and the wave amplitudes increase. Coastal waters may rise as high as 30 metres (100 feet) above normal sea level in 10 to 15 minutes. By a poorly understood process, the continental shelf waters begin to oscillate after the rise in sea level. Between three and five major oscillations generate most of the damage, frequently appearing as powerful "run-ups" of rushing water that uproot trees, pull buildings off their foundations, carry boats far inshore, and wash away entire beaches, peninsulas, and other low-lying coastal formations. Frequently the succeeding outflow of water is just as destructive as the run-up or even more so. In any case, oscillations may continue for several days until the ocean surface reaches equilibrium.

The Pacific Tsunami Warning Center, located near Honolulu, Hawaii, was established in 1949, three years after a tsunami generated by a submarine earthquake near the Aleutian Islands struck the island of Hawaii around Hilo, killing 159 people. Following the disaster of December 2004, UNESCO set a goal of establishing similar systems for the Indian Ocean and eventually the entire globe.

SEICHE WAVES AND INTERNAL WAVES

A freestanding wave may arise in an enclosed or nearly enclosed basin as a free swinging or sloshing of the whole water mass. Such a standing wave is also called a seiche, after the name given to the oscillating movements of the water of Lake Geneva, Switzerland, where this phenomenon first was studied seriously. In addition, gravity waves may also occur on internal "surfaces" within oceans. These surfaces represent strata of rapidly changing water density with increasing depth, and the associated waves are called internal waves.

STANDING, OR SEICHE, WAVES

In seiche waves, the period of oscillation is independent of the force that first brought the water mass out of equilibrium (and that is supposed to have ceased thereafter), but depends only on the dimensions of the enclosing basin and on the direction in which the water mass is swinging. Assuming a simple rectangular basin of constant depth and the most simple lengthwise oscillation, the period of oscillation (T) is equal to two times the length of the basin divided by the wave speed computed from the shallow-water formula above. This relationship may be written: $T = L/C$, in which L equals two times the length of the basin and C is the wave speed found from the formula, using the known depth of the basin. Besides this fundamental tone (or response to stimuli), the water mass also may swing according to an overtone, showing one or more nodal lines across the basin.

The water in an open bay or marginal sea also may perform such a free oscillation as a standing wave, the difference being that in an open bay the greatest horizontal displacements are not in the middle of the bay but at the mouth. For the fundamental period of oscillation, the formula given above is used with a wavelength equal to four times the length (from the mouth to the closed end) of the bay. In practice, of course, it is more difficult than that, because the form of a bay or marginal sea is irregular and the depth differs from place to place. The North Sea has a period of lengthwise swinging of about 36 hours. The cause of such free oscillations may be a temporary wind or pressure field, which brought the sea surface out of its horizontal position and which afterward ceased to act more or less abruptly, leaving the water mass out of equilibrium.

INTERNAL WAVES

Internal waves manifest themselves by a regular rising and sinking of the water layers around which they centre, whereas the height of the sea surface is hardly affected at all. Because the restoring force, excited by the internal deformation of the water layers of equal density, is much smaller than in the case of surface waves, internal waves are much slower than the latter. Given the same wavelength, the period is much longer (the movements of the water particles being much more sluggish), and the speed of propagation is much smaller; the formulas for the speed of surface waves include the acceleration of gravity, g, but those for internal waves include the gravity factor times the difference between the densities of the upper and the lower water layer divided by their sum.

The cause of internal waves may lie in the action of tidal forces (the period then equaling the tidal period) or in the action of a wind or pressure fluctuation. Sometimes, a ship may cause internal waves (dead water) if there is a shallow, brackish upper layer.

OCEAN TIDES

The tides may be regarded as forced waves, partially running waves and partially standing waves. They are manifested by vertical movements of the sea surface (the height maximum and minimum are called high water [HW] and low water [LW]) and in alternating horizontal movements of the water, the tidal currents. The words ebb and flow are used to designate the falling tide and the rising tide, respectively.

TIDE-GENERATING FORCES

The forces that cause the tides are called the tide-generating forces. A tide-generating force is the resultant force of the attracting force of the Moon or the Sun and the force of inertia (centrifugal force) that results from the orbital movement of Earth around the common centre of gravity of the Earth-Moon or Earth-Sun system.

Considering the Earth-Moon system, at any time the tide-generating force is directed vertically upward at the two places on Earth where the Moon is in the vertical (on the same and on the opposite side of Earth); it is directed vertically downward at all places (forming a circle) where the Moon is in the horizon at that moment. At all other places, the tide-generating force also has a horizontal component. Because this pattern of forces is coupled to the position of the Moon with respect to Earth and because for any place on Earth's surface the relative position of the Moon with respect to that place has, on the average, a periodicity of 24 hours 50 minutes, the tide-generating force felt at any place has that same periodicity. When the Moon is in the plane of the equator, the force runs through two identical cycles within this time interval because of the symmetry of the global pattern of forces described above. Consequently, the tidal period is 12 hours 25 minutes in this case; it is the period of the semidiurnal lunar tide. The fact that the Moon is alternately to the north and to the south of the equator causes an inequality of the two successive cycles within the time interval of 24 hours 50 minutes. The effect of this inequality is formally described as the superposition of a partial tide called the diurnal lunar tide, with the period of 24 hours 50 minutes, on the semidiurnal lunar tide.

In the same manner, the Sun causes a semidiurnal solar tide, with a 12-hour period, and a diurnal solar tide, with a 24-hour period. In a complete description of the local variations of the tidal forces, still other partial tides play a role because of further inequalities in the orbital motions of the Moon and Earth.

The interference of the solar-tidal forces with the lunar-tidal forces (the lunar forces are about 2.2 times as strong) causes the regular variation of the tidal range between spring tide, when it has its maximum, and neap tide, when it has its minimum.

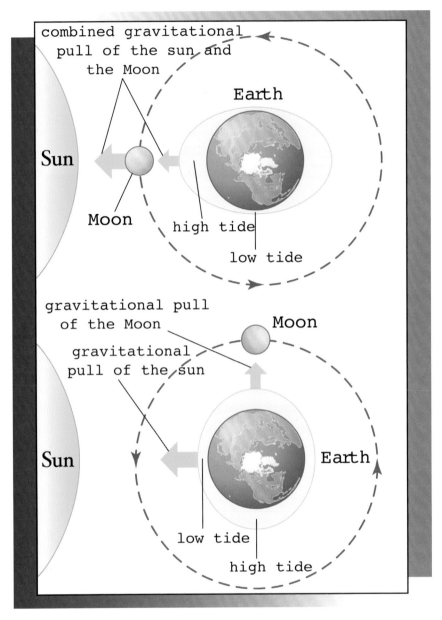

Tides are caused by the gravitational pull of the Sun and the Moon on Earth's water. When the Sun, Moon, and Earth form a straight line (top), higher and lower tides than usual are generated. In contrast, when the lines between the Sun and Earth and the Moon and Earth are perpendicular to one another (bottom), high tides and low tides are moderated. Encyclopædia Britannica, Inc.

Although the tide-generating forces are very small in comparison with Earth's force of gravity (the lunar tidal force at its maximum being only 1.14×10^{-7} times the force of gravity), their effects upon the sea are considerable because of their horizontal component. Since Earth is not surrounded by an uninterrupted envelope of water but rather shows a very irregular alternation of sea and land, the mechanism of the response of the oceans and seas to the tidal forces is extremely complex. A further complication is caused by the deflecting force of Earth's rotation.

In enclosures formed by gulfs and bays, the local tide is generated by interaction with the tides of the adjacent open ocean. Such a tide often takes the form of a running tidal wave that rotates within the confines of the enclosure. In some semi-enclosed seas, such as the Mediterranean, Black, and Baltic seas, a standing wave, or tidal seiche, may be generated by the local tide-raising forces.

In these seas, the tidal range of sea level is only on the order of centimetres. In the open ocean, it generally is on the order of tens of centimetres. In bays and adjacent seas, however, the tidal range may be much greater, because the shape of a bay or adjacent sea may favour the enhancement of the tide inside; in particular, there may be a resonance of the basin concerned with the tide. The largest known tides occur in the Bay of Fundy, where spring tidal ranges up to 15 metres (about 50 feet) have been measured.

TIDAL BORES

Tidal bores form on rivers and estuaries near a coast where there is a large tidal range and the incoming tide is confined to a narrow channel. They consist of a surge of water moving swiftly upstream headed by a wave or series of waves. Such bores are quite common. There is a large one, known as the *mascaret* on the Seine, which forms on spring tides and reaches as far upriver as Rouen. There is a well-known bore on the Severn, in England, and another forms on the Petitcodiac River, which empties into the Bay of Fundy in New Brunswick. The classic example is the bore on the Qiantang (Ch'ien-t'ang) described by Commander W. Usborne Moore of the British navy in 1888 and 1892. He reported heights of 2.5 to 3.5 metres (8.2 to 11.5 feet).

When a tidal bore forms in a river, the direction of flow of the water changes abruptly as the bore passes. Before it arrives, the water may be still or, more usually, a small freshwater current flows outward toward the sea. The tide comes in as a "wall of water" that passes up the river. Behind the bore, the current flows upriver. At the division between the moving water behind the bore and the still water in front, there is a wave, the water surface behind being higher than it is in front. This wave must travel more quickly than the water particles behind it, because, as the advancing water travels upriver, it collects the still water in front and sets it in motion. Upriver, the advancing tide will consist not of salt water from the sea but rather of fresh water that has passed farther down and been collected and returned in front of the incoming tide. It is therefore necessary to distinguish between the velocity of the advancing wave and that of the water particles just behind it.

CHAPTER 4
THE CLIMATIC AND ECONOMIC IMPACTS OF THE OCEANS

Since the oceans are integral parts of Earth's climate, they can influence events deep within the interiors of continents. Major currents, such as the Gulf Stream and Kuroshio, deliver warm water from the tropics to coastal subarctic regions, and these subarctic regions are characterized by milder climates than other areas located at similar latitudes. The oceans are spawning grounds for tropical cyclones, which often bring damaging high winds and flooding to coastal areas. The oceans are also tremendous reservoirs of heat, and the movement of large volumes of warm water can temporarily disrupt normal precipitation and heating patterns. The movement of warm water eastward across the tropical Pacific Ocean as part of the El Niño/Southern Oscillation affects the weather in regions both adjacent to and far from the tropical Pacific.

The oceans are also sites of significant economic activity. Ocean fishes and other organisms are routinely harvested as food by humans. The process of desalinization allows the oceans to provide water resources to thirsty human settlements. Energy resources, such as petroleum and natural gas, and raw materials are also extracted from the oceans, and these bodies of water also serve as media for transportation and communication and sites of waste disposal.

SEASONAL AND INTERANNUAL OCEAN-ATMOSPHERE INTERACTIONS

The notion of a connection between the temperature of the surface layers of the oceans and the circulation of the lowest layer of the atmosphere, the troposphere, is a familiar one. The surface mixed layer of the ocean is a huge reservoir of heat when compared to the overlying atmosphere. The heat capacity of an atmospheric column of unit area cross-section extending from the ocean surface to the outermost layers of the atmosphere is equivalent to the heat capacity of a column of seawater of 2.6-metre (8.5-feet) depth. The surface layer of the oceans is continuously being stirred by the overlying winds and waves, and thus a surface mixed layer is formed that has vertically uniform properties in temperature and salinity. This mixed layer, which is in direct contact with the atmosphere, has a minimum depth of 20 metres (about 66 feet) in summer and a maximum depth exceeding 100 metres (about 330 feet) in late winter in the mid-latitudes. In lower latitudes the seasonal variation in the mixed layer is less marked than at higher latitudes, except in regions such as the Arabian Sea, where the onset of the southwestern Indian monsoon may produce large changes in the depth of the mixed layer. Temperature anomalies (i.e., deviations from the normal seasonal temperature) in the surface mixed layer have a long residence time compared with those of the overlying turbulent atmosphere. Hence they may persist for a number of consecutive seasons and even for years.

Observational studies to investigate the relationship between anomalies in ocean surface temperature and the tropospheric circulation have been undertaken primarily in the Pacific and Atlantic. They have identified large-scale ocean surface temperature anomalies that have similar spatial scales to monthly and seasonal anomalies in atmospheric circulation. The longevity of the ocean surface temperature anomalies, as compared with the shorter dynamical and thermodynamical "memory" of the atmosphere, has suggested that they may be an important predictor for seasonal and interannual climate anomalies.

THE LINK BETWEEN OCEAN SURFACE TEMPERATURE AND CLIMATE ANOMALIES

First, it is useful to consider some examples of the association between anomalies in ocean surface temperature and irregular changes in climate. The Sahel, a region that borders the southern fringe of the Sahara in Africa, experienced a number of devastating droughts during the 1970s and '80s, which can be compared with a much wetter period during the 1950s. Data was obtained that showed the difference in ocean surface temperature during the period from July to September between the "driest" and "wettest" rainfall seasons in the Sahel after 1950. Of particular note were the higher-than-normal surface temperatures in the tropical South Atlantic, Indian, and Southeast Pacific oceans and the lower-than-normal temperatures in the North Atlantic and Pacific oceans. This example illustrates that climate anomalies in one region of the world may be linked to ocean surface temperature changes on a global scale. Global atmospheric modeling studies undertaken during the mid-1980s have indicated that the positions of the main rainfall zones in the tropics are sensitive to anomalies in ocean surface temperature.

Shorter-lived climate anomalies, on time scales of months to one or two years, also have been related to ocean surface temperature anomalies. The equatorial oceans have the largest influence on these climate anomalies because of the evaporation of water. A relatively small change in ocean surface temperature, say, of 1 °C (1.8 °F), may result in a large change in the evaporation of water into the atmosphere. The increased water vapour in the lower atmosphere is condensed in regions of upward motion known as convergence zones. This process liberates latent heat of condensation, which in turn provides a major fraction of the energy to drive tropical circulation and is one of the mechanisms responsible for the El Niño/ Southern Oscillation (ENSO) phenomenon.

Given the sensitivity of the tropical atmosphere to variations in tropical sea surface temperature, there also has been considerable interest in their influence on extratropical circulation. The sensitivity of the tropospheric circulation to surface temperature in both the tropical Pacific and Atlantic oceans has been shown in theoretical and observational studies alike. Figures were prepared to demonstrate the correlation between the equatorial ocean surface temperature in the east Pacific (the location of El Niño) and the atmospheric circulation in the middle troposphere during winter. The atmospheric pattern was a characteristic circulation type known as the Pacific-North American (PNA) mode. Such patterns are intrinsic modes of the atmosphere, which may be forced by thermal anomalies in the tropical atmosphere and which in their turn are forced by tropical ocean surface temperature anomalies.

As noted earlier, enhanced tropical sea surface temperatures increase evaporation into the atmosphere. In the 1982–83 El Niño event a pattern of circulation anomalies occurred throughout the Northern Hemisphere during winter. These modes of the atmosphere, however, account for much less than 50 percent of the variability of the circulation in mid-latitudes, though in certain regions (northern Japan, southern Canada, and the southern United States), they may have sufficient amplitude for them to be used for predicting seasonal surface temperature perhaps up to two seasons in advance.

The response of the atmosphere to mid-latitude ocean surface anomalies has been difficult to detect unambiguously because of the complexity of the turbulent westerly flow between 20° and 60° latitude in both hemispheres. This flow has many properties of nonlinear chaotic systems and thus exhibits behaviour that is difficult to predict beyond a couple of weeks. The atmosphere alone can exhibit large fluctuations on seasonal and longer time scales without any change in external forcing conditions, such as ocean surface temperature. Notwithstanding this inherent problem, some effects of ocean surface temperature anomalies on the atmosphere have been observed and modeled.

The influence of the oceans on the atmosphere in the mid-latitudes is greatest during autumn and early winter when the ocean mixed layer releases to the atmosphere the large quantities of heat that it has stored up over the previous summer. Anomalies in ocean surface temperature are indicative of either a surplus or a deficiency of heat available to the atmosphere. The response of the atmosphere to ocean surface temperature, however, is not random geographically. The circulation over the North Atlantic and northern Europe during early winter has been found to be sensitive to large ocean surface temperature anomalies south of Newfoundland. When a warm positive anomaly exists in this region, an anomalous surface anticyclone occurs in the central Atlantic at a similar latitude to the temperature anomaly, and an anomalous cyclonic circulation is located over the North Sea, Scandinavia, and central Europe. With colder than normal water south of Newfoundland, the circulation patterns are reversed, producing cyclonic circulation over the central Atlantic and anticyclonic circulation over Europe. The sensitivity of the atmosphere to ocean surface temperature anomalies in this particular region is thought to be related to the position of the overlying storm tracks and jet stream. The region is the most active in the Northern

Hemisphere for the growth of storms associated with very large heat fluxes from the surface layer of the ocean.

Another example of a similar type of air-sea interaction event has been documented over the North Pacific Ocean. A statistical seasonal relationship exists between the summer ocean temperature anomaly in the Gulf of Alaska and the atmospheric circulation over the Pacific and North America during the following autumn and winter. The presence of warmer-than-normal ocean surface temperature in the Gulf of Alaska results in increased cyclone development during the subsequent autumn and winter. The relationship has been established by means of monthly sea surface temperature and atmospheric pressure data collected over 30 years in the North Pacific Ocean.

The air-sea interaction events in both the North Pacific and North Atlantic oceans raise questions as to how the anomalies in ocean surface temperature in these areas are initiated, how they are maintained, and whether they yield useful information for atmospheric prediction beyond the normal time scales of weather forecasting (i.e., one to two weeks). Statistical analysis of previous case studies have shown that ocean surface temperature anomalies initially develop in response to anomalous atmospheric forcing. Once developed, however, the temperature anomaly of the ocean surface tends to reinforce and thereby maintain the anomalous atmospheric circulation. The mechanisms thought to be responsible for this behaviour in the ocean are the surface wind drift, wind mixing, and the interchange of heat between the ocean and atmosphere. The question of prediction is therefore difficult to answer, as these events depend on a synchronous and interconnected behaviour between the atmosphere and the surface layer of the ocean, which allows for positive feedback between the two systems.

FORMATION OF TROPICAL CYCLONES

Tropical cyclones represent still another example of sea-air interactions. These storm systems are known as hurricanes in the North Atlantic and eastern North Pacific and as typhoons in the western North Pacific. The winds of such systems revolve around a centre of low pressure in an anticlockwise direction in the Northern Hemisphere and in a clockwise direction in the Southern Hemisphere. The winds attain velocities in excess of 115 km per hour, or 65 knots, in most cases. Tropical cyclones may last from a few hours to as long as two weeks, the average lifetime being six days.

A satellite image shows the approach of Hurricane Andrew toward the Florida coast over the course of three days in August of 1992. NASA Goddard Space Flight Center

The oceans provide the source of energy for tropical cyclones both by direct heat transfer from their surface (known as sensible heat) and by the evaporation of water. This water is subsequently condensed within a storm system, thereby releasing latent heat energy. When a tropical cyclone moves over land, this energy is severely depleted and the circulation of the winds is consequently weakened.

Such storms are truly phenomena of the tropical oceans. They originate in two distinct latitude zones, between 4° and 22° S and between 4° and 35° N. They are absent in the equatorial zone between 4° S and 4° N. Most tropical cyclones are spawned on the poleward side of the region known as the intertropical convergence zone (ITCZ).

More than two-thirds of observed tropical cyclones originate in the Northern Hemisphere, and roughly the same proportion occur in the Eastern Hemisphere. The North Pacific has more than one-third of all such storms, while the southeast Pacific and South Atlantic are normally devoid of them. Most northern hemispheric tropical cyclones occur between May and November, with peak periods in August and September. The majority of southern hemispheric cyclones occur between December and April, with peaks in January and February.

EFFECTS OF TROPICAL CYCLONES ON OCEAN WATERS

A tropical cyclone can affect the thermal structure and currents in the surface layer of the ocean waters in its path. Cooling of the surface layer occurs in the wake of such a storm. Maximum cooling occurs on the right of a hurricane's path in the Northern Hemisphere. In the wake of Hurricane Hilda's passage through the Gulf of Mexico in

1964 at a translational speed of only 5 knots (5.75 miles per hour), the surface waters were cooled by as much as 6 °C (42.8 °F). Tropical cyclones that have higher translational velocities cause less cooling of the surface. The surface cooling is caused primarily by wind-induced upwelling of cooler water from below the surface layer. The warm surface water is simultaneously transported toward the periphery of the cyclone, where it downwells into the deeper ocean layers. Heat loss across the air-sea interface and the wind-induced mixing of the surface water with those of the cooler subsurface layers make a significant but smaller contribution to surface cooling.

In addition to surface cooling, tropical cyclones may induce large horizontal surge currents and vertical displacements of the thermocline. The surge currents have their largest amplitude at the surface, where they may reach velocities approaching 1 metre (3.3 feet) per second. The horizontal currents and the vertical displacement of the thermocline observed in the wake of a tropical cyclone oscillate close to the inertial period. These oscillations remain for a few days after the passage of the storm and spread outward from the rear of the system as an internal wake on the thermocline. The vertical motion may transport nutrients from the deeper layers into the sunlit surface waters, which in turn promotes phytoplankton blooms (i.e., the rapid growth of diatoms and other minute one-celled organisms). The ocean surface temperature normally recovers to its precyclone value within 10 days of a storm's passage.

INFLUENCE ON ATMOSPHERIC CIRCULATION AND RAINFALL

Tropical cyclones play an important role in the general circulation of the atmosphere, accounting for 2 percent of the global annual rainfall and between 4 and 5 percent of the global rainfall in August and September at the height of the Northern Hemispheric cyclone season. For a local area, the occurrence of a single tropical cyclone can have a major impact on the region's annual rainfall. Furthermore, tropical cyclones contribute approximately 2 percent of the kinetic energy of the general circulation of the atmosphere, some of which is exported from the tropics to higher latitudes.

THE GULF STREAM AND KUROSHIO SYSTEMS

The Gulf Stream and the Kuroshio Current are prominent elements of Earth's oceanic circulation system. Geographically, both occur off the eastern coasts of large continents and flow from the tropics toward the poles, bringing tremendous amounts of warm water northward. Both currents influence weather and climate in the Northern Hemisphere.

THE GULF STREAM

This major current system, as described earlier, is a western boundary current that flows poleward along a boundary separating the warm and more saline waters of the Sargasso Sea to the east from the colder, slightly fresher continental slope waters to the north and west. The warm, saline Sargasso Sea, composed of a water mass known as North Atlantic Central Water, has a temperature that ranges from 8 to 19 °C (46 to 66 °F) and a salinity between 35.10 and 36.70 parts per thousand. This is one of the two dominant water masses of the North Atlantic Ocean, the other being the North Atlantic Deep Water, which has a temperature of 2.2 to 3.5 °C (36 to 38.3 °F) and a salinity between

34.90 and 34.97 parts per thousand, and which occupies the deepest layers of the ocean (generally below 1,000 metres [about 3,300 feet]). The North Atlantic Central Water occupies the upper layer of the North Atlantic Ocean between roughly 20° and 40° N. The "lens" of this water is at its lowest depth of 1,000 metres in the northwest Atlantic and becomes progressively shallower to the east and south. To the north it shallows abruptly and outcrops at the surface in winter, and it is at this point that the Gulf Stream is most intense.

The Gulf Stream flows along the rim of the warm North Atlantic Central Water northward from the Florida Straits along the continental slope of North America to Cape Hatteras. There, it leaves the continental slope and turns northeastward as an intense meandering current that extends toward the Grand Banks of Newfoundland. Its maximum velocity is typically between 1 and 2 metres (about 3.3 to 6.6 feet) per second. At this stage, a part of the current loops back onto itself, flowing south and east. Another part flows eastward toward Spain and Portugal, while the remaining water flows northeastward as the North Atlantic Drift (also called the North Atlantic Current) into the northernmost regions of the North Atlantic Ocean between Scotland and Iceland.

The southward-flowing currents are generally weaker than the Gulf Stream and occur in the eastern lens of the North Atlantic Central Water or the subtropical gyre. The circulation to the south on the southern rim of the subtropical gyre is completed by the westward-flowing North Equatorial Current, part of which flows into the Gulf of Mexico; the remaining part flows northward as the Antilles Current. This subtropical gyre of warm North Atlantic Central Water is the hub of the energy that drives the North Atlantic circulation. It is principally forced by the overlying atmospheric circulation, which at these latitudes is dominated by the clockwise circulation of a subtropical anticyclone. This circulation is not steady and fluctuates in particular on its poleward side where extra-tropical cyclones in the westerlies periodically make incursions into the region. On the western side, hurricanes (during the period from May to November) occasionally disturb the atmospheric circulation. Because of the energy of the subtropical gyre and its associated currents, these short-term fluctuations have little influence on it, however. The gyre obtains most of its energy from the climatological wind distribution over periods of one or two decades. This wind distribution drives a system of surface currents in the uppermost 100 metres (about 330 feet) of the ocean.

Nonetheless, these currents are not simply a reflection of the surface wind circulation as they are influenced by the Coriolis force. The wind-driven current decays with depth, becoming negligible below 100 metres. The water in this surface layer is transported to the right and perpendicular to the surface wind stress because of the Coriolis force. Hence an eastward-directed wind on the poleward side of the subtropical anticyclone would transport the surface layer of the ocean to the south. On the equator-ward side of the anticyclone the trade winds would cause a contrary drift of the surface layer to the north and west. Thus surface waters under the subtropical anticyclone are driven toward the mid-latitudes at about 30° N. These surface waters, which are warmed by solar heating and have a high salinity by virtue of the predominance of evaporation over precipitation at these latitudes, then converge and are forced downward into the deeper ocean.

Over many decades this process forms a deep lens of warm, saline North Atlantic Central Water. The shape of the lens of water is distorted by other dynamical effects, the principal one being the change in the vertical component of the Coriolis force with latitude known as the beta effect. This effect involves the displacement of the warm water lens toward the west, so that the deepest part of the lens is situated to the north of the island of Bermuda rather than in the central Atlantic Ocean. This warm lens of water plays an important role, establishing as it does a horizontal pressure gradient force in and below the wind-drift current. The sea level over the deepest part of the lens is about 1 metre (3.3 feet) higher than outside the lens. The Coriolis force in balance with this horizontal pressure gradient force gives rise to a dynamically induced geostrophic current, which occurs throughout the upper layer of warm water. The strength of this geostrophic current is determined by the horizontal pressure gradient through the slope in sea level. The slope in sea level across the Gulf Stream has been measured by satellite radar altimeter to be 1 metre over a horizontal distance of 100 km (about 60 miles), which is sufficient to cause a surface geostrophic current of 1 metre per second at 43° N.

The large-scale circulation of the Gulf Stream system is, however, only one aspect of a far more complex and richer structure of circulation. Embedded within the mean flow is a variety of eddy structures that not only put kinetic energy into circulation but also carry heat and other important properties, such as nutrients for biological systems. The best known of these eddies are the Gulf Stream rings, which develop in meanders of the current east of Cape Hatteras. Though the eddies were mentioned as early as 1793 by Jonathan Williams, a grandnephew of Benjamin Franklin, they were not systematically studied until the early 1930s by the oceanographer Phil E. Church. Intensive research programs were finally undertaken during the 1970s.

Gulf Stream rings have either warm or cold cores. The warm rings are typically 100 to 300 km (about 60 to 186 miles) in diameter and have a clockwise rotation. They consist of waters from the Gulf Stream and Sargasso Sea and form when the meanders in the Gulf Stream pinch off on its continental slope side. They move generally westward, flowing at the speed of the slope waters, and are reabsorbed into the Gulf Stream at Cape Hatteras after a typical lifetime of about six months. The cold core rings, composed of a mixture of Gulf Stream and continental slope waters, are formed when the meanders pinch off to the south of the Gulf Stream. They are a little larger than their warm-core counterparts, characteristically having diameters of 200 to 300 km (about 124 to 186 miles) and an anticlockwise rotation. They move generally southwestward into the Sargasso Sea and have lifetimes of one to two years. The cold-core rings are usually more numerous than warm-core rings, typically 10 each year as compared with five warm-core rings annually.

THE KUROSHIO CURRENT

The Kuroshio Current (Japanese: "Black Current"), which is also called the Japan Current, is a strong surface oceanic current of the Pacific Ocean, the northeasterly flowing continuation of the Pacific North Equatorial Current between Luzon of the Philippines and the east coast of Japan. The temperature and salinity of Kuroshio water are relatively high for the region, about 20 °C (68 °F) and 34.5 parts per thousand, respectively. Only about 400 metres (1,300 feet) deep, the Kuroshio travels at rates ranging between 50 and 300 cm (20 and 120 inches) per second.

Flowing past Taiwan (Formosa) and the Ryukyu Islands, the current skirts the east coast of Kyushu, where, during the summer, it branches west and then northeast through the Korea Strait to parallel the west coast of Honshu in the Sea of Japan as the Tsushima Current. In the vicinity of latitude 35° N (about central Honshu), the bulk of the Kuroshio turns east to receive the southward-flowing Oya Current. This flow, known as the Kuroshio Extension, eventually becomes the North Pacific Current (also known as the North Pacific West Wind Drift). Much of this current's force is lost west of the Hawaiian Islands as a great south-flowing eddy, the Kuroshio countercurrent, joins the Pacific North Equatorial Current and directs the warm water back to the Philippine Sea. The remainder of the original flow continues east to split off the coast of Canada and form the Alaska and California currents. The Kuroshio exhibits distinct seasonal fluctuations. It is strongest from May to August. Receding some in late summer and autumn, it begins to increase from January to February only to weaken in early spring. Similar to the Gulf Stream (Atlantic) in its creation and flow patterns, the Kuroshio has an important warming effect upon the south and southeast coastal regions of Japan as far north as Tokyo.

The existence of the Kuroshio was known to European geographers as early as 1650, as shown by a map drawn by Bernhardus Varenius. It was also noted by Captain J. King, a member of the British expedition under Captain James Cook (1776–80). It is called Kuroshio ("Black Current") because it appears a deeper blue than does the sea through which it flows.

THE POLEWARD TRANSFER OF HEAT

A significant characteristic of the large-scale North Atlantic circulation is the poleward transport of heat. Heat is transferred in a northward direction throughout the North Atlantic. This heat is absorbed by the tropical waters of the Pacific and Indian oceans, as well as of the Atlantic, and is then transferred to the high latitudes, where it is finally given up to the atmosphere.

The mechanism for the heat transfer is principally by thermohaline circulation rather than by wind-driven circulation. Circulation of the thermohaline type involves a large-scale overturning of the ocean, with warm and saline water in the upper 1,000 metres (about 330 feet) moving northward and being cooled in the Labrador, Greenland, and Norwegian seas. The density of the water in contact with the atmosphere is increased by surface cooling, and the water subsequently sinks below the surface layer to the lowest depths of the ocean. This water is mixed with the surrounding water masses by a variety of processes to form North Atlantic Deep Water. The water moves slowly southward as the lower limb of the thermohaline circulation. It is this overturning circulation that is responsible for the warm winter climate of northwestern Europe (notably the British Isles and Norway) rather than the horizontal wind-driven circulation discussed above. The North Atlantic Drift, which is an extension of the Gulf Stream system to the south, provides this northward flow of warm and saline waters into the polar seas. This feature makes the circulation of the North Atlantic Ocean uniquely different from that of the Pacific Ocean, which has a less effective thermohaline circulation. Although there is a northward transfer of heat in the North Pacific, the subtropical wind-driven gyre in the upper ocean is mainly responsible for it. Thus the Kuroshio on the western boundary of the North Pacific gyre is principally driven by the surface wind circulation of the North Pacific.

Studies of the sediment cores obtained from the ocean floor have indicated that the ocean surface temperature was as much as 10 °C (18 °F) cooler than today in the northernmost region of the North Atlantic Ocean during the last glacial maximum some 18,000 years ago. This difference in surface temperature would indicate that the warm North Atlantic Drift was much reduced compared to what it is at present, and hence the thermohaline circulation was considerably weaker. In contrast, the Gulf Stream was probably more intense than it is today and exhibited a large shift from its present path to an eastward flow at 40° N.

EL NIÑO/SOUTHERN OSCILLATION AND CLIMATIC CHANGE

As was explained earlier, the oceans can moderate the climate of certain regions. Not only do they affect such geographic variations, but they also influence temporal changes in climate. The time scales of climate variability range from a few years to millions of years and include the so-called ice age cycles that repeat every 20,000 to 40,000 years, interrupted by interglacial periods of "optimum" climate, such as the present. The climatic modulations that occur at shorter scales include such periods as the Little Ice Age from the early 16th to the mid-19th centuries, when the global average temperature was approximately 1 °C (1.8 °F) lower than it is today. Several climate fluctuations on the scale of decades have occurred in the 20th century, such as warming from 1910 to 1940, cooling from 1940 to 1970, and the warming trend since 1970.

Although many of the mechanisms of climate change are understood, it is usually difficult to pinpoint the specific causes. Scientists acknowledge that climate can be affected by factors external to the land-ocean-atmosphere climate system, such as variations in solar brightness, the shading effect of aerosols injected into the atmosphere by volcanic activity, or the increased atmospheric concentration of "greenhouse" gases (e.g., carbon dioxide, nitrous oxide, methane, and chlorofluorocarbons) produced by human activities. However, none of these factors explain the periodic variations observed during the 20th century, which may simply be manifestations of the natural variability of climate. The existence of natural variability at many time scales makes the identification of causative factors such as human-induced warming more difficult. Whether change is natural or caused, the oceans play a key role and have a moderating effect on influencing factors.

The El Niño Phenomenon

The shortest, or interannual, time scale relates to natural variations that are perceived as years of unusual weather—e.g., excessive heat, drought, or storminess. Such changes are so common in many regions that any given year is about as likely to be considered as exceptional as typical. The best example of the influence of the oceans on interannual climate anomalies is the occurrence of El Niño conditions in the eastern Pacific Ocean at irregular intervals of about 3–10 years. The stronger El Niño episodes of enhanced ocean temperatures (2–8 °C [3.6–14.4 °F] above normal) are typically accompanied by altered weather patterns around the globe, such as droughts in Australia, northeastern Brazil, and the highlands of southern Peru, excessive summer rainfall along the coast of Ecuador and northern Peru, severe winter storminess along the coast of central Chile, and unusual winter weather along the west coast of North America.

The effects of El Niño have been documented in Peru since the Spanish conquest in 1525. The Spanish term "la corriente de El Niño" was introduced by fishermen of the Peruvian port of Paita in the 19th century; it refers to a warm, southward ocean current that temporarily displaces the normally cool, northward-flowing Humboldt, or Peru, Current. (The name is a pious reference to the Christ child, chosen because of the typical appearance of the countercurrent during the Christmas season.) Under normal conditions, coastal winds can induce upwelling of the lower-layer nutrients to the surface, where they support an abundant ecosystem. During an El Niño event, however, the upper layer thickens so that the upwelled water contains fewer nutrients, thus contributing to a collapse of marine productivity.

By the end of the 19th century Peruvian geographers recognized that every few years this countercurrent is more intense than normal, extends farther south, and is associated with torrential rainfall over the otherwise dry northern desert. The abnormal countercurrent also was observed to bring tropical debris, as well as such flora and fauna as bananas and aquatic reptiles, from the coastal region of Ecuador farther north. Increasingly during the 20th century, El Niño has come to connote an exceptional year rather than the original annual event.

As Peruvians began to exploit the guano of marine birds for fertilizer in the early 20th century, they noticed El Niño-related deteriorations in the normally high marine productivity of the coast of Peru as manifested by large reductions in the bird populations that depend on anchovies and sardines for sustenance. The preoccupation with El Niño increased after mid-century, as the Peruvian fishing industry rapidly expanded to exploit the anchovies directly. (Fish meal produced from the anchovies was exported to industrialized nations as a feed supplement for livestock.) By 1971 the Peruvian fishing

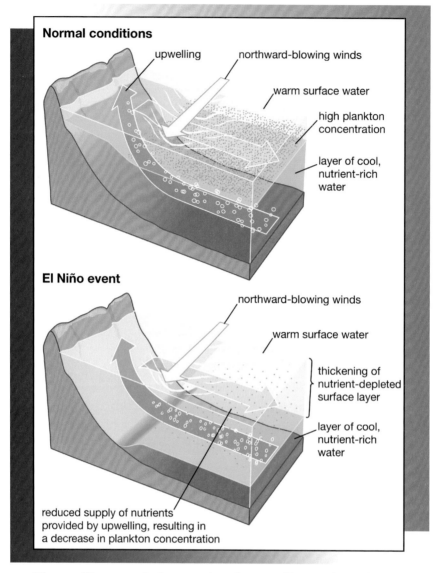

The upwelling process in the ocean along the coast of Peru. A thermocline and a nutricline separate the warm, nutrient-deficient upper layer from the cool, enriched layer below. Encyclopædia Britannica, Inc.

fleet had become the largest in its history; it had extracted very nearly 13 million metric tons (about 14.3 million tons) of anchovies in that year alone. Peru was catapulted into first place among fishing nations, and scientists

Fishing for anchovies off the coast of Peru. Robert Harding Picture Library

expressed serious concern that fish stocks were being depleted beyond self-sustaining levels, even for the extremely productive marine ecosystem of Peru. The strong El Niño of 1972–73 captured world attention because of the drastic reduction in anchovy catches to a small fraction of prior levels. The anchovy catch did not return to previous levels, and the effects of plummeting fish meal exports reverberated throughout the world commodity markets.

El Niño was only a curiosity to the scientific community in the first half of the 20th century, thought to be geographically limited to the west coast of South

America. There was little data, mainly gathered coincidentally from foreign oceanographic cruises, and it was generally believed that El Niño occurred when the normally northward coastal winds off Peru, which cause the upwelling of cool, nutrient-rich water along the coast, decreased, ceased, or reversed in direction. When systematic and extensive oceanographic measurements were made in the Pacific in 1957–58 as part of the International Geophysical Year, it was found that El Niño had occurred during the same period and was also associated with extensive warming over most of the Pacific equatorial zone. Eventually tide-gauge and other measurements made throughout the tropical Pacific showed that the coastal El Niño was but one manifestation of basinwide ocean circulation changes that occur in response to a massive weakening of the westward-blowing trade winds in the western and central equatorial Pacific and not to localized wind anomalies along the Peru coast.

THE SOUTHERN OSCILLATION

The wind anomalies are a manifestation of an atmospheric counterpart to the oceanic El Niño. At the turn of the century, the British climatologist Gilbert Walker set out to determine the connections between the Asian monsoon and other climatic fluctuations around the globe in an effort to predict unusual monsoon years that bring drought and famine to the Asian sector. Unaware of any connection to El Niño, he discovered a coherent interannual fluctuation of atmospheric pressure over the tropical Indo-Pacific region, which he termed the Southern Oscillation (SO). During years of reduced rainfall over northern Australia and Indonesia, the pressure in that region (e.g., at what are now Darwin and Jakarta) was anomalously high and wind patterns were altered.

Simultaneously, in the eastern South Pacific pressures were unusually low, negatively correlated with those at Darwin and Jakarta. A Southern Oscillation Index (SOI), based on pressure differences between the two regions (east minus west), showed low, negative values at such times, which were termed the "low phase" of the SO. During more normal "high-phase" years, the pressures were low over Indonesia and high in the eastern Pacific, with high, positive values of the SOI. In papers published during the 1920s and '30s, Walker gave statistical evidence for widespread climatic anomalies around the globe being associated with the SO pressure "seesaw."

In the 1950s, years after Walker's investigations, it was noted that the low-phase years of the SOI corresponded with periods of high ocean temperatures along the Peruvian coast, but no physical connection between the SO and El Niño was recognized until Jacob Bjerknes, in the early 1960s, tried to understand the large geographic scale of the anomalies observed during the 1957–58 El Niño event. Bjerknes, a meteorologist, formulated the first conceptual model of the large-scale ocean-atmosphere interactions that occur during El Niño episodes. His model has been refined through intensive research since the early 1970s.

During a year or two prior to an El Niño event (high-phase years of the SO), the westward trade winds typically blow more intensely along the equator in the equatorial Pacific, causing warm upper-ocean water to accumulate in a thickened surface layer in the western Pacific where sea level rises. Meanwhile, the stronger, upwelling-favourable winds in the eastern Pacific induce colder surface water and lowered sea levels off South America. Toward the end of the year preceding an El Niño, the area of intense tropical storm activity over Indonesia migrates eastward toward the equatorial Pacific west of the International

Date Line (which corresponds in general to the 180th meridian of longitude), bringing episodes of eastward wind reversals to that region of the ocean. These wind bursts excite extremely long ocean waves, known as Kelvin waves (imperceptible to an observer), that propagate eastward toward the coast of South America, where they cause the upper ocean layer of relatively warm water to thicken and sea level to rise.

The tropical storms of the western Pacific also occur in other years, though less frequently, and produce similar Kelvin waves, but an El Niño event does not result and the waves continue poleward along the coast toward Chile and California, detectable only in tide-gauge measurements. Something else occurs prior to an El Niño that is not fully understood: as the Kelvin waves travel eastward along the equator, an anomalous eastward current carries warm western Pacific water farther east, and the warm surface layer deepens in the central equatorial Pacific (east of the international dateline). Additional surface warming takes place as the upwelling-favourable winds bring warmer subsurface water to the surface. (The subsurface water is warmer now, rather than cooler, because the overlying layer of warmer water is now significantly deeper than before.) The anomalous warming creates conditions favourable for the further migration of the tropical storm centre toward the east, giving renewed vigour to eastward winds, more Kelvin waves, and additional warming. Each increment of anomalies in one medium (e.g., the ocean) induces further anomalies in the other (the atmosphere) and vice versa, giving rise to an unstable growth of anomalies through a process of positive feedbacks. During this time, the SO is found in its low phase.

After several months of these unstable ocean-atmosphere interactions, the entire equatorial zone becomes considerably warmer (2–5 °C [3.6–9 °F]) than normal, and a sizable volume of warm upper ocean water is transported from the western to the eastern Pacific. As a result, sea levels fall by 10–20 cm (4–8 inches) in the west and rise by larger amounts off the coast of South America, where sea surface temperature anomalies may vary from 2 to 8 °C (3.6 to 14.4 °F) above normal. Anomalous conditions typically persist for 10–14 months before returning to normal. The warming off South America occurs even though the upwelling-favourable winds there continue unabated: the upwelled water is warmer now, rather than cooler as before, and its associated nutrients are less plentiful, thereby failing to sustain the marine ecosystem at its prior productive levels.

The current focus of oceanographic research is on understanding the circumstances leading to the demise of the El Niño event and the onset of another such event several years later. The most widely held hypothesis is that a second class of long equatorial ocean waves—Rossby waves with a shallow surface layer—is generated by the El Niño and that they propagate westward to the landmasses of Asia. There, the Rossby waves reflect off the Asian coast eastward along the equator in the form of upwelling Kelvin waves, resulting in a thinning of the upper ocean warm layer and a cooling of the ocean as the winds bring deeper, cooler water to the surface. This process is thought to initiate one to two years of colder-than-average conditions until Rossby waves of a contrary sense (i.e., with a thickened surface layer) are again generated, functioning as a switching mechanism, this time to start another El Niño sequence.

Another goal of scientists is to understand climate change on the scale of centuries or longer and to make projections about the changes that will occur within the next few generations. Yet, determinations of current climatic trends from recent data are made difficult by natural variability at shorter time scales, such as the El Niño phenomenon. Many scientists are attempting to understand the mechanisms of change during an El Niño event from improved global measurements so as to determine how the ocean-atmosphere engine operates at longer time scales. Others are studying prehistoric records preserved in trees, sediments, and fossil corals in an effort to reconstruct past variations, including those like the El Niño. Their aim is to remove such short-term variations so as to be able to make more accurate estimates of long-term trends.

ECONOMIC ASPECTS OF THE OCEANS

The sea is generally accepted by scientists as the place where life began on Earth. Without the sea, life as it is known today could not exist. Among other functions, it acts as a great heat reservoir, leveling the temperature extremes that would otherwise prevail over Earth and expand the desert areas. The oceans provide the least expensive form of transportation known, and the coasts serve as a major recreational site. More importantly, the sea is a valuable source of food and a potentially important source of energy and minerals, all of which are required in ever-increasing quantities by industrialized and developing nations alike.

MEDIUM FOR TRANSPORTATION AND COMMUNICATIONS

From the beginning of recorded history, people have used the sea as a means of transporting themselves and their goods. The bulk of the tonnage of products transported throughout the world today continues to be moved in ocean vessels. The size of these vessels ranges from small boats capable of carrying a few tons to bulk carriers (e.g., supertankers) capable of transporting more than 500,000 tons of oil. The cost of transporting goods on the ocean depends on the product, the form of shipment, and the type of vessel. As the per capita consumption of materials increases, the outlook for marine transportation is one of ever-increasing tonnages and size of carrying vessels.

Since the laying of the transatlantic cable in the 19th century, the oceans have served as a major means of communication between continents and islands. Hundreds of seafloor cables connect many large centres of world population. With the development of satellite communications, seafloor cables as a means of communication have decreased somewhat in importance, but they will continue to carry information for many decades to come.

In addition to communications, cable and pipes laid on the seafloor carry electrical energy, oil, and other commodities in many parts of the world.

Source of Food and Water

Many millions of tons of edible fish and shellfish are taken from the oceans each year. Yet, the food-producing potential of the sea is considerably greater than this. The prevailing methods by which fish are taken from the oceans are inefficient. This problem is compounded by the fact that only a handful of varieties are targeted by commercial fishermen (anchovy, sardine, herring, cod, mackerel, and pollack constitute more than half of the total annual catch). Overfishing of certain varieties and areas along the continental shelves also has resulted in declining numbers and therefore catches.

Several alternatives have been proposed to enhance productivity. One possibility is to extract protein concentrates from all types of fish, promoting the use of varieties formerly ignored for foodstuff. It has been estimated that this procedure could produce a sustained yield of 2 billion tons of food annually for the world's populace. Another alternative would be to use protein derived from algae cultivated on the continental shelf. A more viable course of action would be to develop the continental shelf for fish- and kelp-farming. The Japanese have instituted a substantial research program in this area. They have farmed oysters in their oceanic bays for many years and more recently raised sea bream and shrimp in protected environments. Commercial shrimp and oyster farms also have been developed in the United States in the shallow waters of estuaries and bays. Both commercial and research aquaculture projects have been conducted to raise abalone, Maine lobster, salmon, and edible forms of seaweed under controlled conditions. Limited sea farming has been practiced in France and Italy, both of which raise mussels and certain other shellfish.

Workers clean the harvest at an oyster farm in Point Reyes Station, California. Seafood production can be greatly enhanced by such operations. Justin Sullivan/Getty Images

Various marine organisms have been artificially cultivated as sources for therapeutic drugs. For example, during the early 1980s American researchers isolated a substance called bryostatin 1 from the moss animal *Burgula neritina*; this substance has been shown to slow the development of tumours.

The need for water for domestic and agricultural purposes grew steadily throughout the latter half of the 20th century. As a result, increasing attention has been given to desalting ocean waters and brackish waters in inland seas. Throughout the world, more than 3,500 land-based desalination plants, producing a total of more than 8 billion litres (in excess of 2 billion gallons) per day, were in operation by the early 1990s. In general, the desalination plants are located in areas where the population has outstripped the onshore water supply and where high-cost desalinated water can be afforded. This situation tends to arise in coastal-desert areas or on densely populated islands, because the cost of pumping water through pipelines to interior areas would add prohibitively to the basic cost at the sites of desalination. The United States operates a little more than 30 percent of the world's desalination facilities. Another 20 percent or so are found in the Middle East, chiefly in Israel, Saudi Arabia, Kuwait, and the United Arab Emirates. Together, these Middle Eastern plants produce roughly two-thirds of the world's desalinated water.

A population usually can afford to pay about 10 times as much for water for domestic purposes as it does for agricultural water. Large-scale nuclear desalination facilities promise to lower the cost of desalted water at the desalination sites to a level that most industries and some agricultural enterprises can afford. As yet, however, no such plant has been constructed.

At present desalination is accomplished primarily by distillation and membrane processes. Distillation processes involve some form of evaporation and subsequent condensation. Many of the largest commercial desalination plants use multiple-effect distillation (i.e., multistage-flash distillation). Roughly half of the world's desalting facilities employ distillation processes and account for approximately 75 percent of all desalinated water produced annually.

Membrane processes for desalting include reverse osmosis and electrodialysis. Of the two, reverse osmosis is the more widely used, particularly for desalting brackish waters from inland seas. In this method the natural process of osmosis is reversed by applying pressure to brine that is in contact with an osmotic membrane. The membrane impedes the passage of salt ions while allowing fresh water to move through. In electrodialysis an electric potential is used to drive positive and negative ions of the dissolved salts through membranous filters, thereby sharply reducing the salt content of the water between the filters.

In the future, it can be expected that the ocean will become an increasingly important source of fresh water. If production and transportation costs can be lowered sufficiently, it may be possible to produce fresh water to irrigate large areas that border the oceans in many parts of the world.

ENERGY RESOURCES

There are several recognized techniques by which energy can be extracted from the sea. The major problem in taking energy resources from the sea is that they tend to be diffused over a large lateral area. A point-concentration energy source is necessary if it is to be exploited economically.

TIDAL POWER GENERATION

Hydraulic turbine generator units are used to extract energy from ocean tides. As of the late 1980s, operating tidal units included a 240-megawatt plant in France on the estuary of the Rance River and several smaller installations such as, for example, a 40,000-kilowatt pilot plant in Russia on the Barents Sea. By the early 21st century some of these technologies had become commercially available, and a number of other countries, such as Scotland and South Korea, were expanding their tidal power generation capacity.

Ocean Thermal Energy Conversion

Another more promising technology, known as ocean thermal energy conversion (OTEC), makes use of the temperature differential between the warm surface waters of the oceans, heated by solar radiation, and the deeper cold waters to generate power in a conventional heat engine. The difference in temperature between the surface and lower water layer can be as large as 50 °C (90 °F) over vertical distances of as little as 90 metres (295 feet) in some ocean areas. To be economically practical, the temperature

The La Rance River tidal power plant near Saint Malo, in western France. Marchel Mochet/AFP/Getty Images

differential should be at least 20 °C (36 °F) in the first 1,000 metres (3,300 feet) below the surface.

The OTEC concept was first proposed in the early 1880s by the French engineer Jacques-Arsìne d'Arsonval. His idea called for a closed-cycle system, a design that has been adapted for most present-day OTEC pilot plants. Such a system employs a secondary working fluid (a refrigerant) such as ammonia. Heat transferred from the warm surface ocean water causes the working fluid to vaporize through a heat exchanger. The vapour then expands under moderate pressures, turning a turbine connected to a generator and thereby producing electricity. Cold seawater pumped up from the ocean depths to a second heat exchanger provides a surface cool enough to cause the vapour to condense. The working fluid remains within the closed system, vaporizing and reliquefying continuously.

Some researchers have centred their attention on an open-cycle OTEC system that employs water vapour as the working fluid and dispenses with the use of a refrigerant. In this kind of system warm surface seawater is partially vaporized as it is injected into a near vacuum. The resultant steam is expanded through a low-pressure steam turbogenerator to produce electric power. Cold seawater is used to condense the steam, and a vacuum pump maintains the proper system pressure.

The prospects for the commercial application of OTEC technology seem bright, particularly on islands and in developing nations in the tropical regions where conditions are most favourable for OTEC plant operation. It has been estimated that the tropical ocean waters absorb solar radiation equivalent in heat content to that of about 170 billion barrels of oil each day. Removal of this much heat from the ocean would not significantly alter its temperature, but would permit the generation of about 10 million megawatts of electricity on a continuous basis.

SOURCE OF MINERALS AND OTHER RAW MATERIALS

The ocean floor continues to be the site of petroleum and mineral extraction. Oil and natural gas deposits occur in rock layers beneath the ocean floor, and several countries and multinational corporations spend huge sums of money to extract these resources annually. Minerals recovered from the ocean floor and marine sediments below include phosphorite, from which phosphorus can be extracted, calcareous oozes, which can be used to make cement, and precious metals.

PETROLEUM

In the mid-1950s the production of oil and gas from oceanic areas was negligible. By the early 1980s about 14 million barrels per day, or about 25 percent of the world's production, came from offshore wells, and the amount continues to grow. More than 700 offshore drilling and production rigs were at work by the early 21st century at more than 200 offshore locations throughout the world, drilling, completing, and maintaining offshore oil wells.

It was once thought that only the continental-shelf areas contained potential petroleum resources, but discoveries of oil deposits in deeper waters of the Gulf of Mexico (about 3,000 to 4,000 metres [9,800 to 13,100 feet]) have changed that view. It is now believed that the continental slopes and neighbouring seafloor areas contain large oil deposits, thus enhancing potential petroleum reserves of the ocean bottom.

Offshore drilling is not without its drawbacks, however. Not only is it difficult and expensive to drill on the continental shelf and in deeper water, but there is also the risk of accidental discharges of oil that

DEEPWATER DISASTER

The Deepwater Horizon oil rig, owned and operated by offshore-oil-drilling company Transocean and leased by oil company BP, was situated in the Macondo oil prospect in the Mississippi Canyon, a valley in the continental shelf in the Gulf of Mexico. On the night of April 20, 2010, a surge of natural gas blasted through a concrete cap recently installed to seal the well for later use. The gas traveled up the rig's riser to the platform, where it ignited, killing 11 workers and injuring 17. The rig capsized and sank on the morning of April 22 — ironically, on Earth Day that year — rupturing the riser, through which drilling mud was injected in order to counteract the upward pressure of oil and natural gas. Without the opposing force, oil began to discharge into the gulf.

Although BP attempted to activate the rig's blowout preventer (BOP), a fail-safe mechanism designed to close the channel through which oil was drawn, the device malfunctioned. Several attempts to contain the oil were attempted over the ensuing weeks, including capping the well and drilling two relief wells, which were channels paralleling and eventually intersecting the original well. These efforts had varying rates of success.

Meanwhile, the volume of oil escaping the damaged well formed a slick extending over thousands of square miles of the Gulf of Mexico. To clean oil from the open water, dispersants — substances that emulsified the oil, thus allowing for easier metabolism by bacteria — were pumped directly into the leak and applied aerially to the slick. Booms to corral portions of the slick were deployed, and the contained oil was then siphoned off or burned. As oil began to contaminate Louisiana beaches in May, it was manually removed.

More difficult to clean were the state's marshes and estuaries, where the topography was knit together by delicate plant life. By June, oil and tar balls had made landfall on the beaches of Mississippi, Florida, and Alabama. Thousands of oil-plastered birds, mammals, and sea turtles were transported to rehabilitation centres; countless fish and smaller sea life perished. Various cleanup efforts were coordinated by the National Response Team, a group of government agencies headed by the U.S. Coast Guard and the Environmental Protection Agency (EPA).

With many residents of Gulf Coast states dependent on fishing and tourism to support themselves, economic prospects for the region were dire. More than a third of the gulf was closed to fishing due to fears of contamination, and few travelers were willing to face the prospect of petroleum-sullied beaches. Following demands by U.S. Pres. Barack Obama, BP, which was already spending millions of dollars for cleanup efforts daily, created a $20 billion compensation fund for those affected by the spill.

can cause serious damage to the environment and marine organisms. In spite of technological advances, inadvertent leaks, sometimes on a large scale, continue to occur.

MINERALS

The rivers of the world dump billions of tons of material into the oceans each year. Seafloor springs and volcanic eruptions also add many millions of tons of elements. Even the winds contribute solid materials to the oceans in appreciable quantities. Most of these sediments rapidly settle to the seafloor in nearshore areas, in some cases forming potentially valuable placer mineral deposits. The dissolved load of the rivers, however, mixes with seawater and is gradually dispersed over Earth's total oceanic envelope. Because of the nature of the minerals and their mode of formation, it is convenient to consider the occurrence of ocean deposits in several environments—marine beaches, seawater, continental shelves, sub-seafloor consolidated rocks, and the marine sediments of the deep-sea floor. Minerals are mined from all of these environments except for the deep-sea floor, which was only recently recognized as a repository for mineral deposits of unbelievable extent and significant economic value.

Minerals that resist the chemical and mechanical processes of erosion in nature and that possess a density greater than that of Earth's common minerals have a tendency to concentrate in gravity deposits known as placers. During the Pleistocene glaciations, sea level was appreciably lowered as the ocean water was transferred to the continental glaciers. Because of the cyclical nature of the ice ages and the intervening warm periods, a series of beaches were formed in nearshore areas both above and below present sea level. Also, when sea level was lowered in past ages, the streams that today flow into the sea coursed much further seaward, carrying placer minerals to be deposited in channels that are now submerged. With geophysical exploration techniques, these channels and beaches can be easily delineated, even though these features are totally covered by Holocene sediments—i.e., those deposited during the past 10,000 years.

Sand and gravel are mined from a number of offshore locations around the world, generally with hydraulic dredges. They are used primarily for construction purposes or for beach replenishment or nearshore fills.

Sulfur, which is taken from salt domes in the Gulf of Mexico, is mined by a process in which pressurized hot water is pumped into the sulfur-containing cap of the dome, melting the sulfur and forcing it to the surface. Compressed air is also used to pump sulfur to the surface; the still-molten sulfur is then conveyed to the shore through insulated pipelines.

Of considerable interest are the seafloor phosphorite deposits on the coastal shelves of many nations. The phosphorite off California occurs as nodules that vary in shape from flat slabs a few metres across to small spherical forms termed oolites. The nodules commonly are found as a single layer at the surface of coarse-grained sediments. Phosphorite composition from the California offshore area is surprisingly uniform and contains potentially economically attractive amounts of phosphorus. Another type of phosphate deposit has been discovered off the west coast of Mexico. It contains as much as 40 percent apatite (common phosphate mineral), and some experts have speculated that up to 20 billion tons of recoverable phosphate rock exist in the deposit.

Mineral deposits of enormous size and potential economic significance have been discovered on the deep ocean floor. Minerals formed in the deep sea are frequently found in high concentrations because there is relatively little clastic material generated in these areas to dilute the chemical precipitates.

An estimated 10^{16} tons of calcareous oozes, formed by the deposition of calcareous shells and skeletons of planktonic organisms, cover some 130 million square km (about 50 million square miles) of the ocean floor. In a few instances, these oozes, which occur within a few hundred kilometres of most nations bordering the sea, are almost pure calcium carbonate; however, they often show a composition similar to that of the limestones used in the manufacture of portland cement.

Covering about 39 million square km (about 15 million square miles) of the ocean floor in great bands across the northern and southern ends of the Pacific Ocean and across the southern ends of the Indian and Atlantic oceans are other oozes, consisting of the siliceous shells and skeletons of plankton animals and plants. Normally these oozes could serve in most of the applications for which diatomaceous earth is used, for fire and sound insulation, for lightweight concrete formulations, as filters, and as soil conditioners.

An estimated 10^{16} tons of red clay covers about 104 million square km (about 40 million square miles) of the ocean floor. Although compositional analyses are not particularly exciting, red clay may possess some value as a raw material in the clay-products industries, or it may serve as a source of metals in the future. The average assay for alumina is about 15 percent, but red clays from specific locations have assayed as high as 25 percent alumina; copper contents as high as 0.20 percent also have been found. A few hundredths of a percent of such metals as nickel and cobalt and a percent or so of manganese also are generally present in a micronodular fraction of the clays and in all likelihood can be separated and concentrated from the other materials by a screening process or by some other physical method.

Underlying the hot brines in the Red Sea are basins containing metal-rich sediments that potentially may prove to be of considerable significance. It has been estimated that the largest of several such pools, the Atlantis II Deep, contains several billion dollars worth of copper, zinc, silver, and gold in relatively high grades. These pools lie in about 2,000 metres (about 6,600 feet) of water midway between the Sudan and the Arabian Peninsula. Because of their gellike nature, pumping these sediments to the surface may prove relatively uncomplicated. These deposits are forming today under present geochemical conditions and are similar in character to certain major ore deposits on land.

The discovery, in 1978, of polymetallic sulfides at the mid-ocean spreading centres has aroused much interest. These sulfides include sediments enriched in iron and manganese. Sites of rich deposits have been located at the Galápagos spreading centre in the Gulf of California and at the East Pacific Rise.

From an economic standpoint, the most interesting oceanic sediments are manganese nodules—small, black to brown, friable lumps found to be widely distributed throughout the major oceans in the late 19th century by the Challenger and Albatross expeditions.

Many theories have been proposed to account for the formation of manganese nodules, the best probably being that the ocean is saturated at its present state of acidity-alkalinity in iron and manganese. For this reason, these elements precipitate as colloidal particles that gradually increase in size and filter down to the seafloor. Colloids of manganese and iron oxides collect many metals and tend to agglomerate as nodules at the seafloor rather than settle as particles in the general sediments. An estimated 1.5 trillion tons of manganese nodules lie on the Pacific Ocean floor alone. Averaging about 4 cm (1.6 inches) in diameter and found in concentrations as high as 38,600 tons per square km (100,000 tons per square mile), these manganese nodules contain as much as 2.5 percent copper, 2.0 percent nickel, 0.2 percent cobalt, and 35 percent manganese. In some deposits, the content of cobalt and manganese is as high as 2.5 percent and 50 percent, respectively. Such concentrations would be considered high-grade ores if found on land, and, because of the large horizontal extent of the deposit, they are a potential source of many important industrial metals.

Relatively simple mechanical cable bucket or hydraulic dredges with submerged motors and pumps can effect the mining of the nodules at rates as high as 10,000 to 15,000 tons per day, from depths as great as 6,000 metres (19,700 feet). The estimated costs of mining and processing the nodules indicate that copper, nickel, cobalt, and other metals can be economically produced from this source.

The prospects of mining the manganese nodules and metal-rich sediments have brought home the need to resolve long-standing legal problems relating to the ownership of marine resources. During the 18th century the extent of the territorial sea (and therefore rights) was established as 5.6 km (3 nautical miles) from a nation's shoreline. The area beyond the territorial sea, the so-called high seas, was regarded as open to all nations. By the mid-1940s technological advances had extended offshore oil drilling beyond the territorial limit. This situation, together with the desire of various coastal nations to protect their fishing grounds, eventually resulted in an attempt to codify international law concerning territorial waters, ocean resources, and sea lanes. A 1982 treaty that called for the enactment of the United Nations Law of the Sea Convention was initially signed by 138 countries; some 30 other states, including the United States, the United Kingdom, and West Germany, refused to sign, however. By the end of the first decade of the 21st century, the number of signatories had grown to 159. The treaty extended the territorial limit of each coastal country to a distance of 12 nautical miles and granted it sovereign rights over natural resources—living and nonliving—within an exclusive economic zone (EEZ) of 200 nautical miles. The countries that initially refused to sign the treaty objected to its provisions governing seabed mining. The treaty declared the minerals on the seafloor beneath the high seas the "common heritage of mankind" and stipulated that their exploitation be directed by a global authority. While private and national mining concerns are allowed to conduct exploration and set up extraction operations, the question of seabed mineral ownership and mining rights remains largely unresolved. This situation is viewed in some quarters as the primary obstacle to full and effective utilization of seabed resources.

WASTE DISPOSAL AND OTHER RELATED ACTIONS

One of the least known but most significant uses of the sea is as an enormous dump site. In the past, the oceans were able to assimilate the wastes of society without noticeable adverse effects. However, industrialization and other concomitant developments, along with sharp increases in global population, have given rise to quantities and forms of waste that are now taxing the capacity of the oceans to absorb them. Extensive marginal areas of the oceans have been heavily polluted by human wastes ranging from the raw sewage of urban centres to junked appliances and automobiles. Less apparent but more insidious forms of pollution are toxic chemicals, nuclear wastes, and oily bilges pumped by practically all vessels using petroleum for power.

Some other human activities are equally harmful to the marine environment. Massive oil spills from tanker accidents, such as the 1989 mishap involving the *Exxon Valdez* in Prince William Sound, Alaska, and the 2010 Deepwater Horizon offshore drilling incident have not only disfigured innumerable beaches and estuaries but caused widespread damage to wildlife as well. Large power plants are generally located along coastlines to reduce the costs involved in cooling their condensers by water-circulation systems. Although the whole of the ocean never will be affected by the waste heat dissipated by these plants, detrimental environmental effects can be caused in the immediate area of the power-plant outfall. Herbicides and pesticides (especially the organochlorides still used by some countries) reach the oceans via the wind and rivers and contaminate marine organisms.

The fringes of the oceans—the beaches, lagoons, and bays—are the most sensitive to human action, but the continued dumping of wastes, attended by other abuses, will eventually affect the entire marine environment.

CHAPTER 5

OCEANOGRAPHY

Oceanography is the scientific discipline concerned with all aspects of the world's oceans and seas, including their physical and chemical properties, their origin and geologic framework, and the forms of life that inhabit the marine environment. Traditionally, oceanography has been divided into four separate but related branches: physical oceanography, chemical oceanography, marine geology, and marine ecology. Physical oceanography deals with the properties of seawater (temperature, density, pressure, and so on), its movement (waves, currents, and tides), and the interactions between the ocean waters and the atmosphere. Chemical oceanography has to do with the composition of seawater and the biogeochemical cycles that affect it. Marine geology focuses on the structure, features, and evolution of the ocean basins. Marine ecology, also called biological oceanography, involves the study of the plants and animals of the sea, including life cycles and food production.

Oceanography is the sum of these several branches. Oceanographic research entails the sampling of seawater and marine life for close study, the remote sensing of oceanic processes with aircraft and Earth-orbiting satellites, and the exploration of the seafloor by means of deep-sea drilling and seismic profiling of the terrestrial crust below the ocean bottom. Greater knowledge of the world's oceans enables scientists to more accurately predict, for example, long-term weather and climatic changes and also leads to more efficient exploitation of Earth's resources. Oceanography also is vital to understanding the effect of pollutants on ocean waters and to the preservation of the quality of the oceans' waters in the face of increasing human demands made on them.

Research diver deploying self-contained instrument package. Courtesy of National Oceanic and Atmospheric Administration

ANCIENT OCEANOGRAPHY

The only substance known to the ancient philosophers in its solid, liquid, and gaseous states, water is prominently featured in early theories about the origin and operations of Earth. Thales of Miletus (*c.* 624–*c.* 545 BCE) is credited with a belief that water is the essential substance of the planet, and Anaximander of Miletus (*c.* 610–545 BCE) held that water was probably the source of life. In the system proposed by Empedocles of Agrigentum (*c.* 490–430 BCE), water shared the primacy Thales had given it with three other elements: fire, air, and earth. The doctrine of the four earthly elements was later embodied in the universal system of Aristotle and thereby influenced Western scientific thought until late in the 17th century.

THE DISCOVERY OF THE HYDROLOGIC CYCLE

The idea that the waters of Earth undergo cyclical motions, changing from seawater to vapour to precipitation and then flowing back to the ocean, is probably older than any of the surviving texts that hint at or frame it explicitly.

The idea of the hydrological cycle developed independently in China as early as the 4th century BCE and was explicitly stated in the *Lüshi chunqiu* ("The Spring and Autumn [Annals] of Mr. Lü"), written in the 3rd century BCE. A circulatory system of a different kind, involving movements of water on a large scale within Earth, was envisioned by Plato (*c.* 428–348/347 BCE). In one of his two explanations for the origin of rivers and springs, he described Earth as perforated by passages connecting with Tartarus, a vast subterranean reservoir.

A coherent theory of precipitation is found in the writings of Aristotle. Moisture on Earth is changed to airy vapour by heat from above. Because it is the nature of heat to rise, the heat in the vapour carries it aloft. When the heat begins to leave the vapour, the vapour turns to water. The formation of water from air produces clouds. Heat remaining in the clouds is further opposed by the cold inherent in the water and is driven away. The cold presses the particles of the cloud closer together, restoring in them the true nature of the element water. Water naturally moves downward, and so it falls from the cloud as raindrops. Snow falls from clouds that have frozen.

In Aristotle's system the four earthly elements were not stable but could change into one another. If air can change to water in the sky, it should also be able to change into water underground.

THE INITIAL STUDIES OF THE TIDES

The tides of the Mediterranean, being inconspicuous in most places, attracted little notice from Greek and Roman naturalists. Poseidonius (135–50 BCE) first correlated variations in the tides with phases of the Moon. By contrast, the tides along the eastern shores of Asia generally have a considerable range and were the subject of close observation and much speculation among the Chinese. In particular, the tidal bore on the Qiantang River near Hangzhou attracted early attention; with its front ranging up to 3.7 metres (12.1 feet) in height, this bore is one of the largest in the world. As early as the 2nd century BCE, the Chinese had recognized a connection between tides and tidal bores and the lunar cycle.

EARLY OCEANOGRAPHY

The groundwork for early ocean science can be attributed to Henry the Navigator, the 15th-century Portuguese prince whose school of oceanography at Sagres, Port.,

Areas reached by explorers under the sponsorship of Henry the Navigator.

provided training for hundreds of seamen and advanced substantially the fields of ship design, simulation, and instrumentation. In addition, the idea that there is a circulatory system within Earth, by which seawater is conveyed to mountaintops and there discharged, persisted until early in the 18th century.

Two questions left unresolved by this theory were acknowledged even by its advocates. How is seawater forced uphill? How is the salt lost in the process?

THE RISE OF SUBTERRANEAN WATER

René Descartes supposed that the seawater diffused through subterranean channels into large caverns below the tops of mountains. The Jesuit philosopher Athanasius Kircher in his *Mundus subterraneus* (1664; "Subterranean World") suggested that the tides pump seawater through hidden channels to points of outlet at springs. To explain the rise of subterranean water beneath mountains, the chemist Robert Plot appealed to the pressure of air, which forces water up the insides of mountains. The idea of a great subterranean sea connecting with the ocean and supplying it with water together with all springs and rivers was resurrected in 1695 in John Woodward's *Essay Towards a Natural History of the Earth and Terrestrial Bodies*.

The French Huguenot Bernard Palissy maintained, to the contrary, that rainfall is the sole source of rivers and springs. In his *Discours admirables* (1580; *Admirable Discourses*) he described how rainwater falling on mountains enters cracks in the ground and flows down along these until, diverted by some obstruction, it flows out on the surface as springs. Palissy scorned the idea that seawater courses in veins to the tops of mountains. For this to be true, sea level would have to be higher than mountaintops—an impossibility. In his *Discours* Palissy suggested that water would rise above the level at which it was first encountered in a well provided the source of the groundwater came from a place higher than the bottom of the well. This is an early reference to conditions essential to the occurrence of artesian water, a popular subject among Italian hydrologists of the 17th and 18th centuries.

In the latter part of the 17th century, Pierre Perrault and Edmé Mariotte conducted hydrologic investigations in the basin of the Seine River that established that the local annual precipitation was more than ample to account for the annual runoff.

Evaporation from the Sea

The question remained as to whether the amount of water evaporated from the sea is sufficient to account for the precipitation that feeds the streams. The English astronomer-mathematician Edmond Halley measured the rate of evaporation from pans of water exposed to the air during hot summer days. Assuming that this same rate would obtain for the Mediterranean, Halley calculated that some 5.28 billion tons of water are evaporated from this sea during a summer day. Assuming further that each of the nine major rivers flowing into the Mediterranean has a daily discharge 10 times that of the Thames, he calculated that a daily inflow of fresh water back into that sea would be 1.827 billion tons, only slightly more than a third of the amount lost by evaporation. Halley went on to explain what happens to the remainder. A part falls back into the sea as rain before it reaches land. Another part is taken up by plants.

In the course of the hydrologic cycle, Halley reasoned, the rivers constantly bring salt into the sea in solution, but the salt is left behind when seawater evaporates to replenish the streams with rainwater. Thus the sea must be growing steadily saltier.

OCEANOGRAPHY IN THE 19TH CENTURY

Modern efforts to study systematically the physical and biological properties of the Atlantic began in earnest during the 1800s and were notable for several pioneering research expeditions, the results of which form the basis for present-day scientific understanding of the oceans. While crude sampling and inaccurate measurement techniques led to numerous misconceptions during this time, the period also marked the advent of large-scale, multiyear scientific expeditions.

Incremental advances in both oceanographic theory and technique evolved from early interdisciplinary studies of Atlantic processes. As early as 1770, the American Benjamin Franklin published the first good map of the Gulf Stream, based on data collected by Timothy Folger from the logs of transatlantic mail ships. The work of the American naval officer Matthew Fontaine Maury in the 1840s and '50s paved the way for generations of future

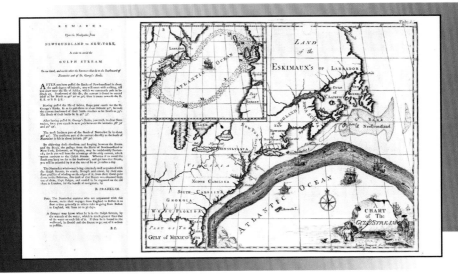

Map of the Gulf Stream drawn by Benjamin Franklin. Library of Congress, Washington, D.C.

researchers. His exhaustive calculations of Atlantic winds and currents, as well as his early seafloor maps, were the beginning of modern oceanography in the United States.

In 1807 Thomas Jefferson ordered the establishment of the U.S. Coast Survey (later Coast and Geodetic Survey and now the National Ocean Survey). Modeled after British and French agencies that had grown up in the 1700s, the agency was charged with the responsibilities of hydrographic and geodetic surveying, studies of tides, and preparation of charts. Beginning in 1842, the U.S. Navy undertook expansive oceanographic operations through its office of charts and instruments. Lieut. Matthew Fontaine Maury promoted international cooperation in gathering meteorologic and hydrologic data at sea. In 1847 Maury compiled the first wind and current charts for the North Atlantic and in 1854 issued the first depth map to 4,000 fathoms (7,300 metres). His *Physical Geography of the Sea* (1855) is generally considered the first oceanographic textbook.

The voyage of the *Beagle* (1831–36) is remembered for Darwin's biological and geologic contributions. From his observations in the South Pacific, Darwin formulated a theory for the origin of coral reefs, which with minor changes has stood the test of time. He viewed the fringing reefs, barrier reefs, and atolls as successive stages in a developmental sequence. The volcanic islands around which the reef-building organisms are attached slowly sink, but at the same time the shallow-water organisms that form the reefs build their colonies upward so as to remain in the sunlit layers of water. With submergence of the island, what began as a fringing reef girdling a land-mass at last becomes an atoll enclosing a lagoon.

The advent of the telegraph and the dream of a trans-atlantic cable required improved knowledge of bathymetry (measurement of ocean depth), currents, topography, and bottom sediments. British and American naval ships were instrumental in conducting hydrographic surveys in support of the early attempts to lay a transatlantic cable; the first successful cable was laid in 1866. A watershed expedition made by HMS *Challenger* in 1872–76 generated thousands of observations in the Atlantic and other ocean basins, culminating in the publication of 50 volumes of data on currents, water depth, temperature, ocean sediments, and animal and plant species. Other important contributions of the late 19th and early 20th centuries include those of Albert I of Monaco and of many Scandinavians, including Bjørn Helland-Hansen and V. Walfrid Ekman. Prince Albert financed a fleet of oceanographic vessels whose efforts led to improved understanding of North Atlantic currents and to the discovery of many new species of mid-depth fishes.

Laying telegraphic cables across the Atlantic called for investigations of the configuration of the ocean floor, of the currents that sweep the bottom, and of the benthonic animals that might damage the cables. The explorations of the British ships *Lightning* and *Porcupine* in 1868 and 1869 turned up surprising oceanographic information. Following closely upon these voyages, the *Challenger* was authorized to determine "the conditions of the Deep Sea throughout the Great Ocean Basins."

The *Challenger* left port in December of 1872 and returned in May 1876, after logging 127,600 km (68,890 nautical miles). Under the direction of Wyville Thomson, Scottish professor of natural history, it occupied 350 stations scattered over all oceans except the Arctic. The work involved in analyzing the information gathered during the expedition was completed by Thomson's shipmate Sir John Murray, and the results filled 50 large volumes. Hundreds of new species of marine organisms were described, including new forms of life from deep waters. The temperature of water at the bottom of the oceans was found to be nearly constant below the 2,000-fathom level, averaging about 2.5 °C (36.5 °F) in the North Atlantic and 2 °C (35 °F) in the North Pacific. Soundings showed wide variations in depths of water, and from the dredgings of the bottom came new types of sediment—red clay as well as oozes made predominantly of the minute skeletons of foraminifera, radiolarians, or diatoms. Improved charts of the principal surface currents were produced, and the precise location of many oceanic islands was determined for the first time. Seventy-seven samples of seawater were taken at different stations from depths ranging downward to about 1.5 km (0.9 mile). The German-born chemist Wilhelm Dittmar conducted quantitative determinations of the seven major constituents (other than the hydrogen and oxygen of the water itself)—namely, sodium, calcium, magnesium, potassium, chloride, bromide, and sulfate. Surprisingly, the percentages of these components turned out to be nearly the same in all samples.

Efforts to analyze the rise and fall of the tides in mathematical terms reflecting the relative and constantly changing positions of Earth, Moon, and Sun, and thus to predict the tides at particular localities, has never been entirely successful because of local variations in configuration of shore and seafloor. Nevertheless, harmonic tidal analysis gives essential first approximations that are essential to tidal prediction. In 1884 a mechanical analog tidal prediction device was invented by William Ferrel of the U.S. Coast and Geodetic Survey, and improved models were used until 1965, when the work of the analog machines was taken over by electronic computers.

OCEANOGRAPHY IN THE 20TH CENTURY

The science of oceanography in the 20th century saw advancements in the understanding of ocean circulation, the measurement of ocean depth (bathymetry), the recognition of the limits of Earth's water resources, and the continued development of the ocean's economic resources. New innovations included the development of desalinization techniques, tidal power, and new methods to extract mineral, oil, and natural gas resources.

A few critical developments early in the century set the stage for later oceanographic investigation. The disaster in 1912 of the *Titanic* catalyzed research efforts concerned with iceberg flows and current patterns in the North Atlantic, accelerated the development of both radio and sonar, and led to the establishment of the International Ice Patrol. In the field of marine communications, the Italian Guglielmo Marconi was demonstrating his new invention—wireless radio—in Europe and the United States during this period, having used it in 1899 to report from sea the results of the America's Cup yacht races. In 1925–27 a series of scientific voyages by the research vessel *Meteor* established Germany as a leader in marine research. Operating in the waters of the South Atlantic, the *Meteor* traversed the basin 14 times, mapping the seafloor by means of sonar and measuring salinity and temperature distributions at various depths.

Ocean Circulation, Currents, and Waves

Results of many investigations suggest that the forces that drive the ocean currents originate at the interface between water and air. The direct transfer of momentum from the atmosphere to the sea is doubtless the most important driving force for currents in the upper parts of the ocean. Next in importance are differential heating, evaporation, and precipitation across the air-sea boundary, altering the density of seawater and thus initiating movement of water masses with different densities. Studies of the properties and motion of water at depth have shown that strong currents also exist in the deep sea and that distinct types of water travel far from their geographic sources. For example, the highly saline water of the Mediterranean that flows through the Strait of Gibraltar has been traced over a large part of the Atlantic, where it forms a deepwater stratum that is circulated far beyond that ocean in currents around Antarctica.

Improvements in devices for determining the motion of seawater in three dimensions have led to the discovery of new currents and to the disclosure of unexpected complexities in the circulation of the oceans generally. In 1951 a huge countercurrent moving eastward across the Pacific was found below depths as shallow as 20 metres (about 66 feet), and in the following year an analogous equatorial undercurrent was discovered in the Atlantic. In 1957 a deep countercurrent was detected beneath the Gulf

Stream with the aid of subsurface floats emitting acoustic signals.

Since the 1970s Earth-orbiting satellites have yielded much information on the temperature distribution and thermal energy of ocean currents such as the Gulf Stream. Chemical analyses from Geosecs makes possible the determination of circulation paths, speeds, and mixing rates of ocean currents.

Surface waves of the ocean are also exceedingly complex, at most places and times reflecting the coexistence and interferences of several independent wave systems. During World War II, interest in forecasting wave characteristics was stimulated by the need for this critical information in the planning of amphibious operations.

A scientist reviews data at the Tsunami Early Warning Centre in Hyderabad, India. Tsunamis are the most destructive of ocean waves. AFP/ Getty Images

The oceanographers H.U. Sverdrup and Walter Heinrich Munk combined theory and empirical relationships in developing a method of forecasting "significant wave height"—the average height of the highest third of the waves in a wave train. Subsequently this method was improved to permit wave forecasters to predict optimal routes for mariners.

Forecasting of the most destructive of all waves, tsunamis caused by submarine quakes and volcanic eruptions, is another recent development. Soon after 159 persons were killed in Hawaii by the tsunami of 1946, the U.S. Coast and Geodetic Survey established a seismic sea-wave warning system. Using a seismic network to locate epicentres of submarine quakes, the installation predicts the arrival of tsunamis at points around the Pacific basin often hours before the arrival of the waves.

Ocean Bathymetry

Modern bathymetric charts show that about 20 percent of the surfaces of the continents are submerged to form continental shelves. Altogether the shelves form an area about the size of Africa. Continental slopes, which slant down from the outer edges of the shelves to the abyssal plains of the seafloor, are nearly everywhere furrowed by submarine canyons. The depths to which these canyons have been cut below sea level seem to rule out the possibility that they are drowned valleys cut by ordinary streams. More likely, the canyons were eroded by turbidity currents, dense mixtures of mud and water that originate as mudslides in the heads of the canyons and pour down their bottoms.

Profiling of the Pacific basin prior to and during World War II resulted in the discovery of hundreds of

BATHYMETRY

Bathymetry is the measurement of ocean depth. The earliest technique involved lowering a heavy rope or cable of known length over the side of a ship, then measuring the amount needed to reach the bottom. Tedious and frequently inaccurate, this method yielded the depth at only a single point rather than a continuous measurement; inaccuracies arose because the rope did not necessarily travel straight to the bottom but instead might be deflected by subsurface currents or movements of the vessel.

A more satisfactory approach, though not without problems, is echo sounding, widely used today, in which a sound pulse travels from the vessel to the ocean floor, is reflected, and returns. By calculations involving the time elapsed between generation of the pulse and its return and the speed of sound in water, a continuous record of seafloor topography can be made. Most echo sounders perform these calculations mechanically, producing a graphic record in the form of a paper chart. Misleading reflections caused by the presence of undersea canyons or mountains plus variations in the speed of sound through water caused by differences in temperature, depth, and salinity limit the accuracy of echo sounding, though these problems can be met somewhat by crossing and recrossing the same area. Sonar has also been employed in bathymetric studies, as have underwater cameras.

isolated eminences rising 1,000 or more metres (about 3,300 feet) above the floor. Of particular interest were seamounts in the shape of truncated cones, whose flat tops rise to between 1.6 km (1 mile) and a few hundred metres below the surface. Harry H. Hess interpreted the flat-topped seamounts (guyots) as volcanic mountains planed off by action of waves before they subsided to their present depths. Subsequent drilling in guyots west of Hawaii confirmed this view; samples of rocks from the tops contained fossils of Cretaceous age representing reef-building organisms of the kind that inhabit shallow water.

WATER RESOURCES AND SEAWATER CHEMISTRY

Quantitative studies of the distribution of water have revealed that an astonishingly small part of Earth's water is contained in lakes and rivers. Ninety-seven percent of all the water is in the oceans, and, of the fresh water constituting the remainder, three-fourths is locked up in glacial ice and most of the rest is in the ground. Approximate figures are also now available for the amounts of water involved in the different stages of the hydrologic cycle. Of the 859 mm (34 inches) of annual global precipitation, 23 percent falls on the lands; but only about a third of the precipitation on the lands runs directly back to the sea, the remainder being recycled through the atmosphere by evaporation and transpiration.

Subsurface groundwater accumulates by infiltration of rainwater into soil and bedrock. Some may run off into rivers and lakes, and some may reemerge as springs or aquifers. Advanced techniques are used extensively in groundwater studies nowadays. The rate of groundwater flow, for example, can be calculated from the breakdown of radioactive carbon-14 by measuring the time it takes for rainwater to pass through the ground, while numerical modeling is used to study heat and mass transfer in groundwater. High-precision equipment is used for measuring down-hole temperature, pressure, flow rate, and water level. Groundwater hydrology is important in studies of fractured reservoirs, subsidence resulting from fluid withdrawal, geothermal resource exploration, radioactive waste disposal, and aquifer thermal-energy storage.

Chemical analyses of trace elements and isotopes of seawater are conducted as part of the Geochemical Ocean Sections (Geosecs) program. Of the 92 naturally occurring elements, nearly 80 have been detected in seawater or in the organisms that inhabit it, and it is thought to be only a matter of time until traces of the others are detected. Contrary to the idea widely circulated in the older literature of oceanography, that the relative proportions of the oceans' dissolved constituents are constant, investigations since 1962 have revealed statistically significant variations in the ratios of calcium and strontium to chlorinity. The role of organisms as influences on the composition of seawater has become better understood with advances in marine biology. It is now known that plants and animals may collect certain elements to concentrations as much as 100,000 times their normal amounts in seawater. Abnormally high concentrations of beryllium, scandium, chromium, and iodine have been found in algae; of copper and arsenic in both the soft and skeletal parts of invertebrate animals; and of zirconium and cerium in plankton.

DESALINIZATION, TIDAL POWER, AND MINERALS FROM THE SEA

For ages a source of food and common salt, the sea is increasingly becoming a source of water, chemicals, and energy. In 1967 Key West, Fla., became the first U.S. city to be supplied solely by water from the sea, drawing its supplies from a plant that produces more than 7,570,000 litres (about 2 million gallons) of refined water daily.

Many ambitious schemes for using tidal power have been devised. The first major hydrographic project of this kind was not completed until 1967, when a dam and electrical generating equipment were installed across the Rance River in Brittany.

The seafloor and the strata below the continental shelves are also sources of mineral wealth. Magnesia was

MARINE GEOLOGY

Marine geology, which is also called geologic oceanography, is the scientific discipline that is concerned with all geological aspects of the continental shelves and slopes and the ocean basins. In practice, the principal focus of marine geology has been on marine sedimentation and on the interpretation of the many bottom samples that have been obtained through the years. The advent of the concept of seafloor spreading in the 1960s, however, broadened the scope of marine geology considerably. Many investigations of mid-oceanic ridges, remanent magnetism of rocks on the seafloor, geochemical analyses of deep brine pools, and of seafloor spreading and continental drift may be considered within the general realm of marine geology.

extracted from the Mediterranean in the late 19th century; at present nearly all the magnesium metal used in the United States is mined from the sea at Freeport, Texas. Concretions of manganese oxide, evidently formed in the process of subaqueous weathering of volcanic rocks, have been found in dense concentrations with a total abundance of 10^{11} tons. In addition to the manganese, these concretions contain copper, nickel, cobalt, zinc, and molybdenum. To date, oil and gas have been the most valuable products to be produced from beneath the sea.

UNDERSEA EXPLORATION

Undersea exploration is the investigation and description of the ocean waters and the seafloor and of layers of rock beneath. The study of the physical and chemical properties of seawater, the various forms of life in the sea, and the geological and geophysical features of Earth's crust are topics typically included within the scope of this endeavour.

Researchers in the field define and measure such properties; prepare maps in order to identify patterns; and utilize these maps, measurements, and theoretical models to achieve a better grasp of how Earth works as a whole. This knowledge enables scientists to predict, for example, long-term weather and climatic changes and leads to more efficient exploration and exploitation of Earth's resources, which in turn result in better management of the environment in general.

The multidisciplinary expedition of the British ship *Challenger* in 1872–76 was the first major undersea survey. Although its main goal was to search for deep-sea life by means of net tows and dredging, the findings of its physical and chemical studies expanded scientific knowledge of temperature and salinity distribution of the open seas. Moreover, depth measurements by wire soundings were carried out all over the globe during the expedition.

Since the time of the *Challenger* voyage, scientists have learned much about the mechanics of the ocean, what it contains, and what lies below its surface. Investigators have produced global maps showing the distribution of surface winds as well as of heat and rainfall, which all work together to drive the ocean in its unceasing motion. They have discovered that storms at the surface can penetrate deep into the ocean and, in fact, cause deep-sea sediments to be rippled and moved. Recent studies also have revealed that storms called eddies occur within the ocean itself and that such a climatic anomaly as El Niño is caused by an interaction of the ocean and the atmosphere.

Other investigations have shown that the ocean absorbs large amounts of carbon dioxide and hence plays a major role in delaying its buildup in the atmosphere. Without the moderating effect of the ocean, the steadily increasing input of carbon dioxide into the atmosphere (due to the extensive burning of coal, oil, and natural gas) would result in the rapid onset of the so-called greenhouse effect—i.e., a warming of Earth caused by the absorption and reradiating of infrared energy to the terrestrial surface by carbon dioxide and water vapour in the air.

The field of marine biology has benefitted from the development of new sampling methods. Among these, broad ranging acoustical techniques have revealed diverse fish populations and their distribution, while direct, close up observation made possible by deep-sea submersibles has resulted in the discovery of unusual (and unexpected) species and phenomena.

In the area of geology, undersea exploration of the topography of the seafloor and its gravitational and magnetic properties has led to the recognition of global patterns of continental plate motion. These patterns form the basis of the concept of plate tectonics, which synthesized earlier hypotheses of continental drift and seafloor spreading. As noted earlier, this concept not only revolutionized scientific understanding of Earth's dynamic features (e.g., seismic activity, mountain-building, and volcanism) but also yielded discoveries of economic and political impact. Earth scientists found that the mid-ocean centres of seafloor spreading also are sites of important metal deposits. The hydrothermal circulations associated with these centres produce sizable accumulations of metals important to the world economy, including zinc, copper, lead, silver, and gold. Rich deposits of manganese, cobalt, nickel, and other commercially valuable metals have been found in nodules distributed over the entire ocean floor. The latter discovery proved to be a major factor in the establishment of the Convention of the Law of the Sea (1982), which calls for the sharing of these resources among developed and developing nations alike. Exploitation of these findings awaits only the introduction of commercially viable techniques for deep-sea mining and transportation.

BASIC ELEMENTS OF UNDERSEA EXPLORATION

Undersea exploration relies on accurate navigation and the use of scientific platforms that operate far from land. Although aircraft, ships, and other vehicles may be used to transport researchers to and from study sites, they can also deploy sensors, tools, and other types of scientific equipment. Some aircraft and ships can even serve as mobile laboratories. It should be noted that exploration of any kind is useful only when the location of the discoveries can be noted precisely. Thus, navigation has always been a key to undersea exploration.

PLATFORMS

Undersea exploration of any kind must be conducted from platforms, in most cases, ships, buoys, aircraft, or satellites. Typical oceanographic vessels capable of carrying out a full complement of underwater exploratory activities range in size from about 50 to 150 metres (about 160 to 500 feet). They support scientific crews of 16 to 50 persons and generally permit a full spectrum of interdisciplinary studies. One example of a research vessel of this kind is the *Melville*, operated by the Scripps Institution of Oceanography. It has a displacement of 2,075 tons and can carry 25 scientists in addition to 25 crew members. It is powered by a dual cycloidal propulsion system, which provides remarkable manoeuvrability.

The *JOIDES Resolution*, operated by Texas A & M University for the Joint Oceanographic Institutions for Deep Earth Sampling, represents a major advance in research vessels. A converted commercial drill ship, it measures 145 metres (475 feet) in length, has a displacement of 18,600 tons, and is equipped with a derrick that extends 62 metres (about 200 feet) above the waterline. A computer-controlled dynamic positioning system enables the ship to remain over a specific location while drilling in water to depths as great as 8,300 metres (about 27,200 feet). The drilling system of the

JOIDES Resolution, *a deep-sea drilling vessel that uses a computer-controlled, acoustic dynamic positioning system to maintain location over the drilling site. The derrick is visible amidships.* Courtesy of Ocean Drilling Program, Texas A & M University

ship is designed to collect cores from below the ocean floor; it can handle 9,200 metres (30,200 feet) of drill pipe. The vessel thus can sample most of the ocean floor, including the bottoms of deep ocean basins and trenches. The *JOIDES Resolution* has other notable capabilities. It can operate in waves as high as 8 metres (about 26 feet), winds up to 23 metres (75 feet) per second, and currents as strong as 1.3 metres (4.3 feet) per second. It has been outfitted for use in ice so that it can conduct drilling operations in high latitudes. The ship can accommodate 50 scientists as well as the crew and drilling team, and its geophysical laboratories total nearly 930 square metres (about 10,000 square feet).

Other specialized vessels include the deep submergence research vehicle known as *Alvin*, which can carry a pilot and two scientific observers to a depth of 4,000 metres (about 13,100 feet). The manoeuvrability of the *Alvin* was pivotal to the discoveries of the mineral deposits at the mid-ocean seafloor spreading centres and of previously unknown biological communities living at those sites. Another versatile vessel is the Floating Instrument Platform (FLIP). It is a long narrow platform that is towed in a horizontal position to a research site. Once on location, the ballast tanks are flooded to flip the ship to a vertical position. Only 17 metres (56 feet) of the ship extend above the waterline, with the remaining 92 metres (about 300 feet) completely submerged. The rise and fall of the waves cause a very small change in the displacement, resulting in a high degree of stability.

New ship designs that promise even greater stability and ease of use include that of the Small Waterplane Area Twin Hull (SWATH) variety. This design type requires the use of twin submerged, streamlined hulls to support a structure that rides above the water surface. The deck shape is entirely unconstrained by the hull shape, as is the case for conventional surface vessels. Ship motion is greatly reduced because of the depth of the submerged hulls. For a given displacement, a SWATH-type vessel can provide twice the amount of deck space that a single-hull ship can, with only 10 percent of the motion of the single-hull design type. In addition, a large centre opening, or well, can be used to display and recover instruments.

Navigation

There are various ways by which the position of a vessel at sea can be determined. In cases where external references such as stars or radio and satellite beacons are unavailable or undetectable, inertial navigation, which relies on a stable gyroscope for determining position, is commonly employed. It is far more accurate than the long-used technique of dead reckoning, which is dependent on a knowledge of the ship's original position and the effects of the winds and ocean currents on the vessel.

Another modern position-fixing method is all-weather, long-range radio navigation. It was introduced during World War II as Loran (long-range navigation) A, a system that determines position by measuring the difference in the time of reception of synchronized pulses from widely spaced transmitting stations. The latest version of this system, Loran C, uses low-frequency transmissions and derives its high degree of accuracy from precise time-difference measurements of the pulsed signals and the inherent stability of signal propagation. Users of Loran C are able to identify a position with an accuracy of 0.4 km (0.25 mile) and a repeatability of 15 metres (about 50 feet) at a distance of up to about 2,220 km (about 1,400 miles) from the reference stations. The Loran C system covers heavily travelled regions in the North Pacific and North Atlantic oceans, parts of the Indian Ocean, and the Mediterranean Sea.

DEAD RECKONING

Dead reckoning is the determination without the aid of celestial navigation of the position of a ship or aircraft from the record of the courses sailed or flown, the distance made (which can be estimated from velocity), the known starting point, and the known or estimated drift.

Some marine navigators differentiate between the dead-reckoning position, for which they use the course steered and their estimated speed through the water, and the estimated position, which is the dead-reckoning position corrected for effects of current, wind, and other factors. Because the uncertainty of dead reckoning increases over time and maybe over distance, celestial observations are taken intermittently to determine a more reliable position (called a fix), from which a new dead reckoning is begun. Dead reckoning is also embedded in Kalman filtering techniques, which mathematically combine a sequence of navigation solutions to obtain the best estimate of the navigator's current position, velocity, attitude angles, and so forth.

A number of devices used for the determination of dead reckoning—such as a plotter (a protractor attached to a straightedge) and computing charts, now chiefly used by operators of smaller vehicles—have been replaced in most larger aircraft and military vessels by one or more dead-reckoning computers, which input direction and speed (wind velocity can be manually inserted). Some of these computers include an inertial guidance system or have a unit that measures Doppler effects, and some can be programmed to pick up signals from electronic or optical sensing units. The use of more than one such device tends to increase reliability.

Satellite navigation has proved to be the most accurate method of locating geographical position. A polar-orbiting satellite system called Transit was established in the early 1960s by the United States to provide global coverage for ships at sea. In this system, a vessel pinpoints its position relative to a set of satellites whose orbits are known by measuring the Doppler shift of a received signal—i.e., the change in the frequency of the received signal from that of the transmitted signal. The Transit system suffers from one major drawback. Because of the limited number of system satellites, the frequency with which position determinations can be made each day is relatively low, particularly in the tropics. The system is being improved to provide nearly continuous positioning capability at sea. This expanded version, the Global Positioning System (GPS), is to have 18 satellites, six in each of three orbital planes spaced 120° apart. The GPS is designed to provide fixes anywhere on Earth to an accuracy of 20 metres (about 66 feet) and a relative accuracy 10 times greater.

METHODOLOGY AND INSTRUMENTATION

The physical, chemical, and biological study of the oceans requires the development of sampling techniques and equipment tailored to the demands of marine environments. Water samplers and chemical analyzers are typically used to study the chemistry of seawater, and acoustic and other types of remote sensors are often used for bathymetry. Although remote-sensing equipment is also used to study marine life and the geologic formations of ocean basins, sometimes researchers must collect samples with nets, dredges, and other tools in order to bring these objects of study to the surface for closer inspection.

WATER SAMPLING FOR TEMPERATURE AND SALINITY

The temperature, chemical environment, and movement and mixing of seawater are fundamental to understanding the physical, chemical, and biological features of the ocean and the geology of the ocean floor. Traditionally, oceanographers have collected seawater by means of specially adapted water-sampling bottles. The most universal water sampler used today, the Nansen bottle, is a modification of a type developed in the latter part of the 19th century by the Norwegian Arctic explorer and oceanographer Fridtjof Nansen. It is a metal sampler equipped with special closing valves that are actuated when the bottle, attached by one end to a wire that carries it to the desired depth, rotates about that end. A mercury thermometer fastened to the bottle records the temperature at the specified depth. The design of the device is such that, when it is inverted, its mercury column breaks. The amount of mercury remaining in the graduated capillary portion of the thermometer indicates the temperature at the point of inversion. This type of reversing thermometer and the Nansen bottle are extensively used by oceanographers because of their accuracy and dependability in a harsh environment.

The temperature and salinity of the ocean have been mapped with data gathered by many ships over many years. This information is used for tracing heat and water movement and mixing, as well as for making density measurements, which are employed in calculating ocean currents. It was noted as early as the *Challenger* Expedition that the salt dissolved in seawater has remarkably constant major constituents. As a consequence, it is possible to map water density patterns within the sea with measurements of only the water temperature and one major property of the sea salt (e.g., the chloride ion content or the electrical conductivity) to arrive at an accurate estimate of the density of a given sample.

Standard laboratory techniques such as titration are routinely used at sea for determining chlorinity. Chlorinity can be briefly defined as the number of grams of chlorine, bromine, and iodine contained in 1 kg (2.2 pounds) of seawater, assuming that the bromine and iodine are replaced by chlorine. Salinity is the total weight of dissolved solids, in grams, found in 1 kg of seawater and may be determined from the concentration of chlorinity because of the constancy of major constituents. In the traditional technique, a solution of silver nitrate of a known strength is added to a sample of seawater to produce the same reaction as with "standard" seawater. The difference in the amounts added gives the degree of chlorinity. To ensure worldwide uniformity in chlorinity and salinity determinations, the International Council for the Exploration of the Sea prepared a universal reference, *Eau de Mer Normale* ("Standard Seawater"), in 1902. A new primary standard, prepared in 1937 and having a chlorinity of 19.381 parts per 1,000, is used to determine the chlorinities of all batches of standard seawater. It also is utilized to calibrate electrical conductivity measurements.

Accurate and continuous measurements of temperature as it changes with depth are required for understanding how the ocean moves and mixes heat. To provide the necessary detail, temperature profilers had to be developed; then, with the introduction of reliable conductivity sensors, salinity profilers were added. An instrument called the bathythermograph (BT), which has been used since the early 1940s to obtain a graphic record of water temperature at various depths, can be lowered from a ship while it is moving at reduced speed. In this instrument a depth element (pressure-operated bellows) drives a slide of smoked glass or metal at right angles to a stylus. Actuated by a thermal element (liquid-filled bourdon tube) that expands and contracts in response to changes in temperature, the stylus scribes a continuous record of temperature and depth.

An expendable bathythermograph (XBT) was developed during the 1970s and has come into increasingly wider use. Unlike the BT, this instrument requires an electrical system aboard the research platform. It detects temperature variations by means of a thermistor (an electrical resistance element made of a semiconductor material) and depends on a known fall rate for depth determination. The sensor unit of the XBT is connected to the research platform by a leak-proof, insulated two-conductor cable. This cable is wound around a pair of large spools in an arrangement resembling that of a fisherman's spinning reel. In operation, the cable is unwound from each of the spools in a direction that is parallel to the axis of the respective spool. As a result, the cable unwinds from both the platform—either a ship or an airplane—and the sensor unit simultaneously but independently. Because of this double-spool arrangement, the sensor unit can free-fall from wherever it hits the sea surface and is completely unaffected by the direction or speed of the craft from which it was deployed. One of the principal reasons why the XBT has proved so useful is that it can provide a record of considerable depth even when it is deployed from a ship moving at full speed.

Until the late 1950s, salinity was universally determined by titration. Since then, shipboard electrical conductivity systems have become widely used. Salinity-Temperature-Depth (STD) and the more recent Conductivity-Temperature-Depth (CTD) systems have greatly improved on-site hydrographic sampling methods. They have enabled oceanographers to learn much about small-scale temperature and salinity distributions.

The most recent version of the CTD systems features rapid-response conductivity and temperature sensors. The conductivity sensor consists of a tiny cell with four platinum electrodes. This type of conductivity cell virtually eliminates errors resulting from the polarization that occurs where the electrodes come in contact with seawater. The temperature sensor combines a tiny thermistor with a platinum-resistance thermometer. Its operations are carried out in such a way as to fully exploit the fast response of the thermistor and the high accuracy of the platinum thermometer. In addition, the system uses a strain gauge as a pressure sensor, the gauge being adjusted to reduce temperature effects to a minimum. This CTD system is extremely reliable. While its temperature precision is greater than 0.001 °C (0.002 °F) over a range of -3 to +32 °C (26.6 to 89.6 °F), its conductivity precision is on the order of one part per million.

Electrical conductivity measurement of seawater salinity has been so effective that it has given rise to a new practical salinity scale, one that is defined on the basis of conductivity ratio. This scale has proved to be a more reliable way of determining density (i.e., the weight of any given volume of seawater at a specified temperature) than the chlorinity scale traditionally used. Such is the case because chlorinity is ion specific while conductivity is sensitive to changes in any ion. Investigators have found that measurements of conductivity ratio make it possible to predict density with a precision almost one order of magnitude greater than was permitted by the chlorinity measurements of the past.

WATER SAMPLING FOR CHEMICAL CONSTITUENTS

Nutrient concentration (e.g., phosphate, nitrate, silicate), the pH (acidity), and the proportion of dissolved gases are used by the ocean chemist to determine the age, origin, and movement of water masses and their effect on marine life. Analysis of dissolved gases, for example, is useful in tracing ocean mixing, in studying gas production in the ocean, and in elucidating the natural cycles of atmospheric pollutants. Many such measurements are conducted aboard ship by autoanalyzers, devices that continually monitor a flow of seawater by spectral techniques. Those analyses that cannot be accomplished by an autoanalyzer are carried out with discrete samples in shipboard or shore-based laboratories.

NANSEN BOTTLE

The Nansen bottle is an ocean-water sampler devised late in the 19th century by the Norwegian oceanographer Fridtjof Nansen and subsequently modified by various workers. The standard Nansen bottle is made of metal and has a capacity of 1.25 litres. It is equipped with plug valves at either end. The bottle is affixed to a winch wire with its valves open, and the winch wire is paid out until the bottle is approximately at its desired sampling depth. A weight, or "messenger," is then allowed to slide down the cable. The upper attachment of the Nansen bottle is disengaged from the cable by the impact of the messenger; and the bottle is reversed end over end, its valves closing in the process to trap the water sample. Thermometers usually are attached to the Nansen bottle to record the temperature and pressure of the sample site. Several Nansen bottles are employed during a single hydrographic cast, each bottle releasing another messenger when tripped, in order to trigger the deeper bottles in turn.

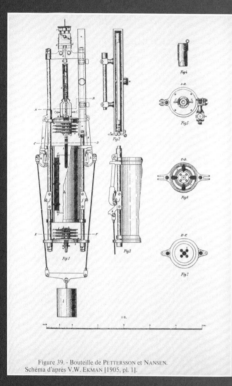

Figure 39. - Bouteille de PETTERSSON et NANSEN. Schéma d'après V.W. EKMAN [1905, pl. 1].

A schematic drawing of the Nansen bottle, one of the first oceanographic water-sampling devices. Oceanographic Museum of Monaco/ National Oceanic and Atmospheric Administration/ Department of Commerce

The Niskin bottle, created by American inventor Shale Niskin in 1966, is more widely used than the Nansen bottle in modern ocean-water sampling activities. Although it is similar to the Nansen bottle in most respects, the Niskin bottle is viewed as an improvement over Nansen's design because of its plastic construction and because it does not require end-over-end movement to collect samples.

Radioactive chemical tracers are of special interest. Radioisotopes serve as time clocks, thus offering a means of determining the age of water masses, the absolute rates of oceanic mixing, and the generation and destruction of plant tissue. The distribution of these time clocks is controlled by the interaction of physical and biological processes, and so these influences must be disentangled before the clocks can be read. A notable example is the use of carbon-14 (^{14}C). Today, a number of oceanographic laboratories make carbon-14 measurements of oceanic dissolved carbon for the study of mixing and transport processes in the deep ocean. Until recently large samples of water—about 200 litres (one litre = 0.264 gallon)— were required for analysis. New techniques use a linear accelerator (a device that greatly increases the velocity of electrically charged atomic and subatomic particles) as a sophisticated mass spectrometer to directly determine abundancy ratios of carbon-14/carbon-13/carbon-12 atoms. The advantage of the newer methodology is that only very small sample amounts—about 250 millilitres (one millilitre = 0.034 fluid ounce)—are required for high accuracy measurements.

MEASUREMENTS OF OCEAN CURRENTS

Ocean currents can be measured indirectly through data on density and directly with current meters. In the indirect technique, water density is computed from temperature and salinity observations, and pressure is then calculated from density. The resulting highs and lows of ocean pressure can be used to estimate ocean currents. The indirect technique establishes currents relative to a particular pressure surface; it is best for large-scale, low-frequency currents.

Direct measurement of currents is used to establish absolute currents and to monitor rapidly varying changes.

In order to measure currents directly, a current meter must accurately record the speed and direction of flow, and the platform or mooring has to be reliable, readily deployable, and extremely sturdy. Researchers are able to make continuous measurements of currents at levels below the surface layer for periods of more than a year.

A typical system for the direct measure of ocean currents has three principal components: a surface or near-surface float; a line consisting of segments of wire and nylon that holds the current meters; and a release mechanism, signalled acoustically, which will drop an anchor when the system is ready to be brought back. A current meter typically employs a rotor equipped with a small direction vane that moves freely in line with the meter.

One of the most important advances in modern instrument design has been the introduction of low-power, solid-state microelectronics. The accuracy of the Vector Averaging Current Meter (VACM), for example, has been improved appreciably by the use of integrated circuits, as has its data-handling capability. Because of the latter, the VACM can sample the direction and speed of currents roughly eight times during each revolution of the rotor. It then computes the north and east components of speed and stores this data, together with direction and time measurements, on a compact cassette recorder. The VACM is capable of making accurate measurements in wave fields as well as from moorings at the ocean surface because of its direct vector-averaging feature.

Currents also can be measured by drifting floats, either at the surface or at a given depth. Tracking the location of the floats is critical. Surface floats can be followed by satellite, but subsurface drifters must be tracked acoustically. A drifter of this sort acts as an acoustical source and transmits signals that can be followed by a ship with hydrophones suspended into the sea. For such tracking, a low sound frequency is crucial because the higher the frequency of sound, the more rapidly is its energy absorbed by the sea. The longest range floats available during the mid-1980s operated at a frequency as low as about 250 hertz. Long-range floats usually drift along channels known as sound fixing and ranging (SOFAR) channels, which occur in various areas of the ocean where a particular combination of temperature and pressure conditions affect the speed of sound. In a sense, the SOFAR channel acts as a type of acoustic waveguide that focusses sound; as a consequence, several watts of sound can be detected as far away as 2,000 km (about 1,200 miles) or so.

Measuring vertical velocity in the ocean posed a major problem for years because of the difficulty of devising a platform that does not move vertically. During the 1960s oceanographers finally came up with a solution: they employed a neutrally buoyant float for measuring vertical velocities. This form of vertical-current meter consists of a cylindrical float on which fins are mounted at an angle. When water moves past the float, it causes the float to turn on its axis. Measurement of the rotation in relation to a compass yields the amount of vertical water movement.

An extension of the neutrally buoyant float is the self-propelled, guided float. One such system, called a Self-Propelled Underwater Research Vehicle (SPURV), manoeuvres below the surface of the sea in response to acoustic signals from the research vessel. It can be used to produce horizontal as well as vertical profiles of various physical properties.

A Doppler-sonar system for measuring upper-ocean current velocity transmits a narrow beam that scatters off drifting plankton and other organisms in the uppermost strata of the ocean. From the Doppler shift of the back-scattered sound, the component of water velocity parallel to the beam can be determined to a range of 1,400 metres (about 5,000 feet) from the transmitter with a precision of 1 cm per 0.1 second (1 cm = 0.394 inch).

Integral to a complete picture of the ocean is a profile of velocity. Various methods have been devised for measuring currents as dependent on and varying with depth or horizontal position. Three techniques have been developed to make such measurements. The first involves acoustically tracking a "sinking float" as it descends toward the seafloor. The second technique entails the use of a free-fall device equipped with a current sensor. The third involves a class of current meter specially designed to move up and down a fixed line attached to a vessel, mooring, or drifting buoy. One such instrument has a roller block that couples the front of the instrument to a wire from the vessel. In this way, the motion of the vessel is decoupled from that of the instrument. Another important component of this instrument is its hull, a structure that not only furnishes buoyancy but also serves as a direction vane. In the bottom of the hull is a device that records velocity, temperature, and depth. The entire system descends at a rate of approximately 10 cm (about 4 inches) per second, resulting in a vertical resolution of several metres for the velocity profile produced.

Acoustic and Satellite Sensing

Remote sensing of the ocean can be done by aircraft and Earth-orbiting satellites or by sending acoustic signals through it. These techniques all offer a more sweeping view of the ocean than can be provided by slow-moving ships and hence have become increasingly important in oceanographic research.

Satellite-borne radar altimeters have proved to be especially useful. A radar system of this type can determine the distance between the satellite and the sea surface to an accuracy of better than 10 cm by measuring the time it takes for a transmitted pulse of radio energy to travel to the surface and return. By combining such a precise distance measurement with information about the satellite's orbit, oceanographers are able to produce maps of sea-surface topography. Moreover, they can deduce the pressure field of the sea surface by combining the distance measurement with knowledge about the geoid. They can in turn extrapolate information about the general circulation of the upper stratum of the ocean from a synoptic view of the surface pressure field.

Another remote-sensing technique involves the use of satellite-borne infrared and microwave radiometers to measure radiant energy released from the surface of the ocean. Such measurements are used to determine sea-surface temperature. High-resolution, infrared images transmitted by polar-orbiting satellites have provided researchers with an effective means of monitoring wave features in ocean currents over a wide area, as, for example, long equatorial waves in the Pacific Ocean and time variations in the flow of the Gulf Stream between Florida and Cape Hatteras, North Carolina.

Acoustic techniques also have many applications in the study of the ocean, particularly of those subsurface processes and physical properties inaccessible to satellite observation. In one such technique, the temperature structure of a water column from a given point on the sea-floor to the surface is studied using an inverted echo sounder. This instrument, which features both an acoustic transmitter and a receiver, measures the time taken by a pulse of sound to travel from the sea bottom to the surface and back again. In most cases, a change in the average temperature of the water column above the instrument causes a fluctuation in the time interval between the transmission and the reception of the acoustic signal.

SONAR

Sonar (from "*so*und *na*vigation *r*anging") is the technique for detecting and determining the distance and direction of underwater objects by acoustic means. Sound waves emitted by or reflected from the object are detected by sonar apparatus and analyzed for the information they contain.

Sonar systems may be divided into three categories. In active sonar systems an acoustic projector generates a sound wave that spreads outward and is reflected back by a target object. A receiver picks up and analyzes the reflected signal and may determine the range, bearing, and relative motion of the target. Passive systems consist simply of receiving sensors that pick up the noise produced by the target (such as a ship, submarine, or torpedo). Waveforms thus detected may be analyzed for identifying characteristics as well as direction and distance. The third category of sonar devices is acoustic communication systems, which require a projector and receiver at both ends of the acoustic path.

Sonar was first proposed as a means of detecting icebergs. Interest in sonar was heightened by the threat posed by submarine warfare in World War I. An early passive system, consisting of towed lines of microphones, was used to detect submarines by 1916, and by 1918 an

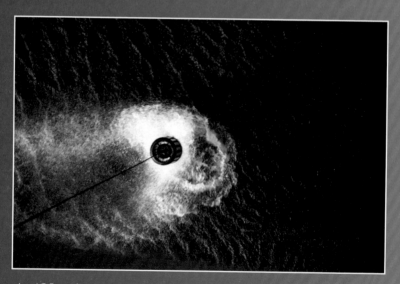

An AQS-13 dipping sonar being deployed in the ocean. C. Yebba/U.S. Navy

operational active system had been built by British and U.S. scientists. Subsequent developments included the echo sounder, or depth detector, rapid-scanning sonar, side-scan sonar, and WPESS (within-pulse electronic-sector-scanning) sonar.

The uses of sonar are now many. In the military field are a large number of systems that detect, identify, and locate submarines. Sonar is also used in acoustic homing torpedoes, in acoustic mines, and in mine detection. Nonmilitary uses of sonar include fish finding, depth sounding, mapping of the sea bottom, Doppler navigation, and acoustic locating for divers.

A major step in the development of sonar systems was the invention of the acoustic transducer and the design of efficient acoustic projectors. These utilize piezoelectric crystals (e.g., quartz or tourmaline), magnetostrictive materials (e.g., iron or nickel), or electrostrictive crystals (e.g., barium titanate). These materials change shape when subjected to electric or magnetic fields, thus converting electrical energy to acoustic energy. Suitably mounted in an oil-filled housing, they produce beams of acoustic energy over a wide range of frequencies.

In active systems the projector may be deployed from an air-launched sonobuoy, hull-mounted on a vessel, or suspended in the sea from a helicopter. Usually the receiving and transmitting transducers are the same. Passive systems are usually hull-mounted, deployed from sonobuoys, or towed behind a ship. Some passive systems are placed on the seabed, often in large arrays, to provide continuous surveillance.

Other acoustic techniques can be utilized to study ocean variables on a large scale. A method known as ocean acoustic tomography, for example, monitors the travel time of sound pulses with an array of echo-sounding systems. In general, the amount of data collected is directly proportional to the product of the number of transmitters and receivers, so that much information on averaged oceanic properties can be gathered within a short period of time at relatively low cost.

COLLECTION OF BIOLOGICAL SAMPLES

Life at the bottom, benthos, is affected by the water column and by the sediment–water interface; the swimmers, or nekton, are influenced by the water that they come in contact with; and the floaters, or plankton— phytoplankton (plant forms) and zooplankton (animal forms)—are influenced by the water and the transfers that occur at the surface of the sea. Thus, in most cases, measurements and sampling of marine life is best done in concert with measurements of the physical and chemical properties of the ocean and the surface effects of the atmosphere.

As a consequence of the close interaction of sea life and its environment, marine biologists and biological oceanographers use most of the techniques mentioned above as well as some specialized techniques for biological sampling. Investigative techniques include the use of sampling devices, remote sensing of surface life-forms by satellite and aircraft, and in situ observation of plants and animals in direct interaction with their environment. The latter is becoming increasingly important as biologists recognize the fragility of organisms and the difficulty of obtaining representative samples. The absence of good sampling techniques means that even today little is known about the distribution, number, and life cycles of many of the important species of marine life.

Some of the most commonly used samplers are plankton nets and midwater trawls. Nets have a mesh size smaller than the plankton under investigation; trawls filter out only the larger forms. The smaller net sizes can be used only when the ship is either stopped or moving ahead slowly; the larger can be used while the ship is travelling at normal speeds. Plankton nets can be used to sample at one or more depths. Qualitative samplers sieve organisms from the water without measuring the volume of water passing through, whereas quantitative samplers measure the volume and hence the concentration of organisms in a unit volume of seawater.

The Clark-Bumpus sampler is a quantitative type designed to take an uncontaminated sample from any desired depth while simultaneously estimating the filtered volume of seawater. It is equipped with a flow meter that monitors the volume of seawater that passes through the net. A shutter opens and closes on demand from the surface, admitting water and spinning the impeller of the meter while catching the plankton. When the impeller is stopped by closing the shutter, the sampler can be raised without contamination from plankton in the waters above.

The midwater trawl is specially designed for rapid collection at depths well below the surface and at such a speed that active, fast-swimming fish are unable to escape from the net once caught. Trawls can be towed at speeds up to 9 km (5.6 miles) per hour. To counteract the tendency of an ordinary net to surface behind the towing vessel, a midwater trawl of the Isaacs-Kidd variety uses an inclined-plane surface rigged in front of the net entrance to act as a depressor. The trawl is shaped like an asymmetrical cone with a pentagonal mouth opening and a round closed end. Within the net, additional netting is attached as lining. A steel ring is fastened at the end of the net to maintain shape. A large perforated can is fastened by drawstrings on the end of the net to retain the sample in relatively undamaged condition.

The use of acoustics to record and measure the distribution of biological organisms is becoming a widely adopted practice. Some organisms can be tracked directly by their distinctive sounds. By recording and analyzing these sounds, biologists are able to chart the behaviour and distribution of such life-forms.

Organisms that passively affect various electronic systems are large mammals, schools of fish, and plankton that either scatter sound and so appear as false targets or background reverberation, or that attenuate the acoustic signal. Some fishes and invertebrates make up layers of acoustic-scattering material, which may exhibit daily vertical movement related to daily changes in light.

Light in the upper layers of the ocean is crucial to maintaining marine life. The penetration and absorption of light and the colour and transparency of the ocean water are indicative of biological activity and of suspended material. In situ measurements of water transparency and absorption include the submarine photometer, the hydrophotometer, and the Secchi disk. The submarine photometer records directly to depths of about 150 metres (about 500 feet) the infrared, visible, and ultraviolet portions of the spectrum. The hydrophotometer has a self-contained light source that allows greater latitude in observation because it can be used at any time of night or day and measures finer gradations of transparency. The Secchi disk, designed to measure water transparency, is a circular white disk that is lowered on a cable into the sea. In practice, the depth at which it is barely visible is noted. The greater the depth reading, the more transparent is the water.

The primary productivity of the ocean, which occurs in the upper layers, can be monitored by continuous measurement of absorption by chlorophyll molecules. This occurs in the red and blue portions of the spectrum, leaving the green to represent the characteristic colour of biological activity. Satellite measurements of ocean colour that span a number of wavelengths in the visible and infrared portions of the spectrum are used to give a large-scale view of the biological activity and suspended material in the ocean.

EXPLORATION OF THE SEAFLOOR AND THE EARTH'S CRUST

The ocean floor has the same general character as the land areas of the world: mountains, plains, channels, canyons, exposed rocks, and sediment-covered areas. The lack of weathering and erosion in most areas, however, allows geological processes to be seen more clearly on the seafloor than on land. Undisturbed sediments, for example, contain a historical record of past climates and the state of the ocean, which has enabled geologists to find a close relation between past climates and the variation of the distance of Earth from the Sun (the Milankovich effect).

Because electromagnetic radiation cannot penetrate any significant distance into the sea, the oceanographer uses acoustic signals, explosives, and earthquakes, as well as gravity and magnetic fields, to probe the seafloor and the structure beneath. Such techniques—which now include the capability to produce a swath, or two-dimensional, description of the seafloor beneath a ship—are providing increasingly accurate data on the shape of the ocean, its roughness, and the structure beneath. Satellite techniques are a more recent development. Because the shape of the sea surface is closely related to that of the seafloor due to gravity, satellite measurements of surface topography have been used to provide a global view of the ocean bottom. They also have provided data for an accurate mapping of such features as seamounts.

Research on marine sedimentation involves the study of deposition, composition, and classification of organic and inorganic materials found on the seafloor. Samples of such materials are thoroughly examined aboard research vessels or in shore-based laboratories, where investigators analyze the size and shape of constituent particles, determine chemical properties such as pH, and identify and categorize the minerals and organisms present. From thousands of reported classifications and collected samples, bottom-sediment charts are prepared.

Various kinds of equipment are used to obtain samples from the seafloor. These include grabbing devices, dredges, and coring devices.

Grabbing devices, commonly known as snappers, vary widely in size and design. One general class of such devices is the clamshell snapper, which is used to obtain small samples of the superficial layers of bottom sediments. Clamshell snappers come in two basic varieties. One measures 76 cm (about 30 inches) in length, weighs roughly 27 kg (60 pounds), and is constructed of stainless steel. The jaws of this device are closed by heavy arms, which are actuated by a strong spring and lead weight. It is capable of trapping about a pint of bottom material. The second type of clamshell snapper is appreciably smaller. Commonly called the mud snapper, this device is approximately 28 cm (11 inches) long and weighs 1.4 kg (3.1 pounds). Other grabbing devices include the orange peel bucket sampler, which is used for collecting bottom materials in shallow waters. A small hook attached to the end of the lowering wire supports the sampler as it is lowered and also holds the jaws open. When contact is made with the bottom, the sampler jaws sink into the sediment and the wire tension is released, allowing the hook to swing free of the sampler. Upon hoisting, the wire takes a strain on the closing line, which closes the jaws and traps a sample. The underway bottom sampler, or scoopfish, is designed to sample rapidly without stopping the ship. It is lowered to depths less than 200 metres (about 660 feet) from a ship moving at speeds no more than 28 km (about 17 miles) per hour. The sampler weighs 5 kg (11 pounds) and can capture samples ranging from mud to coral.

The second major category of bottom sampler is the dredge, which is dragged along the seafloor to collect materials. Bottom-dredging operations require very sturdy gear, particularly when dredging for rock samples. A typical dredge is constructed of steel plate and is 30 cm (12 inches) deep, 60 cm (24 inches) wide, and 90 cm (35 inches) long. The forward end is open, but the aft end has a heavy grill of round steel bars that is designed to retain large rock samples. When finer sized material is sought, a screen of heavy hardware cloth is placed over the grill.

Coring devices typically have three principal components: interchangeable core tubes, a main body of streamlined lead weights, and a tailfin assembly that directs the corer in a vertical line to the ocean bottom. The amount of sediment collected depends on the length of the corer, the size of the main weight, and the penetrability of the bottom. One type of coring device, the lightweight Phleger corer, takes samples only of the upper layer of the ocean bottom to a depth of about 1 metre (3.3 feet). Deeper cores are taken by the piston corer. In this device, a closely fitted piston attached to the end of the lowering cable is installed inside the coring tube. When the coring tube is driven into the ocean floor, friction exerts a downward pull on the core sample. The hydrostatic pressure on the ocean bottom, however, exerts an upward pressure on the core that will work against a vacuum being created between the piston and the top of the core. The piston, in effect, provides a suction that overcomes the frictional forces acting between the sediment sample and the inside of the coring tube. The complete assembly of a typical piston core weighs about 180 kg (about 400 pounds) and can be used to obtain samples as long as 20 metres (about 66 feet). An improved version of this device, the hydraulic piston corer, is used by deep-sea drilling ships such as the *JOIDES Resolution*. Essentially undisturbed cores of lengths up to 200 metres (about 660 feet) have been obtained with this type of corer.

Investigators may also make use of wire-line logging tools that are capable of measuring electrical resistance, acoustic properties, and magnetic and gravitational effects in the holes drilled. The *JOIDES Resolution* is equipped with tools of this sort, including a remote television camera, which are lowered into a drill hole after the core has been removed. Such wire-line logging apparatus make data immediately available for scientific analysis and decision making.

Acoustic techniques have reached a high level of sophistication for geological and geophysical studies. Such multifrequency techniques as those that employ Seabeam and Gloria (Geological Long-Range Inclined Asdic) permit mapping two-dimensional swaths with great accuracy from a single ship. These methods are widely used to ascertain the major features of the seafloor. The Gloria system, for example, can produce a picture of the morphology of a region at a rate of up to 1,000 square km (about 400 square miles) per hour. Techniques of this kind are employed in conjunction with seismic reflection techniques, which involve the use of multichannel receiving arrays to detect sound waves triggered by explosive shots (e.g., dynamite blasts) that are reflected off of interfaces separating rocks of different physical properties. Such techniques make it possible to measure the structure of Earth's crust deep below the seafloor.

CONCLUSION

Covering the majority of Earth's surface, the oceans are the planet's most prominent features, and in many ways, they are among the most important ones. The oceans are critical components of Earth's climate. They are tremendous absorbers of solar energy and dispersers of heat. Ocean currents move masses of warm and cold water from their source regions in an attempt to equilibrate surface heating across the globe. As this water moves, it interacts with processes in the atmosphere that drive temperature and rainfall patterns across the globe.

Life began in the oceans billions of years ago. Since then, the earliest living things have evolved into more and more complex forms. Although some of the descendants of early organisms left the oceans to live on land, many remained. Today, the oceans teem with crustaceans, corals, mollusks, and other invertebrates, as well as fishes, mammals, and other vertebrates. From this bounty, a large number of species are harvested by humans for food.

Like other parts of the living Earth, the oceans are frequently harmed by human activities. Though populations of many fish species have declined due to overharvesting, many other fishes and other marine life face the scourge of pollution. Since Earth's water courses terminate in the oceans, they are often the final resting places for trash and other forms of pollution released into rivers and streams. In addition, the oceans are traversed by large vessels carrying petroleum and other harmful chemicals. When these vessels are damaged or sink, their cargoes may be released into the surrounding water. Oil released from damaged tankers or oil drilling equipment does not sink harmlessly to the ocean floor. It rises to the surface. Driven by wind and waves toward the shorelines of continents and other landmasses, it fouls beaches and coastal wetlands, killing wildlife and threatening the livelihoods of local human residents.

CHAPTER 6
MARINE EXPLORERS AND OCEANOGRAPHERS

The modern scientific understanding of the oceans owes much to the work of oceanographers and marine explorers. Some of the more influential personages include Jacques-Yves Cousteau, noted explorer and inventor of the Aqua-Lung, submersible pioneer Robert Ballard, and celebrated Arctic explorer Fridtjof Nansen.

ALEXANDER AGASSIZ

(b. Dec. 17, 1835, Neuchâtel, Switz.—d. March 27, 1910, at sea),

Swiss-born American marine zoologist, oceanographer, and mining engineer Alexander Emmanuel Rodolphe Agassiz made important contributions to systematic zoology, to the knowledge of ocean beds, and to the development of a major copper mine.

Son of the Swiss naturalist Louis Agassiz, he joined his father in 1849 in the U.S., where he studied engineering and zoology at Harvard University. His early research on echinoderms (e.g., starfish) resulted in his most significant work in the area of systematic zoology, the *Revision of the Echini* (1872–74).

From 1866 to 1869 Agassiz was the superintendent of a copper mine near Lake Superior, at Calumet, Mich.; he eventually became president of the mine, retaining that position until his death, by which time he had changed an initially unprofitable operation into the world's foremost copper mine. Agassiz instituted modern machinery and safety devices, pension and accident funds for miners, and sanitary measures for surrounding communities. He donated large sums to the Harvard Museum, of which he was curator from 1874 to 1885, and to other institutions engaged in advancing the study of biology.

Agassiz opened a private biological laboratory at Newport, R.I., soon after closing his father's experimental school of biology on Penikese Island, off the coast of Massachusetts, following the death of Louis Agassiz (1873). On a trip along the west coast of South America (1875), he discovered a coral reef 3,000 feet above sea level, an observation that

Alexander Agassiz. National Oceanic and Atmospheric Administration

appeared to contradict Charles Darwin's theory of coral-reef formation, in which he postulated a rate of coral formation identical with the rise of sea level. He continued his marine and coral-reef studies for more than 25 years, making expeditions in various waters, including the Caribbean, the South Pacific, and the Great Barrier Reef of Australia.

PRINCE ALBERT I OF MONACO
(b. Nov. 13, 1848, Paris, France—d. June 26, 1922, Paris)

Albert-Honoré-Charles Grimaldi was prince of Monaco from 1889 to 1922. He was also a seaman, an amateur oceanographer, and a patron of the sciences, whose contributions to the development of oceanography included innovations in oceanographic equipment and technique and the founding and endowment of institutions to further basic research.

Albert's love of the sea developed at an early age, and as a young man he served in the Spanish Navy. Later, he conducted his own oceanographic surveys on a series of increasingly large and well-equipped ships. His active involvement in oceanography continued even after he became ruler of Monaco—upon the death of his father, Charles III (1889)—and culminated in his establishment of the Oceanographic Museum of Monaco (1899) and the Oceanographic Institute in Paris (1906).

Albert was succeeded as prince of Monaco by his son, Louis II (1870–1949).

ROBERT BALLARD

(b. June 30, 1942, Wichita, Kan., U.S.)

Robert Duane Ballard is an American oceanographer and marine geologist whose pioneering use of deep-diving submersibles laid the foundations for deep-sea archaeology. He is best known for discovering the wreck of the *Titanic* in 1985.

Ballard grew up in San Diego, California, where he developed a fascination with the ocean. He attended the University of California in Santa Barbara, earning degrees in chemistry and geology in 1965. As a member of the Reserve Officers Training Corps, he entered the army following graduation, serving a two-year tour before requesting a transfer to the navy. In 1967 he was assigned to the Woods Hole (Massachusetts) Oceanographic Research Institution, where he became a full-time marine scientist in 1974 after completing his doctoral degrees in marine geology and geophysics at the University of Rhode Island.

In the early 1970s Ballard helped develop *Alvin*, a three-person submersible equipped with a mechanical arm. In 1973–75 he dived 2,750 metres (9,000 feet) in *Alvin* and in a French submersible to explore the Mid-Atlantic Ridge, an underwater mountain chain in the Atlantic Ocean. In 1977 and 1979 he was part of an expedition that uncovered thermal vents in the Galápagos Rift. The presence of plant and animal life within these deep-sea warm springs led to the discovery of chemosynthesis, the chemical synthesis of food energy.

To advance deep-sea exploration, Ballard designed a series of vessels, most notably the *Argo*, a 5-metre (16-foot) submersible sled equipped with a remote-controlled camera that could transmit live images to a monitor. Ballard called this new technology "telepresence." To test the *Argo*, he searched for the *Titanic*, which had sunk in 1912 and remained undiscovered despite numerous attempts to locate it. Working with the Institut Français de Recherche pour l'Exploitation de la Mer (IFREMER; French Research Institute for the Exploitation of the Sea), Ballard began the mission in August 1985 aboard the U.S. Navy research ship *Knorr*. The *Argo* was sent some 4,000 metres (13,000 feet) to the floor of the North Atlantic, sending video to the monitors on the *Knorr*. On Sept. 1, 1985, the first images of the ocean liner were recorded as its giant boilers were discovered. Later video revealed that the *Titanic* was lying in two pieces, with the hull upright and largely intact. Ballard returned to the site in 1986, traveling to the underwater wreckage in the submersible *Alvin*.

In 1989 Ballard established the JASON project, an educational program that used video and audio satellite feeds and later the Internet to allow students to follow various expeditions. In 1997 Ballard, then a commander in the navy, left Woods Hole to head the Institute for Exploration in Mystic, Conn., a centre for deep-sea archaeology that he founded. In 2002 he joined the faculty of the University of Rhode Island's Graduate School of Oceanography. He continued to search for shipwrecks, and his notable discoveries include ancient vessels and World War II ships, including the *Bismarck* (sunk 1941). A prolific writer, Ballard described his expeditions in a number of books and articles.

JACQUES-YVES COUSTEAU

(b. June 11, 1910, Saint-André-de-Cubzac, France — d. June 25, 1997, Paris)

Jacques-Yves Cousteau was a French naval officer and ocean explorer, known for his extensive underseas investigations.

After graduating from France's naval academy in 1933, he was commissioned a second lieutenant. However, his plans to become a navy pilot were undermined by an almost fatal automobile accident in which both his arms were broken. Cousteau, not formally trained as a scientist, was drawn to undersea exploration by his love both of the ocean and of diving. In 1943 Cousteau and French engineer Émile Gagnan developed the first fully automatic compressed-air Aqua-Lung. Cousteau helped to invent many other tools useful to oceanographers, including the diving saucer (an easily maneuverable small submarine for seafloor exploration) and a number of underwater cameras.

Cousteau served in World War II as a gunnery officer in France and was a member of the French Resistance. He later was awarded the Legion of Honour for his espionage work. Cousteau's experiments with underwater filmmaking began during the war. Cousteau helped found the French navy's Undersea Research Group in 1945. He also was involved in conducting oceanographic research at a centre in Marseille, France. When the war ended, he continued working for the French navy, heading the Undersea Research Group at Toulon.

To expand his work in marine exploration, he founded numerous marketing, manufacturing, engineering, and research organizations, which were incorporated in 1973 as the Cousteau Group. In 1950 Cousteau converted a British minesweeper into the *Calypso*, an oceanographic research ship, aboard which he and his crew carried out numerous expeditions. Cousteau eventually popularized oceanographic research and the sport of scuba diving in the book *Le Monde du silence* (1952; *The Silent World*), written with Frédéric Dumas. Two years later he adapted the book into a documentary film that won both the Palme d'Or at the 1956 Cannes international film festival and an Academy Award in 1957, one of three Oscars his films received.

Also in 1957, Cousteau became director of the Oceanographic Museum of Monaco. He led the Conshelf Saturation Dive Program, conducting experiments in which men live and work for extended periods of time at considerable depths along the continental shelves. The undersea laboratories were called Conshelf I, II, and III.

Cousteau produced and starred in many television programs, including the American series "The Undersea World of Jacques Cousteau" (1968–76). In 1974 he formed the Cousteau Society, a nonprofit environmental group dedicated to marine conservation. In addition to *The Silent World*, Cousteau also wrote *Par 18 mètres de fond* (1946; *Through 18 Metres of Water*), *The Living Sea* (1963), *Three Adventures: Galápagos, Titicaca, the Blue Holes* (1973), *Dolphins*

(1975), and *Jacques Cousteau: The Ocean World* (1985). His last book, *The Human, the Orchid, and the Octopus: Exploring and Conserving Our Natural World* (2007), was published posthumously.

ROBERT S. DIETZ

(b. Sept. 14, 1914, Westfield, N.J., U.S.—d. May 19, 1995, Tempe, Ariz.)

Robert Sinclair Dietz was an American geophysicist and oceanographer who set forth a theory of seafloor spreading in 1961.

Dietz was educated at the University of Illinois (B.S., 1937; M.S., 1939; Ph.D., 1941). After serving as an officer in the U.S. Army Air Corps during World War II, he became a civilian scientist with the U.S. Navy. In this capacity, he supervised the oceanographic research on Admiral Richard E. Byrd's last Antarctic expedition (1946–47). He subsequently served as oceanographer with several organizations, including the U.S. Coast and Geodetic Survey (1958–65) and the Atlantic Oceanography and Meteorology Laboratories (1970–77). He became professor of geology at Arizona State University, Tempe, in 1977.

Dietz's discovery in 1952 of the first fracture zone in the Pacific, which he related to deformation of Earth's crust, led him to hypothesize that new crustal material is formed at oceanic ridges and spreads outward at a rate of several centimetres per year. Subsequent work confirmed this suggestion. He helped to redevelop the bathyscaphe *Trieste* of Swiss engineer Jacques Piccard, who descended about 7 miles (11 km) into the Pacific Ocean in it in 1960. Dietz also became known for his work in the fields of selenography (study of the Moon's physical features) and meteoritics, particularly for his suggestion that certain shock effects in rocks are indicative of meteorite impact.

VAGN WALFRID EKMAN

(b. May 3, 1874, Stockholm, Swed.—d. March 9, 1954, Gostad, near Stockaryd, Swed.)

Swedish physical oceanographer Vagn Walfrid Ekman was best known for his studies of the dynamics of ocean currents. The common oceanographic terms Ekman layer, denoting certain oceanic or atmospheric layers occurring at various interfaces; Ekman spiral, used in connection with vertical oceanic velocity; and Ekman transport, denoting wind-driven currents, derive from his research.

Ekman was the youngest son of Fredrik Laurentz Ekman, a Swedish physical oceanographer. After finishing secondary school in Stockholm, Ekman studied at the University of Uppsala, where he majored in physics. But lectures on hydrodynamics in 1897 by Vilhelm Bjerknes, one of the founders of meteorology and oceanography, definitely decided the direction of Ekman's work.

While still a student at Uppsala, Ekman made important contributions to oceanography. When it was observed, during the Norwegian North Polar Expedition, that drift ice did not follow the wind direction but deviated by 20° to 40°, Bjerknes chose Ekman to make a theoretical study of the problem. In his report, published in 1902, Ekman took into account the balance of the frictions between the wind and sea surface, within layers of water, and the deflecting force due to Earth's rotation (Coriolis force).

After taking his degree at Uppsala in 1902, he joined the staff of the International Laboratory for Oceanographic Research in Oslo, where he remained until 1909. During those years he proved to be a skilled inventor and experimentalist. The Ekman current meter, an instrument with a simple and reliable mechanism, has been used, with subsequent improvements, to the present, while the Ekman reversing water bottle is used in freshwater lakes and sometimes in the ocean to obtain water samples at different depths with a simultaneous measurement of water temperatures. He displayed his theoretical and experimental talents in his study of so-called dead water, which causes slow-moving boats to become stuck because of a thin layer of nearly fresh water spreading over the sea from melting ice. This phenomenon, frequently occurring in fjords, seriously impeded the Norwegian explorer Fridtjof Nansen in Arctic waters. Ekman demonstrated by experiments in a wave tank that the resistance to the motion of the vessels is increased by the waves that are formed at the interface between layers of water of different densities.

He also derived an empirical formula for the mean compressibility (compression ratio divided by pressure) of seawater as a function of pressure and temperature. This formula is still in use today to determine density of deep seawater which is compressed by hydrostatic pressure.

From 1910 to 1939, Ekman was professor of mechanics and mathematical physics at the University of Lund in Sweden, where he pursued his main interest, the dynamics of ocean currents. He published theories on wind-driven ocean currents, including the effects of coasts and bottom topography, and on the dynamics of the Gulf Stream. He also tried, with partial success, to solve the complex problem of ocean turbulence.

In 1925 Ekman participated in a cruise of a German research ship to the Canary Islands. On finding that data on currents obtained for several days at several marine stations between the Bay of Biscay and the Canary Islands were not sufficient to obtain an average figure, he and a colleague, during the years 1922–29, improved the technique for measuring currents for a prolonged period by collecting data from an anchored ship. After several preparatory cruises for that purpose off the Norwegian coast aboard a Norwegian research vessel, they made a cruise to the trade-wind region off northwestern Africa in the summer of 1930 to determine the average current at various ocean depths at stations occupied for two weeks or longer. Preliminary reports were published soon after the cruise, but Ekman wrote the final report in 1953 at the age of 79. The long delay in publication, partly owing to the loss of important data during the German occupation of Norway, also indicates the unparalleled care he took with his work.

Although his name and achievements were well known among oceanographers, he rarely attended international meetings — but his genuine kindliness prevented him from becoming a recluse. Most of his teachers and friends, such as Nansen and Bjerknes, were Norwegian; he spent many vacations in Bergen. He sang a beautiful bass, spent much time at the piano, and occasionally composed music. In the fall of 1953, he began a study of turbid currents, which he continued until a few days before his death.

RICHARD H. FLEMING

(b. Sept. 21, 1909, Victoria, B.C., Can. — d. Oct. 25, 1989, Seattle, Wash., U.S.)

Canadian-born American oceanographer Richard Howell Fleming conducted wide-ranging studies in the areas of chemical and biochemical oceanography, ocean currents (particularly those off the Pacific coast of Central America), and naval uses of oceanography.

Fleming joined the Scripps Institution in La Jolla, Calif., in 1931 and served as assistant director from 1946 to

1950, when he left to become professor of oceanography at the University of Washington.

Fleming measured the amounts of chemical elements in sea water and in marine life. His work on ocean currents included measurement of tidal-current velocities, description of upwelling of seawater, and observations of seasonal variations in currents. He also explored sedimentation in moving and stagnant bodies of water. With H.U. Sverdrup and Martin W. Johnson, Fleming wrote *The Oceans* (1942).

BJØRN HELLAND-HANSEN
(b. Oct. 16, 1877, Christiania, Nor.—d. Sept. 7, 1957, Bergen)

Bjørn Helland-Hansen was a Norwegian pioneer of modern oceanography whose studies of the physical structure and dynamics of the oceans were instrumental in transforming oceanography from a science that was mainly descriptive to one based on the principles of physics and chemistry.

Most of Helland-Hansen's work was done in Bergen, where he was successively director of the Marine Biological Station, professor at the Bergen Museum, and first director of the Geophysical Institute, which was established in 1917 largely through his efforts. He was active in international scientific affairs and in 1945 was elected president of the International Union of Geodesy and Geophysics.

COLUMBUS O'DONNELL ISELIN
(b. Sept. 25, 1904, New Rochelle, N.Y., U.S.—d. Jan. 5, 1971, Vineyard Haven, Mass.)

American oceanographer Columbus O'Donnell Iselin served as director of the Woods Hole Oceanographic

Institution (1940–50; 1956–57) in Massachusetts, expanded its facilities tenfold and made it one of the largest research establishments of its kind in the world.

The scion of a New York banking family (his greatgrandfather had helped found the Metropolitan Opera House and the Metropolitan Museum of Art), Iselin attended Harvard University (A.B., 1926; A.M., 1928). From 1926 on, he made a series of summer sea excursions toward Labrador and the Arctic with his own schooner and crew, collecting material and data for Harvard's Museum of Comparative Zoology. For Harvard he served as assistant curator of oceanography (1929–48) and research oceanographer of the Museum of Comparative Zoology. Concurrently, in 1932 he joined the newly established Woods Hole institution and, from 1936, taught oceanography at Harvard.

In 1940 he was named director of Woods Hole and, with wartime funds from the U.S. Navy, vastly increased the institution's budget and size. Wartime studies—factors in seaborne invasions, ocean currents, underwater explosions, and other matters—turned in 1946 to peacetime studies of fisheries, the dynamics of currents, the profiles of ocean floors, and other oceanographic concerns. Later, Iselin was professor of oceanography at the Massachusetts Institute of Technology (1959–70) and Harvard University (1960–70).

MATTHEW FONTAINE MAURY

(b. Jan. 14, 1806, Spotsylvania County, Va., U.S.—d. Feb. 1, 1873, Lexington, Va.)

Matthew Fontaine Maury was a U.S. naval officer and pioneer hydrographer. He is considered to be one of the founders of oceanography.

Maury entered the navy in 1825 as a midshipman, circumnavigated the globe (1826–30), and in 1836 was

Matthew Fontaine Maury. Harris & Ewing Collection/Library of Congress, Washington, D.C. (Digital File Number: LC-DIG-hec-07970)

promoted to the rank of lieutenant. In 1839 he was lamed in a stagecoach accident, which made him unfit for active service. In 1842 he was placed in charge of the Depot of Charts and Instruments, out of which grew the U.S. Naval Observatory and Hydrographic Office. To gather information on maritime winds and currents, Maury distributed to captains specially prepared logbooks from which he compiled pilot charts, enabling ships to shorten the time of sea voyages. In 1848 he published maps of the main wind fields of Earth. Maury's work inspired the first international marine conference, held in Brussels in 1853. He was U.S. representative at the meeting that led to the establishment of the International Hydrographic Bureau. Provided with worldwide information, Maury was able to produce charts of the Atlantic, Pacific, and

Indian oceans. He also prepared a profile of the Atlantic seabed, which proved the feasibility of laying a transatlantic telegraph cable. In 1855 he published the first modern oceanographic text, *The Physical Geography of the Sea*. In that year his *Sailing Directions* included a section recommending that eastbound and westbound steamers travel in separate lanes in the North Atlantic to prevent collisions.

On the outbreak (1861) of the American Civil War, Maury returned to Virginia to become head of coast, harbour, and river defenses for the Confederate Navy, for which he attempted to develop an electric torpedo. In 1862 he went to England as a special agent of the Confederacy, and at the war's end (1865) he went to Mexico, where the emperor Maximilian made him imperial commissioner of immigration so that Maury could establish a Confederate colony there. In 1866, when the emperor abandoned this scheme, Maury went back to England. He returned to the United States in 1868 and accepted the professorship of meteorology at Virginia Military Institute, a post he held until his death. Maury Hall at Annapolis, Md., is named in his honour, and his birthday is a school holiday in Virginia.

WALTER MUNK
(b. Oct. 19, 1917, Vienna, Austria)

Austrian-born American oceanographer Walter Heinrich Munk pioneered studies of ocean currents and wave propagation and laid the foundations for contemporary oceanography.

The child of a wealthy family, Munk was born and raised in Vienna. He moved to Lake George, N.Y., in 1932 to attend boarding school, as his parents hoped to prepare him for a career in banking. He worked in banking for several years but grew dissatisfied and left to take classes at Columbia University. After earning a bachelor's degree (1939) in physics from the California Institute of Technology, Munk convinced Harald Sverdrup, director of the Scripps Institution of Oceanography at the University of California, Los Angeles, to give him a summer job. By 1940 he had earned a master's degree in geophysics from the California Institute of Technology and by 1947 had completed a doctorate in oceanography at Scripps. After graduation Scripps hired him as an assistant professor of geophysics. He became a full professor there in 1954 and was made a member of the University of California's Institute of Geophysics.

Distressed by the 1938 occupation of Austria by Germany, Munk had applied for U.S. citizenship and enlisted in the U.S. Army prior to completing his doctorate. From 1939 to 1945 he joined several of his colleagues from Scripps at the U.S. Navy Radio and Sound Laboratory, where they developed methods related to amphibious warfare. Their method for predicting and dealing with waves was carried out successfully by the Allied forces on D-Day (June 6, 1944) during the Normandy invasion. In 1946 Munk helped to analyze the currents, diffusion, and water exchanges at Bikini Atoll in the South Pacific, where the United States was testing nuclear weapons. Funded by a Guggenheim Fellowship, he spent a portion of 1949 at the University of Oslo studying the dynamics of ocean currents. Throughout the 1950s Munk studied the effect of geophysical processes on the wobble in Earth's rotation, publishing the seminal results in *The Rotation of the Earth: A Geophysical Discussion* (with G.J.F. MacDonald, 1960).

In 1959 Munk began campaigning for the creation of what would become the Cecil H. and Ida M. Green

Institute of Geophysics and Planetary Physics (IGPP) at Scripps. He directed the institute until 1982. Munk worked on the Mid-Ocean Dynamics Experiment (MODE) from 1965 to 1975; it resulted in significant improvement in the accuracy of tide prediction. *Waves Across the Pacific*, a 1967 documentary, depicted his study of how waves generated by storms in the Southern Hemisphere travel through the rest of the world's oceans. In 1968 he became a member of JASON, a panel of scientists who advised the U.S. government.

Beginning in 1975, Munk had begun experimenting with the use of acoustic tomography, which uses sound waves to generate images of water. This culminated in the 1991 Heard Island experiment, in which sound signals were transmitted from instruments 150 metres (492 feet) below the ocean's surface to receivers around the world. The project used the speed at which the signals transmitted to measure the temperature of the water. He cowrote the definitive volume on the subject, *Ocean Acoustic Tomography* (1995). Munk was named Secretary of the Navy Research Chair in Oceanography in 1984 and continued to research the implications of global warming for the oceans as part of the Acoustic Thermometry of Ocean Climate (ATOC) project from 1996 to 2006.

Munk was the recipient of the Royal Astronomical Society's 1968 Gold Medal and the American Geophysical Union's 1989 William Bowie Medal, among others. He became the first recipient of the annual Walter Munk Award, given in his honour by The Oceanography Society and several naval offices, in 1993. In 1999 he won the 15th annual Kyoto Prize in Basic Sciences for his work in physical oceanography and geophysics; he became the first in his field to be honoured with this award.

SIR JOHN MURRAY

(b. March 3, 1841, Cobourg, Ont., Can.—d. March 16, 1914, near Kirkliston, West Lothian [now in Edinburgh], Scot.)

Scottish Canadian naturalist Sir John Murray was one of the founders of oceanography. His particular interests were ocean basins, deep-sea deposits, and coral-reef formation.

In 1868 Murray began collecting marine organisms and making a variety of oceanographic observations during an expedition to the Arctic islands of Jan Mayen and Spitsbergen, off Norway. Murray did much to organize the *Challenger* Expedition (1872–76), which made extremely valuable contributions in charting, surveying, and biological investigation, and he helped outfit it with equipment for conducting oceanographic studies. As a naturalist with the expedition, he was placed in charge of the biological specimens collected. Kept at Edinburgh, they attracted the attention of marine biologists from around the world for 20 years.

After the death of the expedition's leader, Sir Wyville Thomson (1882), Murray completed the publication of the 50-volume *Report on the Scientific Results of the Voyage of H.M.S. Challenger* (1880–95). He also directed biological investigations of Scottish waters (1882–94), surveyed the depths of Scottish lakes (1906), and took part in a North Atlantic oceanographic expedition (1910). He was knighted in 1898. His writings include the paper "On the Structure and Origin of Coral Reefs and Islands" (1880) and, with Johan Hjort, *The Depths of the Ocean* (1912).

FRIDTJOF NANSEN

(b. Oct. 10, 1861, Store-Frøen, near Kristiania [now Oslo], Nor.—d. May 13, 1930, Lysaker, near Oslo)

Fridtjof Nansen was a Norwegian explorer, oceanographer, statesman, and humanitarian who led a number of expeditions to the Arctic (1888, 1893, 1895–96) and ocean-ographic expeditions in the North Atlantic (1900, 1910–14). For his relief work after World War I he was awarded the Nobel Prize for Peace (1922).

Nansen's success as an explorer was due largely to his careful evaluation of the difficulties that might be encountered, his clear reasoning, which was never influenced by the opinions of others, his willingness to accept a calculated risk, his thorough planning, and his meticulous attention to detail. Many of these traits can be recognized in his scientific writings. In 1882 he was appointed curator of zoology at the Bergen museum. He wrote papers on zoological and histological subjects, illustrated by excellent drawings. For one of his papers, "The Structure and Combination of Histological Elements of the Central Nervous System" (1887), the University of Kristiania conferred upon him the degree of doctor of philosophy. Though the paper contained so many novel interpretations that the committee that had to examine it accepted it with doubt, it is now considered a classic.

On his return from the *Fram* expedition in 1896, a professorship in zoology was established for Nansen at the University of Kristiania, but his interests shifted from zoology to physical oceanography, and in

Fridtjof Nansen, 1896. © Photos.com/ Jupiterimages

1908 his status was changed to professor of oceanography. During 1896–1917 he devoted most of his time and energy to scientific work. He edited the report of the scientific results of his expedition and himself wrote some of the most important parts. He participated in the establishment of the International Council for the Exploration of the Sea and for some time directed the council's central laboratory in Kristiania. In 1900 he joined the *Michael Sars* on a cruise in the Norwegian Sea. In 1910 he made a cruise in the *Fridtjof* through the northeastern North Atlantic; in 1912 he visited the Spitsbergen waters on board his own yacht *Veslemoy;* and in 1914 he joined B. Helland-Hansen on an oceanographic cruise to the Azores in the *Armauer Hansen.* In 1913 Nansen traveled through the Barents Sea and the Kara Sea to the mouth of the Yenisey River and back through Siberia. He published the results of his cruises in numerous papers, partly in cooperation with Helland-Hansen. His lasting contributions to oceanography comprise improvement and design of instruments, explanation of the wind-driven currents of the seas, discussions of the waters of the Arctic, and explanation of the manner in which deep- and bottom-water is formed.

Nansen also dealt with other subjects: for instance, his *Nord i tåkeheimen,* 2 vol. (1911; *In Northern Mists*) gave a critical review of the exploration of the northern regions from early times up to the beginning of the 16th century.

JACQUES PICCARD

(b. July 28, 1922, Brussels, Belg.—d. Nov. 1, 2008, La Tour-de-Peilz, Switz.)

Jacques-Ernest-Jean Piccard was a Swiss oceanic engineer, economist, and physicist, who helped his father, Auguste Piccard, build the bathyscaphe for deep-sea exploration and who also invented the mesoscaphe, an undersea vessel for exploring middle depths.

Jacques Piccard was born in Brussels while his Swiss-born father was a professor at the University of Brussels. After graduating from the École Nouvelle de Suisse Romande in Lausanne, Switz., in 1943, he studied at the University of Geneva, taking a year off in 1944–45 in order to serve with the French First Army. Upon receiving his licentiate in 1946, he taught at the university for two years before entering private teaching.

Meanwhile, he was helping his father to design bathyscaphes and in 1953 accompanied him in the *Trieste* on a dive of 10,168 feet (3,099 m) off the island of Ponza, Italy. In 1956 Jacques Piccard went to the United States seeking funding; two years later the U.S. Navy bought the *Trieste* and retained him as a consultant. On Jan. 23, 1960, he and Lieutenant Don Walsh of the U.S. Navy set a new submarine depth record by descending 10,916 metres (35,810 feet) into the Mariana Trench in the Pacific Ocean using the *Trieste*. He recounted this feat in *Seven Miles Down* (1961), written with Robert Dietz. In the early 1960s, working with his father, he designed and built the first of four mesoscaphes. His first mesoscaphe, the *Auguste Piccard*, capable of carrying 40 passengers, transported some 33,000 tourists through the depths of Lake Geneva during the 1964 Swiss National Exhibition in Lausanne. In 1969 he drifted some 3,000 km (1,800 miles) along the east coast of North America in the mesoscaphe *Ben Franklin*, conducting research on the Gulf Stream for the U.S. Navy.

In his later career Piccard was a consultant scientist for several private American organizations for deep-sea research, including the Grumman Aircraft Engineering Corporation, New York (1966–71). In the 1970s he founded the Foundation for the Study and Protection of

Seas and Lakes, based in Cully, Switz. In 1999 his son Bertrand Piccard, together with Englishman Brian Jones, completed the first nonstop circumnavigation of the globe in a balloon.

FRANCIS P. SHEPARD

(b. May 10, 1897, Brookline, Mass., U.S.—d. April 25, 1985, La Jolla, Calif.)

Francis Parker Shepard was an American marine geologist whose pioneering surveys of submarine canyons off the coast of California near La Jolla marked the beginning of Pacific marine geology.

Shepard studied geology at Harvard under R.A. Daly and at the University of Chicago (Ph.D., 1922). Most of Shepard's professional life was spent at the Scripps Institution of Oceanography, where he was appointed professor of submarine geology in 1948. Central to his research was the search for an explanation of the origin of submarine canyons. His series of observations of depth changes (begun in the early 1950s) at the head of submarine canyons gave concrete evidence, although not positive proof, of their formation by turbidity currents (submarine flows of muddy suspensions) and sediment slumping. Among his principal works are *Submarine Geology* (1948) and, with R.F. Dill, *Submarine Canyons and Other Sea Valleys* (1966).

HENRY MELSON STOMMEL

(b. Sept. 27, 1920, Wilmington, Del., U.S.—d. Jan. 17, 1992, Boston, Mass.)

American oceanographer and meteorologist Henry Melson Stommel became internationally known during the 1950s for his theories on circulation patterns in the

Atlantic Ocean. Stommel suggested that Earth's rotation is responsible for the Gulf Stream along the coast of North America, and he theorized that its northward flow must be balanced by a stream of cold water moving southward beneath it. He proposed a global circulation in which surface water sinks in the far north to feed the deep, south-flowing current, while water rises in the Antarctic region to supply a northward flow along the eastern coasts of North and South America. Much of this "conveyor belt" theory has been confirmed. In addition to his work on ocean currents, Stommel did research on a variety of problems in oceanography and meteorology.

An anomaly among modern scientists, Stommel became a full professor without an earned doctorate. He received his B.S. from Yale University (1942) and served there as instructor in mathematics and astronomy (1942–44). A research associate at the Woods Hole (Mass.) Oceanographic Institution from 1944 to 1959, he became professor of oceanography at the Massachusetts Institute of Technology in 1959 and remained there except for the years 1960–63, when he taught at Harvard. Stommel established several stations to study ocean currents, including the PANULIRUS station (begun in 1954) in Bermuda. He was elected to the National Academy of Sciences in 1962 and received the National Medal of Science in 1989.

GEORG WÜST

(b. June 15, 1890, Posen, Ger. [now Poznán, Pol.]—d. Nov. 8, 1977, Erlangen, W.Ger.)

Georg Adolf Otto Wüst was a German oceanographer who, by collecting and analyzing many systematic observations, developed the first essentially complete understanding of the physical structure and deep circulation of the Atlantic Ocean.

Wüst received his doctorate from the University of Berlin in 1919. After the death of his teacher Alfred Merz, Wüst took over as chief oceanographer on the German Atlantic (1925–27) expedition. He was also in charge of the International Gulf Stream (1938) expedition. The Atlantic expedition, conducted from the research vessel *Meteor*, was the first study of an entire ocean, and it remains one of the most extensive oceanographic surveys ever undertaken. From the wealth of data amassed, Wüst constructed cross-sectional profiles that revealed the Atlantic's complex temperature and salinity stratification and its deep-current structure.

After World War II Wüst built up again the Institute for Oceanography, at Kiel, so that it flourished as a research centre. He was the institute's director from 1946 until he retired in 1959.

APPENDIX

AVERAGE NET PRIMARY PRODUCTION OF THE EARTH'S MAJOR HABITATS	
HABITAT	**NET PRIMARY PRODUCTION (GRAM PERSQUARE METRE PER YEAR)**
Forests	
tropical	1,800
temperate	1,250
boreal	800
Other Terrestrial Habitats	
swamp and marsh	2,500
savanna	700
cultivated land	650
shrubland	600
desert scrub	70
temperate grassland	500
tundra and alpine	140
Aquatic Habitats	
algal beds and reefs	2,000
estuaries	1,800
lakes and streams	500
continental shelf	360
open ocean	125

Source: Adapted from Robert E. Ricklefs, *Ecology*, 3rd edition (1990), by W.H. Freeman and Company, used with permission.

GLOSSARY

bathymetry The measurement of ocean depth.

benthos A collection of organisms that live on or at the bottom of a body of water.

capillary waves Tiny waves at the ocean surface that are direct products of the wind stress exerted on the sea surface.

desalination A water treatment method that involves the separation of freshwater from salt water or brackish water.

divergence A meteorological term used to describe the drawing apart of air, as well as the rate at which each takes place.

downwelling A region of oceanic convergence that forces surface water downward.

eddy A current in a body of water such as a river that swirls in a different direction than the main current.

El Niño The anomalous appearance, every few years, of unusually warm ocean conditions along the tropical west coast of South America associated with adverse effects on fishing, agriculture, and weather systems.

Gulf Stream A warm ocean current flowing in the North Atlantic northeastward off the North American coast, which produces a warming effect upon the climates of adjacent land areas.

gyre A system of ocean currents that spirals around a central zone.

hydrologic cycle The continuous circulation of water through Earth's atmosphere, surface, and oceans.

isobaric characterized by constant or equal pressure.

Kuroshio Current A strong surface oceanic current of the northwestern Pacific Ocean that dramatically affects atmospheric conditions on Earth.

nekton The assemblage of pelagic animals that swim freely, independent of water motion or wind.

phytoplankton A flora of freely floating, often minute photosynthetic organisms that drift with water currents.

seiche A rhythmic oscillation of water in a lake or a partially enclosed coastal inlet, such as a bay, gulf, or harbour.

swell A long often massive and crestless wave or succession of waves often continuing beyond or after its cause, such as a gale wind.

Southern Oscillation A coherent interannual fluctuation of atmospheric pressure over the tropical Indo-Pacific region.

thermocline A layer in a thermally stratified body of water that separates an upper, warmer, lighter, oxygen-rich zone from a lower, colder, heavier, oxygen-poor zone.

thermohaline circulation The component of general oceanic circulation that is controlled by horizontal differences in temperature and salinity.

tidal bore A surge of swiftly moving water traveling upstream and headed by a wave or series of waves.

transpiration A plant's loss of water, mainly through the stomates of leaves.

tsunamis Catastrophic ocean waves usually caused by submarine earthquakes, underwater or coastal landslides, or volcanic eruptions.

upwelling The process of upward movement to the ocean surface of deeper, cold, usually nutrient-rich waters especially along some shores due to the offshore movement of surface waters.

BIBLIOGRAPHY

GENERAL CONSIDERATIONS

Broad overviews of the oceans are provided by David A. Ross, *Introduction to Oceanography*, 4th ed. (1988); Alyn C. Duxbury and Alison B. Duxbury, *An Introduction to the World's Oceans*, 3rd ed. (1991); Ellen J. Prager and Sylvia A. Earle, *The Oceans* (2001); Sylvia A. Earle, *The World Is Blue: How Our Fate and the Ocean's Are One* (2009); Deborah Cramer, *Smithsonian Ocean: Our Water, Our World* (2008); and M. Grant Gross, *Oceanography, a View of the Earth*, 5th ed. (1990). Alastair Couper (ed.), *The Times Atlas and Encyclopedia of the Sea* (1989), provides a graphic look at all aspects of the ocean. *Ocean Yearbook* (annual), contains essays on resources, transportation, and marine science, among other topics.

CHEMICAL AND PHYSICAL PROPERTIES OF SEAWATER

As an excellent starting point for the reader interested in an integrated account of ocean chemistry, physics, and biology, the classic work by H.U. Sverdrup, Martin W. Johnson, and Richard H. Fleming, *The Oceans* (1942, reissued 1970), is highly recommended. An in-depth, but quite readable, account of the general field of marine chemistry is provided by J.P. Riley and R. Chester, *Introduction to Marine Chemistry* (1971). Kenneth W. Bruland, "Trace Elements in Sea-water," vol. 8, ch. 45 (1983), pp. 157–220, is another readable account. Modern treatments include Anthony Gianguzza, Ezio Pelizzetti, and Silvio Sammartano (eds.), *Chemistry of Marine Water and Sediments* (2002); R.E. Hester and R.M. Harrison (eds.), *Chemistry in the Marine Environment* (2000); and Anthony Gianguzza, Ezio Pelizzetti, and Silvio Sammartano (eds.), *Chemical Processes in Marine Environments* (2000).

OCEAN BASINS AND CONTINENTAL MARGINS

Overviews of the geologic features of the deep-sea floor are given in Eugen Seibold and Wolfgang H. Berger, *The Sea Floor: An Introduction to Marine Geology* (2010); H. Kuenen, *Marine Geology* (2007); and Alan E.M. Nairn and Francis G. Stehli (eds.), *The Ocean Basins and Margins*, 7 vol. in 9 (1973–88). Specific topics and geographic areas are studied by C.M. Powell, S.R. Roots, and J.J. Veevers, "Pre-breakup Continental Extension in East Gondwanaland and the Early Opening of the Eastern Indian Ocean," *Tectonophysics*, 155:261–283 (1988); David B. Rowley and Ann L. Lottes, "Reconstructions of the North Atlantic and Arctic: Late Jurassic to Present," *Tectonophysics*, 155:73–120 (1988); T. Simkins et al., (1989); and two essays in E.L. Winterer, Donald M. Hussong, and Robert W. Decker (eds.), *The Eastern Pacific Ocean and Hawaii* (1989), vol. N of the series "The Geology of North America": Tanya Atwater, "Plate Tectonic History of the Northeast Pacific and Western North America," ch. 4, pp. 21–72; and Ken C. MacDonald, "Tectonic and Magnetic Processes on the East Pacific Rise," ch. 6, pp. 93–110.

CIRCULATION OF OCEAN WATERS

Useful books include those by Open University Oceanography Course Team, *Ocean Circulation* (1989); George L. Pickard and William J. Emery, *Descriptive Physical Oceanography: An Introduction*, 5th enlarged ed.

(1990); Rui Xin Huang, *Ocean Circulation: Wind-Driven and Thermohaline Processes* (2009); Stephen Pond and George L. Pickard, *Introductory Dynamical Oceanography*, 2nd ed. (1983); Henry Stommel, *A View of the Sea* (1987); and Henry Stommel and Dennis W. Moore, *An Introduction to the Coriolis Force* (1989). Joseph Pedlosky, *Ocean Circulation Theory* (2010), is an advanced treatment.

WAVES OF THE SEA

Books discussing waves and tides include Joseph Pedlosky, *Waves in the Ocean and Atmosphere: Introduction to Wave Dynamics* (2010); Open University Oceanography Course Team, *Waves, Tides, and Shallow-water Processes* (1989); Albert Defant, *Ebb and Flow: The Tides of Earth, Air, and Water* (1958; originally published in German, 1953); Blair Kinsman, *Wind Waves: Their Generation and Propagation on the Ocean Surface* (1965, reprinted 1984); M. Grant Gross, *Oceanography*, 5th ed. (1990), ch. 8, "Waves," and ch. 9, "Tides," pp. 193–241; and David T. Pugh, *Tides, Surges, and Mean Sea-level* (1987). C. Garrett and W. Munk, "Internal Waves in the Ocean," *Annual Review of Fluid Mechanics*, vol. 11, pp. 339–369 (1979), is also of interest. Highly technical treatments of ocean waves are provided in Leo H. Holthuijsen, *Waves in Oceanic and Coastal Waters* (2010); and Michel K. Ochi, *Ocean Waves: The Stochastic Approach* (2007).

DENSITY CURRENTS IN THE OCEANS

An introductory treatment to the topic of density currents is provided in Marius Ungarish, *An Introduction to Gravity Currents and Intrusions* (2009). Other studies include Gerard V. Middleton and Monty A. Hampton,

"Subaqueous Sediment Transport and Deposition by Sediment Gravity Flows," ch. 11 in Daniel Jean Stanley and Donald J.P. Swift (eds.), *Marine Sediment Transport and Environmental Management* (1976), pp. 197–218, which describes and discusses turbidity currents, grain flows, fluidized sediment flows, and debris flows; Gary Parker, Yusuke Fukushima, and Henry M. Pantin, "Self-accelerating Turbidity Currents," *Journal of Fluid Mechanics*, 171:145–181 (1986); and Richard J. Seymour, "Nearshore Auto-suspending Turbidity Flows," *Ocean Engineering*, 13(5):435–447 (1986).

IMPACT OF OCEAN-ATMOSPHERE INTERACTIONS ON WEATHER AND CLIMATE

Overviews of the general relationship between air and ocean may be found in John Marshall and R. Alan Plumb, *Atmosphere, Ocean and Climate Dynamics: An Introductory Text* (2007); Grant R. Bigg, *The Oceans and Climate* (2004); Y. Toba (Ed.), *Ocean-Atmosphere Interactions* (2003); Adrian E. Gill, *Atmosphere-Ocean Dynamics* (1982); and Neil Wells, *The Atmosphere and Ocean: A Physical Introduction* (1986).

Studies of the El Niño/Southern Oscillation phenomena and their effect on climatic change are found in P.W. Glynn (ed.), *Global Ecological Consequences of the 1982–83 El Nino-Southern Oscillation* (1990); S. George Philander, *El Niño, La Niña, and the Southern Oscillation* (1990); Warren S. Wooster and David L. Fluharty (eds.), *El Niño North: Niño Effects in the Eastern Subarctic Pacific Ocean* (1985); Brian Fagan, *Floods, Famines, and Emperors: El Niño and the Fate of Civilizations* (2009); Richard T. Barber and Francisco P. Chavez, "Biological Consequences of El Niño," *Science*, 222(4629):1203–1210 (Dec. 16, 1983); Thomas Y. Canby, "El Niño's Ill Wind," *National*

Geographic, 165(2):144–183 (February 1984); M.A. Cane, "El Niño," *Annual Review of Earth and Planetary Sciences*, 14:43–70 (1986); David B. Enfield, "El Niño, Past and Present," *Reviews of Geophysics*, 27(1):159–187 (1989); Nicholas E. Graham and Warren B. White, "The El Niño Cycle: A Natural Oscillator of the Pacific Ocean-Atmosphere System," *Science*, 240:1293–1302 (June 3, 1988); S. George Philander and E.M. Rasmusson, "The Southern Oscillation and El Niño," *Advances in Geophysics*, vol. 28, part A, pp. 197–215 (1985); and E.M. Rasmusson, "El Niño and Variations in Climate," *American Scientist*, 73(2):168–177 (March–April 1985). In addition, the entire issue of *Oceanus*, vol. 27, no. 2 (Summer 1984), is devoted to El Niño studies.

ECONOMIC ASPECTS OF THE OCEANS

An entire issue of *Oceanus*, vol. 21, no. 4 (Winter 1984/85), is devoted to the impact of the Exclusive Economic Zone, especially as it pertains to the United States; coastal fishing, multiple-use management, marine pollution, and nonliving resources are some of the topics covered. Giulio Pontecorvo, *The New Order of the Oceans: The Advent of a Managed Environment* (1986), deals with the new ocean regime and with the research and technology of marine resources from a global perspective, particularly emphasizing the international effects of the 1982 United Nations Law of the Sea Convention. The evolution of international marine policy and shipping law is compellingly discussed in Edgar Gold, *Maritime Transport* (1981), and "Ocean Shipping and the New Law of the Sea: Toward a More Regulatory Regime," *Ocean Yearbook*, vol. 6, pp. 85–96 (1986).

Discussions of the managed production of aquatic organisms include J.F. Muir, "Aquaculture—Towards the

Future," *Endeavour*, 9(1):52–55 (1985); and John Bardach, "Aquaculture: Moving from Craft to Industry," *Environment*, 30(2):6–11, 36–41 (March 1988). Desalinization processes are discussed and illustrated in Alan D.K. Laird, "The Potable Sea: Taking the Salt from Saltwater," *Oceans*, 15(5):25–29 (September–October 1982); and Roberta Friedman, "Salt-free Water from the Sea," *Sea Frontiers*, 36(3):49–54 (May–June 1990).

Overviews of various ocean energy resources and technologies may be found in Maxwell Bruce, "Ocean Energy: Some Perspectives on Economic Viability," *Ocean Yearbook*, vol. 5, pp. 58–78 (1985); and Terry R. Penney and Desikan Bharathan, "Power from the Sea," *Scientific American*, 256(1):86–92 (January 1987). Tidal power generation is covered by B. Count (ed.), *Power from Sea Waves* (1980), based on conference proceedings; and Michael E. McCormick, *Ocean Wave Energy Conversion* (1981). Summaries of ocean thermal energy conversion techniques and future prospects are provided by R. Cohen, "Energy from the Ocean," *Philosophical Transactions of the Royal Society of London*, Series A, 307:405–437 (1982); and D.E. Lennard, "Ocean Thermal Energy Conversion—Past Progress and Future Prospects," *IEE Proceedings*, vol. 134, part A, no. 5, pp. 381–391 (May 1987).

Current and future petroleum and mineral resources in the ocean environment and the technologies necessary to recover them are addressed in Gerard J. Mangone (ed.), *The Future of Gas and Oil from the Sea* (1983); Elisabeth Mann Borgese, *The Mines of Neptune: Minerals and Metals from the Sea* (1985); David Cronan, "A Wealth of Sea-floor Minerals," *New Scientist*, 106:34–38 (June 6, 1985); and James M. Broadus, "Seabed Materials," *Science*, 235:853–860 (Feb. 20, 1987).

Discussions of the use of the ocean as a site for waste disposal, and the problems of marine pollution, include

Iver W. Duedall et al. (eds.), *Wastes in the Ocean*, 6 vol. (1983–85), on industrial, sewage, radioactive, and energy wastes, dredged-material disposal, and deep-sea and nearshore waste disposal; R.B. Clark, *Marine Pollution*, 2nd ed. (1989); Wesley Marx, *The Oceans: Our Last Resource* (1981); David K. Bulloch, *The Wasted Ocean* (1989); and a complete issue of *Oceanus*, vol. 33, no. 2 (Summer 1990).

UNDERSEA EXPLORATION

The classical tools of the oceanographer are described by H.U. Sverdrup, Martin W. Johnson, and Richard H. Fleming, *The Oceans* (1942, reissued 1970). More recent texts on oceanography and marine biology include Tom S. Garrison, *Oceanography: An Invitation to Marine Science*, 7th ed. (2009); Alan P. Trujillo and Harold V. Thurman, *Essentials of Oceanography*, 10th ed. (2010); John A. Knauss, *Introduction to Physical Oceanography*, 2nd ed. (2005); M. Grant Gross, *Oceanography, a View of the Earth*, 5th ed. (1990); George L. Pickard and William J. Emery, *Descriptive Physical Oceanography*, 5th enlarged ed. (1990); James P. Kennett, *Marine Geology* (1982); Bruce A. Warren and Carl Wunsch (eds.), *Evolution of Physical Oceanography* (1981); James L. Sumich, *An Introduction to the Biology of Marine Life*, 5th ed. (1992); M.N. Hill et al. (eds.), *The Sea* (1962); and J.P. Riley and G. Skirrow (eds.), *Chemical Oceanography*, 2nd ed., 8 vol. (1975–83).

Exploration and discovery are chronicled in Rachel L. Carson, *The Sea Around Us*, special ed. (1989); Wolf H. Berger and E.N. Shor, *Ocean: Reflections on a Century of Exploration* (2009); and Martin W. Sandler, *Atlantic Ocean: The Illustrated History of the Ocean That Changed the World* (2008). Also informative are the documentaries of famous explorers, such as the books by William Beebe, *Half Mile Down* (1934, reissued 1951); Jacques Piccard and

Robert S. Dietz, *Seven Miles Down* (1961); George Stephen Ritchie, *Challenger: The Life of a Survey Ship* (1957); Helen Raitt, *Exploring the Deep Pacific*, 2nd ed. (1964); Willard Bascom, *A Hole in the Bottom of the Sea: The Story of the Mohole Project* (1961); Francis P. Shepard, *The Earth Beneath the Sea*, rev. ed. (1967); and Daniel Behrman, *The New World of the Oceans* (1969).

Other treatments include Jacques Cousteau and Alexis Siverine, *Jacques Cousteau's Calypso* (1983; originally published in French, 1978); R. Frank Busby, *Manned Submersibles* (1976), on their design and operation; and Kenneth J. Hsü, *Challenger at Sea*, trans. from German (1992).

Modern undersea explorers are strongly dependent on innovative engineering and technology, such as that treated in *Jane's Ocean Technology, 1979–80* (1979); John J. Myers (ed.), *Handbook of Ocean and Underwater Engineering* (1969); John F. Brahtz (ed.), *Ocean Engineering* (1968); and Robert L. Wiegel, *Oceanographical Engineering* (1964). Other treatments include John Brackett Hersey (ed.), *Deep-Sea Photography* (1967); J.F.R. Gower (ed.), *Oceanography from Space* (1981); G.A. Maul, *Introduction to Satellite Oceanography* (1985); and F. Dobson, L. Hasse, and R. Davis (eds.), *Air-Sea Interaction: Instruments and Methods* (1980).

INDEX

A

abyssal hills, 49, 52, 63–64, 102
abyssal plains, 70, 80, 193
Agassiz, Alexander, 226–227
Albert I, Prince of Monaco, 188, 227–228
Antarctica, 2, 3, 31, 58, 59, 60, 80, 91, 96, 99, 113, 120, 123, 191
Antarctic Bottom Water, 31, 123
Antarctic Circumpolar Current, 118–119, 122, 123, 124
Antarctic Intermediate Water, 122, 123, 124
Arctic Ocean, 2, 78, 113
Atlantic Ocean, 60, 64, 65, 79, 95–96, 116, 117, 121, 122, 142, 144, 148, 149, 151, 154, 175, 203, 229
atmosphere, 1, 2, 9, 10, 15, 16, 19, 28, 29, 37, 40, 41, 42, 43, 44, 45, 104, 105, 118, 119, 140, 141, 142, 143, 144, 147, 153, 155, 161, 162, 164, 180, 191, 195, 198, 218, 225
atmospheric circulation, 5, 140, 142, 144, 147–148, 149, 150

B

Ballard, Robert, 226, 228–230
baroclinic field of mass, 107, 114
bathymetry, 188, 190, 193–194, 205
Beagle, 188

Beaufort, Sir Francis, 126
Beaufort scale, 126
Beer's law, 34, 35, 36
benthos, 218
Blake Plateau, 68, 76, 90

C

Cambrian Period, 9
capillary waves, 125
carbon dioxide, 9, 10, 15, 16, 19, 40, 41, 42, 44, 45, 46, 156, 198, 199
Challenger (HMS), 52, 188, 189, 198, 206, 242
Challenger Expedition, 52, 99, 206, 242
chemical evolution of oceans
    early oceans, 28, 39–44
    modern oceans, 47–48, 122
    the transition stage, 44–47
chemosynthesis, 103, 229
chimneys, 121
chlorofluorocarbons, 119, 156
circulation of the ocean waters, 104–105
climate anomalies, 141–144
climate change, 155, 163
composition of seawater
    dissolved inorganic substances, 11–17
    dissolved organic substances, 17–19
    effects of human activities, 19–20
continental drift, 92, 197, 199